THE
PARADIGM

JONATHAN CAHN

FRONT
LINE

Scripture quotations marked NLT are from the Holy Bible, New Living Translation, copyright © 1996, 2004, 2007. Used by permission of Tyndale House Publishers, Inc., Wheaton, IL 60189. All rights reserved.

Scripture quotations marked YLT are taken from Young's Literal Translation.

Cover design by Justin Evans

Visit the author's website at www.jonathancahn.com.

Library of Congress Cataloging-in-Publication Data:
An application to register this book for cataloging has been submitted to the Library of Congress.
International Standard Book Number: 978-1-62999-476-5
Walmart Special Edition ISBN: 978-1-62999-484-0
E-book ISBN: 978-1-62999-478-9

17 18 19 20 21—987654321
Printed in the United States of America

CONTENTS

Preface

A WORD of PREPARATION

I DON'T USUALLY WRITE prefaces. But I must do so here. A word of preparation is needed. *The Paradigm* is of such an explosive nature, its revelations so specific and so connected to specific figures and events of our times and to such highly charged subjects and concerning the powers that be, that its intent can easily be misinterpreted and its purpose misperceived. Thus what I write here I will echo in the book. It is important enough to be stated more than once.

The Paradigm is not directed against any person or persons. As much as it touches on any figures in the modern world, they are cited as part of letting the chips fall where they may according to the unfolding of the mystery. And so while it will speak of world figures, it will not ultimately be about them. Its ultimate focus will be the larger picture that involves an entire nation and civilization. The importance of the figures involved is in the roles they've played in that larger picture and in the unfolding of the ancient template.

The Paradigm is, above all, the revealing of a mystery, a blueprint, an ancient paradigm, that uncannily and amazingly has everything to do with our times.

It is also the revealing of a warning to a nation and a civilization concerning its present course and the ultimate end of that course.

As far as the figures cited, there is no place in God's kingdom for malice, only love. We are charged to oppose what is wrong but to love all, even those engaged in what is wrong. There is only one right response and action—to love them, to pray for them, and to speak truth in love. None of those involved had any idea of any connection or mystery. They acted without knowing.

Though the book will deal with the political realm and many other realms, it is not political but spiritual and prophetic. If one is to see its revelations, one must, before going forward, put away all preconceptions and presumptions, all politics and related opinions and judgments. One must approach it with complete openness, especially if one is unfamiliar with or alien to that which is scriptural. One can, of course, take them up again at the end, but it is crucial that such things be put aside for now, at the outset— if one is to uncover the mystery.

The mystery will hold unique dynamics and amazing properties. One could seek to explain away a few facts, but what we are about to open up will not be a matter of a few facts, or even several facts. It will be overwhelming in its scope, in its breadth, in its consistency, and in the magnitude of its details. It is something no human being could have orchestrated or woven together.

I pray, above all, that God will use this book to accomplish His purposes, prophetically and sovereignly, for awakening, for illuminating, for empowering, for encouraging, for turning, for restoring, for reviving, for saving, and for such a time as this.

Chapter 1

The MASTER BLUEPRINT

- Is it possible that there exists a master blueprint that lies behind the events of the modern world?

- Is it possible that this blueprint originated in ancient times and yet reveals the events of the twenty-first century?

- Could this blueprint foretell the rise and fall of modern leaders and governments?

- Could events that took place nearly three thousand years ago now be determining the course of our world and with it the course of our lives?

- Could this mystery reveal not only the events of the modern world but the *timing* of those events—revealing the *year* when an event is to take place and in some cases pinpointing the *exact date*—and in at least one case even the *exact hour*?

- Could a template of the ancient Middle East even foretell the outcome of a presidential election?

- Could the ancient figures within the paradigm hold the keys and mysteries behind the rulers and leaders of modern times, with each modern figure having an ancient prototype and each ancient figure having a modern antitype?

- Could it give the exact parameters of time that modern world leaders are allotted to remain on the national and world stage?
- Is it possible that we are all part of the replaying of the mystery?
- And what would happen if we were able to uncover the paradigm and open up the master blueprint?
- What would it reveal to us, or warn us of, concerning our future?

THIS BOOK WILL be the uncovering and opening up of the ancient blueprint, the mystery that came into being ages before the people it concerns were born and millennia before the events it reveals took place. The template is objective and fixed. It has no animus against anyone with whom it corresponds or involves. Nor have I. If the paradigm concerned different peoples or powers, I still would have written it. It is above all the unveiling of a mystery that has operated behind and affected our lives and times. Any connection to any figure or event of the modern world will be a matter of letting the chips of the ancient mystery fall where they may. Because of its explosive nature I was tempted to hold back from writing it. But because of its critical nature I could not hold back. For contained in the mystery is not only a revelation but a critical warning.

The paradigm touches not only those in power but every life on this planet and every realm of life—from politics to spirituality, economics, history, law, religion, culture, international relations, morality, even the course of nations. Though it has touched or determined the realm of politics, that fact is incidental to its ultimate concern, which is not political but something much larger. It is the revelation of where we have been and where we are and a warning as to where we are heading.

We must first identify and then open up the paradigm. To do that, we will begin a journey of nearly three thousand years, from the sands of an arid Middle Eastern landscape to the soil and streets of present-day America, from ancient palaces to the White House. We will see ruthless kings and queens, mysterious priests and priestesses, secrets and scandals, idols and gods, prophets and holy men, signs, portents, wonders, and harbingers.

In the end we will see two mysteries interweave and coalesce, that of *The Paradigm* with that of *The Harbinger*. For *The Paradigm* is the other dimension and realm of *The Harbinger*. They each arise from the same ground. Each was forged in the matrix of the same civilization. If *The Harbinger* opened up prophetic revelations and warnings in the forms of objects and actions, in *The Paradigm* people themselves become prophetic revelations—leaders on the modern world stage become the harbingers.

We will see ancient monarchs and modern presidents merging together, the reigns and actions of ancient kings governing the reigns and actions of modern leaders, ancient scandals lying behind modern scandals, and the events of ancient times determining the course, the direction, and the timing of the events of the modern world.

And in all this we will see our days in a new light and from an eternal vantage point.

With each of the paradigm's mysteries, the revealing will take place in three parts:

- The opening up of the ancient events
- The paradigm itself
- The manifestation of the paradigm in the modern world

The paradigm itself will be distinguished by the fact that it will appear in indented form in a box.

In order to open up the mystery, we must first lay the foundation. To uncover the blueprint, we must go back to ancient times and to the land of the paradigm.

Chapter 2

METAMORPHOSIS

THE IDEA THAT there could exist a blueprint from ancient times in which are contained and revealed the events of the modern world, even the timing of those events, and the people who would take part in those events sounds, of course, too incredible to be true.

But what if it were true? What if it reveals all this as well as the course we are presently on, the ultimate end of that course, and a warning concerning the future? If such a thing existed, we would want to know it and could not afford not to know it.

In this chapter we will set the stage of the mystery of the paradigm, a mystery that begins almost three thousand years ago.

The Paradigm

What exactly is a paradigm?

A *paradigm* is defined as a pattern, a model, a template, a prototype, an exemplar, an archetype.

Paradigms appear throughout the Bible. On Mount Sinai, Moses was given a pattern, or paradigm, from which to build the ark of the covenant and the Tent of God's Presence. So too there was a paradigm, or blueprint, for the building of the Temple of Jerusalem in later days. But other paradigms and other kinds of paradigms appeared in the Scriptures as well.

The prophets used paradigms. They performed prophetic acts, or acts of prophetic symbolism, the tearing of a robe, the breaking of a clay jar, the burying of a deed in the ground. These were prophetic paradigms, models of events yet to come. The tearing of the robe would foretell the tearing away of a kingdom from its king; the breaking of the jar, the destruction of a city; and the burying of the deed, the restoration of a nation.

Paradigms appear as well in the accounts of biblical characters—the life of the patriarch Joseph, a man rejected by his brothers, falsely accused, and suffering for the sins of others—yet ending up the savior of a nation—a foreshadow of the coming Messiah. Beyond this, paradigms appear also in the biblical chronicles of Israel's history—patterns, warnings, and examples for generations yet to come. Concerning this last realm, the apostle Paul wrote this:

> "Now all these things happened to them as examples, and they were written for our admonition..."[1]

In other words, not only were ancient events *recorded* for the sake of future generations, but they actually *happened* for the sake of future generations. In the phrase *all these things* Paul is specifically referring to Israel's ancient apostasy, its falling away from God, its embracing of immorality. It was all to serve as an example and warning to future generations.

Behind the word *example* is the Greek *tupos*. It is from *tupos* that we get the word *type*. The word can also be translated as pattern and model. The same Greek word is used elsewhere in the New Testament to speak of the pattern, or blueprint, Moses received on Mount Sinai. The word *tupos* can also be translated as paradigm. Thus the passage could be rendered this way:

> "Now all these things happened to them as *paradigms*, and they were written for our warning..."

So too the paradigm we are about to open will not only reveal but also warn. Its warning concerns a fatal mistake made in ancient times that is now being reenacted in our time.

But how could an ancient template speak of modern events, much less reveal their details? The answer is that God is sovereign. He knows every event before it takes place. Further, He works all events, every action and reaction, together for the outworking of His purposes. It is not that the paradigm came about as a prophecy of future events but rather that God is able to interweave and interconnect any one event with any other event and any moment with any other moment and thus join two worlds together, the ancient and the modern, even when the two are separated by a chasm of ages.

The Metamorphosis

The paradigm will reveal a nation, a civilization, undergoing a dangerous metamorphosis. It will concern America, in particular, and Western civilization and world civilization, in general. As America has been the center and leader of Western and modern civilization, it will function as the paradigm's central stage—yet the revelation will concern the entire world.

This metamorphosis taking place in our day is following the course of an ancient transformation—that of ancient Israel. Why Israel? Israel is the paradigm nation, the nation that stands as the pattern, or model, for good or bad, to the rest of the world. Israel is the exemplar nation. Beyond that every nation and culture of Western civilization is in some way connected to Israel. They are joined to the ancient nation first through their spiritual, moral, and cultural foundations. American civilization is especially connected, as it was founded by the Puritans to be an Israel of the New World.

The paradigm is formed from what took place in ancient Israel. But there were two Israels in ancient times, the northern kingdom, known as Israel and also Samaria, and the southern kingdom, known as Judah. Our focus will be on the northern kingdom.

So what exactly happened?

Israel had been founded for the will and purposes of God. But in time the nation began falling away from the God of its foundation and the foundation on which it had been established. It turned from God and to idols. In the northern kingdom this began with the worship of the golden calf. The replacing of God with idols of wood and stone and the invisible with the visible, physical, and tangible represented as well a descent into materialism, carnality, and sensuality.

And since they themselves were now creating their own gods, the metamorphosis would also represent a turning away from absolute truth and an embrace of subjectivity. If they could create their own truth, then there could be no more absolute truth. Thus they could now overrule the Word of God and create new laws to nullify the laws of God and a new morality to nullify the standards they had once viewed as immutable. And so they did.

They began driving God out of their public squares, out of their government, out of the instruction of their children, out of their culture, and out of their lives. They expunged His Word from their public discourse and His law from their collective consciousness. And by driving God out, they created a vacuum. Into that vacuum they brought in still more gods. Their lives were now permeated with idols and increasingly carnal, materialistic, and fragmented. And their civilization was now at war against the foundation on which it stood.

There had always been those among them who took part in pagan rites and practices and who lived at war with biblical morality. But they did so from the sidelines of their society. Their practices were taboo, prohibited by law or custom, and performed in the shadows. But as the nation's departure from God continued, such things began emerging from the shadows. In time they would be tolerated and then accepted and then established and then enforced. What the nation had once opposed and shunned it had now become. The metamorphosis was complete.

Of those things that emerged from the shadows, the most pivotal was a Canaanite deity that would eventually dominate the nation's culture. There would even come a time when the nation's monarchs would bow their knees before him. His name was *Baal*. He would become the embodiment of the nation's fall.

Baal was the most prominent god of the Canaanite pantheon. His images depict him wearing a conical helmet and holding a spear in his raised right hand in readiness for combat. He was the god of war, lord of the sky, master of wind, lightning, rains, and storms. He was the god of fertility and thus of increase and prosperity. The Canaanites would implore Baal to make their fields fruitful and their lives prosperous. To invoke his favor, the Canaanites built altars on their high places, in their valleys, and in the middle of their groves. And around his altars they gathered to worship in pagan rites and to offer up sacrifices of grain and livestock and even more precious offerings.

As their apostasy progressed, the worship of Baal grew less and less subtle and more and more blatant and brazen. That which in earlier times would have shocked the nation's moral sensibilities no longer did so. As time went on, they found it less necessary to pretend or disguise the transformation that was overtaking them.

They had exchanged their God. And having done so, they would witness the transformation of everything they had known, their culture, their leaders, their principles, their laws, their ways, their children, their values, their nature, their history, their identity, and ultimately their future. That which at the beginning appeared to them as freedom turned out to be something very different in the end. Having departed from the light, they would now be mastered by the darkness. Baal had promised them freedom, but he would give them degradation and in the end national destruction.

The Sacred Desecration

With their new god came a new morality. In the eyes of any true follower of God the worship of Baal could only be viewed as vile and debased. And as that worship and cult began permeating the nation, its culture grew increasingly coarse, harsh, and crude. In the cult of Baal, life was not sacred but debased. And if even his religion and worship were vile, then what could be sacred? Nothing was now sacred. If values could be overturned, then there could be no more absolute right or wrong. Then life itself could have no absolute value, worth, meaning, or purpose. Then life could be and would be debased.

In the biblical faith worldview that Israel had once followed, man was sacred, woman was sacred, and the union between the two was sacred. It was to be contained in the sacred vessel of marriage. But in the cult of Baal, marriage and sexuality had no absolute value and therefore no absolute sanctity. Therefore these also could be debased.

Baal was carnal, a deity of impulse and passion. He dwelt in a pantheon marked by sexual licentiousness. His female consorts were personifications of unbridled sexual passion. In His temples and shrines were priests and priestesses who officiated over acts of sexual immorality and took part in them. In the worship of Baal, sexuality was divorced from the sanctity of marriage and became the possession of the cult, the temple, and the culture. Sexuality was thus transferred from the private realm of the marriage bed and placed on public display. And as the sacred hedge of marriage was broken down, sexuality would increasingly saturate the public realm. Idols of the Canaanite fertility goddesses, clay images of naked women, were now everywhere. The culture became sexualized. This would, in turn, weaken and erode the institution of marriage. If sexuality could be separated from the realm of marriage in pagan rites, then it could be separated from marriage in other ways. One could have sexual relations with those other than one's spouse. One could have sexual relations apart from marriage altogether. Thus sexual immorality proliferated.

It was a spiral. With the proliferation of sexual immorality marriage was weakened. And as marriage was weakened, sexual immorality further proliferated, further weakening marriage and further encouraging sexual immorality. And in a civilization that had once revered the covenant of marriage as ordained by God, the effect was all the more dramatic and destructive.

But that wasn't the end of it. Baal's war against God's order would go further. If nothing was sacred or of any absolute value, neither were the natures and distinctions of male and female—gender. And if gender had no absolute value or purpose, then one could do with it whatever one wanted. In the first attack sexuality was divorced from marriage. In the second it was removed from gender, biology, and nature.

In the shrines of Baal and the gods of Canaan was a class of people known as the *kadeshote*. The word comes from the Hebrew root *kadesh*, which means holy or consecrated. But the term is ironic. The kadeshote were prostitutes consecrated to pagan deities. It was their "ministry" to perform sexual acts in the temples and shrines of Canaan.

There was another class of people closely related to the kadeshote called the *kadeshim*. They were likewise consecrated to the Canaanite gods and likewise dedicated to performing sexual acts. They were in many ways identical to the kadeshote but with one difference: they were male. The kadeshim were male prostitutes. They performed homosexual acts in the Canaanite shrines and temples. In the ancient translation of the Hebrew Scriptures into Greek made by Aquila Ponticus, the kadeshim are called the *endiellagmenoi*, or the changed ones. So the religion of Baal would involve the confusion of male and female, the obliteration of the distinction between the two. And the kadeshim were the priests of confusion, men in the place of women. They were also a sign. There had always been sin. But in the days of Baal sin became enshrined in Israel's culture. The nation that had once known God was now celebrating transgression, declaring it kadesh, holy. Thus the kadeshim were the sign of a civilization that had departed from God and was now departing from His order.

The Altar

Baal demanded sacrifices, more precious sacrifices than grain and livestock. He demanded human life. If they would offer up their own children, then their god would bless them with increase and prosperity. That was the price of the new morality—the lives of their children.

What exactly did this involve? The writings of ancient historians give us graphic glimpses. They describe parents offering up their child to Baal by placing him or her in the bronze hands of the idol. Underneath its arms raged a fire in which the child would be engulfed and consumed. They would then hope to receive the blessings of their god.

This was the religion and worship that Israel embraced after it turned away from God, and the horror of the new morality. It would be this act that would bring about the nation's judgment. After that judgment fell, the biblical chronicle would sum up the depth of the nation's depravity in just one verse:

> "And they caused their sons and daughters to pass through the fire…"[2]

The offering up of children would become so pervasive that at times it would be given official sanction. It would go from a forbidden pagan practice performed in the shadows to a right endorsed from the highest echelons of society and government. Even kings would offer up their royal children. Though it would be championed first in the northern kingdom, the worship of Baal and the sacrificing of children would become so prevalent that it would spread even to the southern kingdom of Judah.

That which would by the most basic measures of ethics be judged as a grave evil, the murder of their most innocent, would now be proclaimed an incontestable right. Life was no longer sacred. Death was. The sacrifice of children would become a sacrament.

But in the eyes of God and of His people, such a thing could never be viewed as acceptable or as anything else but the most horrific of acts. The prophets would expose their evil and warn them of its consequences:

> "Because they have forsaken Me and made this an alien place, because they have burned incense in it to other gods whom neither they, their fathers, nor the kings of Judah have known, and have filled this place with the blood of the innocents (they have also built the high places of Baal, to burn their sons with fire for burnt offerings to Baal…)"[3]

Their hands were covered with blood. They had deafened their ears to their children's cries. But heaven would hear it. And the destruction they had performed on the altars of Baal would become their own.

Could the metamorphosis that took place in ancient Israel be replaying in our own day? We will now begin the opening up of the paradigm.

Chapter 3

DAYS of the GODS

COULD WHAT TOOK place in ancient times in a Middle Eastern land hold the secret of what is now taking place before our eyes in America and throughout the world?

To begin the opening of the mystery, we will take the template of the metamorphosis that overtook ancient Israel, the paradigm, and hold it up against the modern world.

Days of Metamorphosis

The paradigm begins this way:

> The nation, culture, and civilization that had been established on the Word of God and dedicated to the ways of God will begin to depart from the God of its foundation. It will begin subtly at first, but as time goes on, the departure will become more and more blatant and brazen.

American civilization was dedicated from its inception to the will and purposes of God, established after the ideal and pattern of ancient Israel. But in the mid-twentieth century a critical metamorphosis began—a departure from the God of its foundation. The transformation was subtle at first but in time would become increasingly blatant and brazen.

The metamorphosis was not limited to America. European civilization had also been built on the foundation stone of biblical faith. But in the twentieth century it became increasingly obvious that it was undergoing the same metamorphosis. Churches emptied out, and a post-Christian secularism took hold.

> As the nation and civilization turns away from God, it will turn to idolatry to fill the void. It will deify the material world. Thus it will grow increasingly materialistic and increasingly obsessed with the sensual.

As it happened in ancient Israel, so too it happened in the modern world. In America and in much of the West the turning away from God led to an embrace of idolatry. The idols would not be called idols or gods. And they would assume modern forms—the idols of money, success, pleasure, prosperity, comfort, addictions, materialism, self-obsession, self-indulgence, self-worship. As in the ancient metamorphosis, with the turning away from God and the turning to idolatry, the culture became increasingly materialistic and increasingly obsessed with and addicted to the sensual.

> Paralleling its progressive descent into idolatry will be an increasing movement toward moral relativism—the discarding of absolute truth. Out of this will come the redefining of truth, reality, and values. A "new morality" will be introduced that will overrule the values and ways of God and the biblical moral grounding that had long served as its foundation.

So too the modern turning away from God to idolatry has led to the embracing of moral relativism, apostasy, and the rejection of absolute truth. In America the idea of a nation "under God" eroded. The culture and state redefined what was true, what was real, and what was right and wrong. As in the ancient apostasy, a "new morality" was introduced. The new morality was invariably anti-biblical and anti-Christian and was in reality a revived version of ancient paganism. It overruled the ways and standards of God and recast them as outdated and restrictive.

> As the apostasy continues, the culture will begin progressively driving God out of its public square, out of its government, out of its public discourse, out of the education of its children—out of life.

In the early 1960s America began noticeably driving God out of its public life, out of its educational system, out of its government, out of its culture. Prayer was increasingly banned from public events, Bibles were removed from public schools, and the Ten Commandments were ripped down from the walls and monuments of the public square. The overall phenomenon could be seen as well in other nations and cultures of the West.

> That which had once only been practiced in secret, rites of pagan morality and acts that warred against biblical morality, will now begin emerging from the culture's shadows into the open.

As in the ancient metamorphosis, with the modern apostasy advanced, that which had once been done in secret began emerging from the shadows and came out into the open, from hedonism and sexual immorality to atheism and godlessness. Each was a manifestation of a pagan or anti-biblical morality. As the culture grew increasingly anti-Christian, what had once been taboo was increasingly embraced and that which only existed on its fringes now entered its mainstream.

Just as few in the modern world would ever admit to serving idols, far fewer would ever admit to serving Baal. Yet when a civilization that has once known the ways of God turns away from those ways, it inevitably turns to Baal. The name of Baal will never be spoken; nevertheless he will be served—in one form or another. When a culture or life gives itself to serve the spirit of increase, gain, profit, materialism, prosperity, and self-interest above all things—it has given itself to Baal. He is the zeitgeist, the spirit of the age, the god of increase and materialism, the principle that inhabits and possesses modern civilization. As in ancient times, a civilization that had once known God had turned away from Him and had turned to Baal. And as in ancient times, he remains the god of the modern apostasy—the god of the metamorphosis.

Days of Desecration

> As the metamorphosis progresses, the culture will turn increasingly coarse, base, harsh, and crude. More and more it will be marked and permeated by vulgarity, profanity, and debasement.

As it was in the ancient apostasy, so the modern apostasy has witnessed a coarsening of culture. American and Western culture has grown increasingly crude, harsh, vulgar, and profane. If a person living in 1950s America was given the power to see into the future as to what would be shown on the television screens of present-day America, it would appear to them as apocalyptic. And if we are not equally shocked, it is only a measure of how desensitized we have become—as undoubtedly were the generations of Israel's apostasy.

> As the departure from God continues, that which was once held as sacred, as in marriage, will no longer be held to be so. Increasingly marriage will be divorced from sexuality. The marital bond will weaken and erode. The weakening will further open the door to the proliferation of sexual immorality. And the proliferation will further weaken the bonds of marriage.

So it is no accident that the modern departure from God has witnessed a parallel erosion of marriage and the growing divorce of marriage from sexuality. Where once even the depiction of sexuality outside of marriage was virtually unthinkable, it has now become the norm. And as the marital bond has eroded, sexual immorality has proliferated—which has, in turn, further weakened the bond of marriage.

> As sexuality is divorced from marriage, it will be increasingly transferred from the bedroom to the realm of popular culture. And thus the culture will become increasingly sexualized.

As in the ancient apostasy, we too have witnessed the transference of sexuality out of the bounds of the private realm. Thus what was once the private and sacred possession of the marital chamber was now exhibited on the stage of popular culture, in motion pictures, on television, in popular music, in virtually every facet of media and the entertainment industry—and on the Internet. The culture became increasingly sexualized.

> Carnal and erotic images and objects of sexual desire will multiply and be put on display. The culture will become saturated with them. A civilization founded on a spirit of consecration will increasingly give itself to a spirit of desecration.

As in the days of Israel's fall from God, when the erotic images of Canaanite goddesses were everywhere, so too in the modern apostasy erotic and pornographic images have saturated the culture. This is evident in the mainstreaming of pornography and in the pornification of mainstream culture.

In the temples and shrines of Israel's apostasy were the prostitutes of Baal. In biblical Greek the word for *prostitute* is *porne*. From *porne* we get the word *pornography*. America, the civilization consecrated and dedicated at its inception to be a light to the nations, now fills the world with pornographic images instead.

> As the apostasy deepens, it enters its next stage—the divorcing of sexuality from gender. It will embrace the confusing of male and female. It will enshrine the practice of homosexuality, celebrate that which the Word of God declares as sin, and hold sexual immorality as sacred—kadesh.

As it was in the ancient case, so the modern apostasy has moved from the divorcing of sexuality from marriage to the divorcing of sexuality from gender. In the ancient case this principle was embodied by the kadeshim. In the modern replaying it has manifested in the mainstreaming, celebration, and enshrinement of homosexuality. And yet the modern war against gender is many-pronged and involves everything from sexual immorality to social engineering. But the confusion of gender is as distinctive a part of the modern apostasy as it was of the ancient apostasy.

Days of the Altar

Could the darkest part of the ancient paradigm speak to us as well over two and a half thousand years later? Could the altars of Baal have in our own day a modern parallel? If so, what are the modern-day altars of Baal?

An altar is an instrument of death and destruction. The altars of Baal were the consequence of the ancient apostasy and its logical conclusion, the dark underside of the new morality. Thus the paradigm:

> As the civilization turns away from God and the sanctity of life is lost, it will embrace and commit the darkest of acts, the destruction of its most innocent, the killing of its children.

It is no accident that the first civilization in the modern age to embody a total rejection of God and biblical morality, the Soviet Union, was also the first to legalize the killing of unborn children. It is also no accident that it was at the same time that America began dramatically turning away from God and its biblical foundations, in the mid– and late twentieth century, that it also embraced the killing of its most innocent. Only then did it legalize abortion. This same convergence took place throughout much of the Western world.

> As the apostasy progresses, the killing of children will move from an act performed in secret and against the law to a practice endorsed from the highest echelons of society and legalized by those in power.

As in the ancient case, the practice of killing unborn children took place at first in secret and against the law. But as the apostasy progressed, the act emerged from the shadows to become public policy. It was now endorsed from the highest echelons of society and culture and legalized by those in power. America and the West turned to the altars of Baal.

> The murder of the innocent will now be championed as an unquestionable right, a sacred right, even a sacred act—a sacrament.

That any culture could permit the sacrificing of children is hard to fathom. But that such a thing could be considered a sacred act stretches the limits of comprehension. But this is exactly what took place in the ancient apostasy. Could even this facet of the paradigm correspond to the present day?

The priests of Baal were the ones who oversaw and participated in the sacrifice of children. Their modern-day equivalents would be those who oversee the killing of unborn children in abortions. The following is a quote from a woman who literally oversaw the killing of tens of thousands of unborn children, Patricia Waird-Bindle:

> "Abortion is a major blessing, and a *sacrament* in the hands of women..."[1]

The link of abortion to paganism, as in the sacrifices of Baal, Molech, Artemis, and the other bloody deities of the ancient world, is made clear in the words of feminist author Ginette Paris. In her book, amazingly titled *The Sacrament of Abortion*, she writes:

> "It is not immoral to choose abortion; it is simply another kind of morality, a *pagan* one."[2]

She continues:

> "Our culture needs new rituals as well as laws to restore abortion to its *sacred* dimension..."[3]

So what exactly is the sacred dimension that abortion, the killing of one's child, once possessed and must now be restored to? Lest the connection remain in any way ambiguous, Paris spells it out:

> "Abortion is a sacrifice to Artemis. Abortion [is] a sacrament for the gift of life to remain pure."[4]

Paris is not alone. Other proponents of the new morality, radical feminist authors, have spoken of abortion as the sending of the slain child to the mother goddess, connecting abortion to the pagan child sacrifices of ancient times—as on the altars of Baal. And though many advocates of abortion would never use such terminology, they will unwittingly speak of the practice and the right to perform it as sacred.

When Israel's children were sacrificed on the altars of Baal, the nation deafened its ears to their cries. But God did not. The blood of the innocent would lead to the nation's judgment. So in the modern case we have likewise lifted up our children on the altars of our apostasy and have likewise deafened our ears to their cries. But even by the most basic measures of morality the clear and unavoidable truth remains: the killing of an unborn child, the taking of an innocent life, is as wrong and horrific as any human act could be wrong and horrific. And as in ancient times, no amount of words, legislation, or rulings can alter that fact. That we have sanctioned such a thing or have done nothing to stop it is an indictment not only of our present civilization but of each of us who have sanctioned it or done nothing.

For those who have taken part in this act or in any act spoken of in this chapter, the love of God is greater than any sin, and His mercy, stronger than any guilt. All who seek His forgiveness will find it.

But as for a civilization that wars against the ways of God, sanctions evil, and sacrifices millions of its children on the altars of its transgressions, it stands as did the ancient kingdom—it stands on dangerous ground and under the shadow of God's judgment.

The Paradigm of Kings

We have entered the paradigm. We have seen its big picture, its wide-angle and macro view, the overall prophetic template of our times. The stage is set.

We are now about to enter another realm of the ancient mystery, a realm in which lie specific revelations concerning the days in which we live—a realm in which are found specific details, specific people, specific events, and even the times in which specific events had to take place. Though it may seem surreal or impossible, it is all there and has been there for over two and a half thousand years.

Its ramifications will be explosive. We must therefore prepare accordingly before entering.

In order to open up this other realm of the paradigm, it is crucial that we understand what we are now dealing with. When the prophet Jeremiah smashed a clay vessel before the elders of Israel, the smashing was an act of prophetic symbolism foretelling or corresponding with the smashing or destruction of Jerusalem. The prophetic act, the symbol, the model, or the paradigm corresponded to a future event or reality.

But a clay jar is not Jerusalem—but *corresponds* to Jerusalem. The Hebrew patriarch Joseph is seen by Jewish rabbis and Christians as a prophetic prototype of the Messiah. That doesn't mean that the Messiah must then be thrown into a pit and imprisoned in an Egyptian dungeon. Nor does the fact the Passover lamb is a shadow or prototype of the sacrifice of the Messiah mean that the Messiah will have wool. So when we deal with prophetic symbols, types, templates, and paradigms, we are dealing with the correspondence. The template, or paradigm, can never be exactly the same as the reality or event it foreshadows or corresponds with. Nor can every element, detail, or characteristic of a prophetic symbol or type match up with every element and detail of the reality it foretells or represents.

So it is with the paradigm. It could never be that every element, detail, or characteristic of the ancient case would or could manifest or be replayed in the modern case. If it did, it would *be* the ancient case. It is rather that some elements, some details, and some characteristics of the ancient case will manifest in the modern.

To understand the paradigm, one must understand the realm of prophetic signs and symbolism. In the realm of signs two corresponding events may have no natural connection between them. Elements that in the ancient case are intrinsically and naturally bound to each other may each reappear in the modern case with no natural connection between them. And since signs operate in the realm of appearances, an event in the modern case may correspond to an event in the ancient case not because it shares the same nature but because it shares the same outward form or appearance or is joined together in the realm of perception. Further, a single event from the ancient case, a single element of the paradigm, may relate to more than one event or element in the modern case. Conversely, several events or elements of the ancient case may connect or relate to a single event or element in the modern replaying.

———————

There are of course critical differences between the ancient world and the modern. The ancient world was ruled by kings, and their reigns were most often begun and ended by death and sometimes bloodshed. But in the world of modern democracies the reigns of leaders are most often begun and ended by political elections. So the ancient kings of the paradigm will correspond with modern leaders. And the sometimes bloody rise and fall of ancient kings will correspond with the political rise, fall, defeat, and victory of modern leaders. The means will differ, but the ends will remain the same.

As we open up this dimension of the paradigm, the mystery will zero in on specific leaders and players on the modern world stage. Behind each modern leader or player will lie a mystery—an ancient figure, a ruler, a player, a king or queen, from the paradigm. The ancient figure will be the prototype of the modern figure. The modern figure will be the antitype of the ancient figure. Both the ancient and modern figures will serve as signs.

Lastly, the modern leaders are not to be viewed as exact equivalents to the ancient figures. Nor can we presume that the modern figures are operating from the same motives or nature as did their predecessors. That there is a correspondence in role and function does not mean that there must be a correspondence of motive. Undoubtedly the modern players have acted with no concept of the ancient template and/or of the consequences of their decisions and actions in light of the Word and judgment of God. But they are joined to their predecessors inasmuch as they have played a corresponding role and function in relation to the modern apostasy, inasmuch as they have stepped into their predecessor's template.

And we must make sure to never make the mistake of viewing any man or woman as an enemy. We are instructed by the Scriptures to love without condition or distinction and to pray for and even bless those who persecute us. All the more we must love and pray for those who oppose the ways of God. This is the one and only godly response. Anything outside of it is sin. We must, on one hand, strongly stand against any agenda that wars against the will of God and yet, on the other, pray for those who advance and execute such agendas.

The paradigm is ancient. The template cannot change. But people can change. That is the hope. And so the message, warning, and call of the paradigm are to these as much as to anyone. As much as they have stepped into their predecessor's paradigm, we must pray they step out.

So now we begin. We will embark on a journey from Middle Eastern cities to the American capital, from ancient palaces to the White House, of mysterious priests and priestesses, of ruthless kings and queens, of invaders and assassins, of prophets and holy men, of signs, portents, wonders, and harbingers, and to the mystery of our times.

We now open up a realm that will yield revelations both eerie and stunning. We begin with the first of the paradigm's figures, one who in many ways will set everything else in motion. The mystery will involve an ancient monarch and a modern president. We enter the paradigm of the king.

Chapter 4

The KING

THE APOSTASY OF ancient Israel had taken place over generations. It was a long and continuous fall. It would only end in the nation's judgment and destruction. But in between its beginning and its end was a specific period of time when it radically accelerated and deepened. During that time lines would be crossed that had never before been crossed and moral hedges would be broken that had previously been held as sacrosanct.

It was during this period that the culture underwent a dramatic transformation. Up to this time, though many had transgressed God's standards, there was still an understanding that such things were transgressions. In other words, one could break the law, but one realized that one was a lawbreaker. But now all that changed. It was no longer a matter of transgressing standards or breaking the law—now the standards themselves would be overturned.

Before this period the most egregious of pagan practices would be performed in secret. Now they would be performed from the culture's highest grounds, in public temples and royal palaces. Pagan morality now became the nation's governing morality. Immorality now became the nation's code of morality. Transgression became its law. For the first time the morality of the pagan world would completely supplant the biblical morality on which the nation had been founded.

Baal had always been worshipped in secret on society's fringes. But now his cult would become the official religion of the land. For the first time in the nation's history the government would fully ally itself with the Phoenician god. For the first time the practices of his cult would be sponsored by the state. So the government established Baal and his worship and disestablished God and His ways. Everything was turned upside down.

It didn't happen overnight. It was again the intensification and acceleration of a long-term departure. And it didn't happen without a fight. It would involve a war of culture: the new morality against traditional morality and the ways of God, those who sought to overturn the nation's biblical foundation against those who sought to preserve it.

Who was it that initiated these things? Who pioneered them? Who served as the catalyst for this transformation of society? Who was king?

The king was called *Akhav*. We know him as Ahab. He was the son of the military commander Omri who had by force risen to the throne. The biblical chronicle records that Omri did evil in the sight of the Lord, worse than those kings that had preceded him. Ahab was thus raised in the shadow of an ungodly father. It would undoubtedly impact his ways and actions as king.

But the most critical event in Ahab's life was his marriage to a foreign woman. He married the princess of Phoenicia, Israel's neighboring kingdom. The princess had been raised in a pagan culture and was hostile to the worship of God. She served the god of the Phoenicians—Baal.

When she came to Israel and then to its throne, she was determined to resist the faith of her new homeland. More than that she would wage war against it and attempt to wipe it out of existence. Ahab would translate her fury into a political, cultural, and spiritual war against the God of Israel and those who followed Him.

The biblical record presents Ahab as a man divided. Unlike his wife, Ahab came from a culture that had known God. So to embrace and champion the worship of Baal was to go against his heritage and the faith of his ancestors. His wife was pagan. But Ahab was apostate. Perhaps it was because of his upbringing, the influence or lack of influence of his father, together with the pagan influence of his wife, that he succumbed.

Though he battled the God whose name was *Jehovah*, or *Yahweh*, he named his children *Ahaziah*, meaning Jehovah has seized; *Joram*, meaning

Jehovah has exalted; and *Athaliah*, meaning Jehovah has constrained. Even if he named them before waging his war, it speaks of a man in the midst of two conflicting worlds. On one hand, he would fight those who stood for God, even the prophets of the Lord. On the other, he would consult prophets who would counsel him in the name of the Lord. He would commit great evil against God's ways. Yet he would then publicly express sorrow and repentance over his sins and seek the Lord's mercy. Ahab was a complicated man, compromised, fallen—a man divided.

He was divided in other ways as well. On one hand, he appears to have been adept as a commander, tactical, strategic, and calculated in his leading. On the other, he appears as a man of weakness, weakness in his morals and weakness in his will. He could vacillate from one position to the next and one emotion to another in an instant. He was a complicated man, self-contradictory, an enigma. He could show courage on the battlefield one moment and cowardice the next, begin the construction of a city and then act like a child. One Bible commentary sums up Ahab as:

> "…morally weak, and concerned with luxuries of this world. Though he could display real bravery and at times even heeded God's Word, nevertheless he was basically a compromiser as far as the will of God was concerned. The divine estimation of his character stands as a tragic epitaph…"[1]

In many ways Ahab epitomized the nation's fall. He was compromised. So too was the nation. He was divided. So too was the nation. He was apostate. And so too was the nation. He had been born in the midst of its apostasy, but as king he took it to another level. He was the catalyst to accelerate and deepen its progression. He did what no other king of Israel had ever done. He led a spiritual, cultural, and political war against the nation's biblical faith and traditional values. He oversaw the rise of a new pagan morality and presided over its enshrinement.

He was the first king of Israel to actually build a temple to Baal. He would do so in the capital city. It was a sign. Ahab was wholly joining the state to a pagan religion and allying the nation to a new and foreign morality. The apostasy would now be state-sponsored, and the immorality would become the law of the land. Under his rule government would become an instrument to be used against the ways and people of God.

What did all this mean for Israel? It meant that everything Baal represented would now permeate the culture. It would mean the weakening of absolutes and the altering and redefining of values. Thus the king became an agent of a form of moral relativism.

Baal was the Canaanite god of fertility and material prosperity. His worship was sensual and vulgar. So under Ahab's rule the nation's culture would grow increasingly materialistic, sensual, vulgar, profane, and debased. Ahab would become an agent of cultural debasement.

The worship of Baal involved the divorcing of sexuality from marriage and its transfer from the private realm of marriage to the public realm of the temple cult. Thus as Ahab multiplied the shrines of Baal, he became an agent of sexual immorality, and his reign would witness the transfer of sexuality to the public square.

What else was the worship of Baal? Most horrifically it was parents killing their children. So in advocating for Baal, Ahab became an agent for the shedding of innocent blood, the killing of the nation's children. Under his reign the government would endorse the killing of children, and the restraints against their murder would be swept away.

The Paradigm of the King

This next part of the paradigm takes place within a specific period of time with peculiar characteristics.

> The nation's long-term apostasy will enter a period of acceleration and deepening. During this period a pagan and anti-biblical morality will gain ascendancy over the culture's traditional and biblical morality.

Was there any such period of acceleration in the apostasy of American and Western civilization? There was. The long-term apostasy was noticeable from the mid– to late twentieth century onward. The 1980s saw the "Reagan Revolution," a movement that included a call to return to traditional values. But in the quarter century beginning in the early 1990s the departure of American civilization from its biblical Judeo-Christian foundation not only deepened and accelerated but entered into new territory, crossing critical thresholds that had never before been crossed. In that same period of time there would be a statistically massive defection from the faith, specifically of those who had formerly identified as "Christian." Thus the paradigm:

> During this period of deepening apostasy anti-biblical morality will become the governing morality. Thus anti-biblical or pagan values will supplant the biblical moral foundation on which the nation and civilization had been founded.

So beginning in the early 1990s there would be an all-encompassing redefining of values and morality. That which in earlier ages would have been identified as pagan ethics and practices would now become the culture's mainstream practices, its guiding principles, and its ruling ethics. Moral codes that had been foundational to Western civilization for ages would in this period be overturned. Those who remained faithful to the Word and ways of God now found themselves marginalized, denigrated, and in danger of persecution. By the end of this period there was increasing talk of the end of Christian America and the end of the Christian West.

> The transformation will not happen without a fight. There will be a war of culture. The new morality will war against the ways of God, and those who seek to overturn the culture's biblical foundation against those who vie to protect it—a *culture war.*

So it happened that in America and the West a phrase that had held various meanings in history was now specifically applied to this conflict of traditional, or biblical, values and the values that sought to supplant them. The phrase was *culture war.* When was the phrase applied to this specific conflict? It happened in the early 1990s, the exact beginning of this specific period.[2]

The period of deepening apostasy contained in the paradigm concerns the days of King Ahab and his house. This leads to the unavoidable question. If these are the times of Ahab, then where is the Ahab of the times?

We must now keep in mind the keys and principles given in the previous chapter. We must also keep in mind that unlike the ancient case, modern leaders are elected by the people, do not wield absolute authority, and do not reign indefinitely. Therefore we cannot lay the blame for a nation's apostasy on any single leader. Ultimately the people must themselves bear the responsibility for their course.

Nevertheless leaders are responsible for leading, and their actions carry great weight for good or evil. Keeping all that in mind, we must now ask the question "Does the Ahab of the paradigm or the paradigm of Ahab have a parallel in the modern world? Is there a King Ahab of American and Western civilization, an antitype to the ancient king? And if so, who?" We will refer to this part of the paradigm as "the king."

> The king will reign over a culture in the midst of a long-term apostasy. But he will preside over the beginning of a specific era in which the apostasy will greatly deepen and accelerate.

It was American and Western culture that was in the midst of a long-term apostasy. Who was presiding over it? For most of the twentieth century onward there can only be one answer—the president of the United States, the modern-day equivalent to the king of ancient Israel. The period of accelerating apostasy begins in the early 1990s. Who came to power at that time? There is only one candidate: Bill Clinton. He will preside as "king," or ruler, over the start of this period, the era of deepening apostasy.

> The king will stand at the forefront of a culture war that will mark the years of his reign.

It is not only the timing of his presidency that matches the template but its nature. Bill Clinton's presidential career was joined to the culture war from its outset. The term *culture war* in its modern application was coined in 1991.[3] Clinton's campaign for the presidency was announced the same year. In fact, the two events, the beginning of the modern application of the term and the beginning of Clinton's presidential campaign, took place within two months of each other.

In the paradigm Ahab not only stands at the forefront of the culture war dividing his nation but clearly on one side of it—the side of the new morality, the side that acts against traditional and biblical morality. So too there was no question as to which side of the culture war Clinton stood on. He stood on the side of change and specifically for the overturning of traditional and biblical morality.

As with Ahab, Clinton would be linked to a culture war throughout his days in power. In fact, in the most famous speech ever given concerning the culture war, the focus was specifically on Bill Clinton and the agenda he intended to execute in America.[4]

Does the paradigm reveal anything about the man himself?

> The king will be a divided man. On one hand, he will come from a culture founded on faith in God. On the other, he will embrace and champion a culture and an ethos that wars against the God of his heritage. He will oppose those who stand for God and against his agenda. Yet at times he will seek godly counsel. He will war and sin against the ways of God yet will publicly express sorrow and repentance. He will be a man in conflict, compromised, complicated, and divided.

So too the picture we have of Bill Clinton is that of a complicated man and a man divided. He was raised as a Southern Baptist and growing up regularly attended church and Sunday school.[5] Though Clinton was raised with a biblical foundation, he would embrace an ethos and morality that warred against biblical morality. As was his prototype, King Ahab, Clinton was a man divided. As for those who opposed his agenda on biblical grounds, he would lash out at them. And yet he would at times seek godly counsel—as did his ancient prototype. He would sin against the ways of God and then express repentance and sorrow—just as did Ahab.

The paradigm of Ahab reveals yet other divisions:

> He will be a tactical, calculated, and strategic leader. At the same time, he will appear to be a man of weaknesses—moral weakness and weakness of will. He will be a man of profound contradictions—an enigma.

So too Bill Clinton was a man of not one but many divisions. He was, on one hand, a talented politician, a tactical, strategic, and calculated leader. On the other, he was a man of moral weakness and weakness of will. It was these weaknesses that would haunt him throughout his career. He would remain a man of profound contradictions throughout his time in power— as did King Ahab.

> The king will in many ways epitomize the apostasy of his nation.

As Ahab epitomized Israel's apostasy, Bill Clinton epitomized the American apostasy. His divided nature with regard to God and morality would embody America's spiritually divided and morally compromised condition.

> The king will advocate for the altering of morality. He will become an agent for moral relativism, the weakening of absolutes, and the redefining of values.

As was the age of Ahab, the presidency and age of Bill Clinton would likewise be characterized by the altering of standards—from moral ambiguity to governance by polls to the redefining of morality and truth and the meaning of words. The president would serve as an agent for moral relativism, the weakening of absolutes, and the redefining of values.

> Under the king the nation's culture will grow increasingly profane, vulgar, and debased.

As in the days of Ahab, so too in the days of Bill Clinton, American culture grew increasingly profane, debased. Most prominent in this debasing were the scandals that took place in the White House itself. The eyes and ears of the nation were continually fixed on the profane. The king's reign furthered the vulgarization of the nation's culture.

> He will become an agent for the divorcing of sexuality from marriage and its transference from the private realm of marriage to the public realm of national culture. He will thus become an agent of sexual immorality.

Bill Clinton would become the first president in American history to be exposed while in office for committing adultery in the White House. It seemed to many that his presidency had a corrosive effect on culture by legitimizing sexual sin. The scandal took sexual sin out of the private realm and placed it on the most public platform of display conceivable. The president became an agent for sexual immorality.

Above and beyond all of Ahab's other sins and his complicity in his nation's apostasy was the bloodshed that marked his agenda. By spreading the cult of Baal, Ahab was facilitating the killing of children and thus became an agent of murder.

> The king and the king's government will support and champion the practice of child killing.

As it was with King Ahab, President Clinton was especially connected to the blood of the innocent. It was this above all the rest that exposed the darkness of his agenda. Under his presidency the government supported and championed the killing of the unborn. As it was in the reign of King Ahab, it was in Clinton's time in office that the state now became an active agent in the nation's apostasy.

> The king will cause the restraints against the practice of child killing to be swept away.

So in the very first days of his presidency, in a celebratory ceremony in the Oval Office, Clinton signed a series of executive orders wiping away the protections that had been put into place by former leaders in an attempt to protect the unborn. Clinton's first executive orders as president empowered the practice of abortion in America and around the world. That these things were at the center of the new president's agenda was evidenced by the speed at which it was accomplished:

"Now Ahab the son of Omri did evil in the sight of the LORD, more than all who were before him."[6]

The biblical account presents Ahab as a pioneer in the darkest sense of the word. He breaks new ground. He does what no king of Israel had done before.

> The king's reign will be historic in that he will be the first ruler in his nation's history to fully champion the practice involving the putting to death of children. He will employ the apparatus of state to advance this practice.

So Clinton became the first president in American history to publicly champion and advocate for the killing of the unborn. Despite what he said publicly on making abortion rare, his actions regarding the practice were clear and starkly consistent. Not only was he the first American president to sweep away the protections that had been put in place regarding the unborn, but he was the first as well to seek to expand the practice in other nations. He would be the first as well to use American tax dollars to pressure other nations to engage in the practice and the first to open up America to drugs that would by chemical means kill the unborn child. As with Ahab, the president seemed almost obsessed with championing the act that had taken the lives of millions of the nation's children.

Both Ahab and Clinton were catalysts of national apostasy. Both would operate as agents of societal change. Both would be pioneers. Both would go where none of their predecessors had gone before. Each would lead his nation away from biblical morality. The reign of each would accelerate the debasing and vulgarization of culture, the weakening of absolutes, the divorcing of sexuality from marriage, the infusing of sexuality into the public square, and the promoting of immorality. Each would be involved in a campaign that held the killing of children as sacrosanct. Each would cause an anti-biblical morality to become for the first time in history the nation's governing ethos. And as much as they were able to use it, the government would in their reign become an instrument to advance that morality and to weaken or overturn biblical values. The machinery of state would now be employed to further the apostasy.

Even though there would be reversals of their actions in subsequent years, they had broken the ground and had breached moral parameters that had never before been breached. And because of these breaches the repercussions would be far-reaching, not only into the future but into other lands.

Each had opened the door.

But neither of the two acted alone. In each case there was another. And the other is the next mystery of the paradigm: the queen.

Chapter 5

The QUEEN

S HE WAS A stranger to the land and faith of Israel. She was a Canaanite woman, born of Ithobaal the first, or *Ethbaal* in the biblical account, high priest of the Canaanite goddess Astarte. Ancient history records that Ithobaal murdered the Phoenician king Phelles and became king in his place. So his daughter became a Phoenician princess. He gave her the name Izevel. We know her as Jezebel.

Jezebel would have known little of the God of Israel. As the daughter of the high priest of Astarte and then the Phoenician king she was raised in the center of pagan culture, steeped in its tenets, its worship, its practices, and its morality. In her eyes the faith of Israel with its focus on an invisible God with no connection to any idol would have appeared entirely foreign.

Yet Jezebel would be given in marriage to Israel's king, or to the prince who would become Israel's king—Ahab. Undoubtedly it was a political marriage. Ahab's father, Omri, would seek to strengthen Israel's security by forming strategic alliances with the surrounding kingdoms. One of those kingdoms was Phoenicia. The marriage of his son Ahab to the daughter of

King Ithobaal of Phoenicia would have seemed a masterstroke of foreign policy and diplomacy. It would cement the political, military, and economic alliance between the two nations.

But instead of strengthening Israel, it would corrupt it, divide it, and send it into a violent cultural upheaval that would threaten its very existence. Jezebel left her native land of Phoenicia to live in a kingdom she would have found entirely alien. As a princess she would have been accustomed from a young age to the trappings of royalty. Undoubtedly she possessed a strong sense of entitlement to privilege and power. That she would find in her new land. But what she wouldn't find was the culture and religion she had known in her homeland.

Phoenicia was one of the great commercial and trading empires of ancient times. Its culture centered on the coastlands, the seaports. It was thus brought into contact with a wide variety of peoples and kingdoms. Thus Jezebel grew up in a cosmopolitan culture and would have undoubtedly held a decidedly cosmopolitan outlook. Beyond that she represented the elite of that culture. Yet she would leave all that behind to go to the land of Israel to marry Ahab.

Israel's culture, on the other hand, was founded on holiness and thus on separation from the ways of the nations. To Jezebel it would have appeared unbearably conservative, backward, and insular. Undoubtedly she held it in contempt and looked down on her new subjects.

But her conflict with her new land would be much more specific than that. The thrust of her contempt was reserved for Israel's faith. The Phoenicians worshipped a pantheon of gods and a multitude of idols. The faith of Israel declared that there was only one true God and that the gods of the pagan world were false. The gods of Phoenicia could be seen and touched. Their worship was sensual. But the God of Israel could neither be seen nor touched, and His worship was based not on the sensual or the sensory but on faith. Phoenician religion involved temple prostitution and the sacrifice of children. The Scriptures of Israel declared such things to be immoral, the abominations of the pagan world. And Jezebel would undoubtedly judge the faith of Israel as restrictive, narrow-minded, religiously conservative, parochial, exclusive, and intolerant.

To make matters worse, Phoenician monarchs wielded near absolute power. They could do as they wished. But in Israel, even in its fallen state, no one but God had absolute power and no king was above His authority. To Jezebel such a situation would have presented an unbearable conflict. In Phoenicia the line between the throne and the temple, the monarchy and the priesthood, was ambiguous, if not nonexistent. The king and queen could, and often did, serve as priest and priestess. The royal family would likely be a priestly family, the keepers of the cult of the gods. And since Jezebel was the daughter of a pagan high priest, she would have been profoundly entrenched in the cult and worship of the Phoenician gods. So Jezebel came to the throne of Israel not just as queen but as priestess, the representative of pagan gods.

It was an explosion waiting to happen. Jezebel refused to adapt to the ways of her new nation. She would fully maintain her old and pagan identity. Instead of seeking to change her ways to that of her new kingdom, she would seek to change the kingdom to adapt to her ways. So the kingdom of Israel now had as queen a pagan priestess. And she came with an agenda, a mission. She would be an activist queen, an agent for societal and cultural change.

To those of Israel who were faithful to the Lord and His ways and to those who simply were in favor of the "traditional values" that had long guided their lives, Jezebel would pose a dangerous threat. From the beginning there would be suspicion surrounding her intentions and her agenda. Though she sat on the throne as Israel's queen, she was an outsider. It was not so much because of her origins. There had been others who had come to Israel from pagan lands. But they had joined themselves to the nation and had embraced its faith and calling. But Jezebel never did. She represented values that would war against the biblical and traditional values at the nation's core. Her championing of the "new morality" of paganism would divide the culture. We don't know when Ahab and Jezebel first acted on their plans to wipe out biblical faith and values, but in view of the queen's background and nature it would not have been hard to have to surmise such an agenda from the start.

She would attempt to change Israel into the image of Phoenicia. She would import from her homeland hundreds of pagan priests to begin the transformation. Her goal was to eradicate Israel's faith and replace it with the cult and worship of the Phoenician gods.

And what were those gods? The foremost among them we have already met—Baal, lord of the Phoenician pantheon. Jezebel would become his emissary to her new land. Thus she would become the apostle of the new morality that came with him.

We cannot assume that she was insincere. She undoubtedly believed herself to be an agent of enlightenment, bringing to Israel a form of liberalism, the cosmopolitan open-mindedness of the new morality. There would be many gods, not just one, and not just one truth but many. One could make one's own idols and forge one's own versions of the gods and create one's own truth. Rather it was the idea that truth was absolute or that it could be contained in the revelation of a single faith that she found abhorrent.

But as time went on, the open-minded tolerance of the new morality would reveal itself as more intolerant than anything it opposed. Those who remained faithful to God would find themselves on the receiving end of its fury. At the center of that fury was the Phoenician monarch. She was its raging fire. She would declare all-out war against the conservative stands and practices of biblical faith. She would vow to overturn the deep-seated religious beliefs that still existed among many of its people.

Her views regarding men and women and her ambitions for political power would also strike most of her new subjects as radical. In Phoenicia it was customary for a royal woman to officiate as priestess of the goddesses. It is not unlikely that Jezebel herself, as princess and daughter of the high priest, had been officially installed as priestess. In Canaanite worship, as we have seen, the distinctions of gender were often confused and nullified. In Phoenician society a woman of royal or priestly class could take on roles that in other societies were fulfilled by men. In this they could wield much power. Jezebel would apply this to Israel's throne.

She would not only maneuver and battle on behalf of her husband's authority; she would maneuver and battle to obtain her own. Israel had never seen anything like it—a queen hungry for political power. Jezebel not only influenced her husband but at times appeared to dominate him. She did that which the people of Israel might have expected of a tyrannical king but not of his wife. She waged war against those who had offended her or whom she deemed a threat to her authority—as in the prophets of God who stood against her agenda.

As Baal's emissary she would have been a zealous proponent for the most chilling and distinctive rite of his worship—the sacrificing of children on his altars. Thus Jezebel would have been Israel's chief advocate and ambassador of child sacrifice. For those who remained faithful to the ways of God, it was Jezebel's impact in this realm of Israel's culture that had to have been the most horrifying. The ultimate effect of her rule and advocacy was that multitudes of Israel's children would be killed. As a member of the priestly family she would champion the practice as a sacred right and sacrament.

Jezebel would never be fully trusted by her subjects. Her motives and ambitions would always be suspect. To the faithful and those attuned to the signs of the times, the rise of Ahab and Jezebel portended disaster. It would set the culture at war against itself and, much more ominously, against God.

The Paradigm of the Queen

We must now open the paradigm of Jezebel. The name *Jezebel* has become so loaded with associations, connotations, baggage, and emotions that it becomes a challenge to deal with it objectively. But with regard to the template we are not presuming any evil motive or character of any modern figure. We are dealing with something much more profound: Jezebel's role in the nation's apostasy from God, her agenda and war against biblical and traditional values, and her championing of a most horrific act, that which would ultimately lead to the nation's destruction.

We must here ask the inevitable question: If there is a modern parallel to Israel's ancient king, an Ahab of the modern apostasy, then who is his counterpart? Who in our time has played a parallel role in the modern apostasy? Who has walked in the footsteps of her paradigm?

There is no choice in the matter. If the modern equivalent to the king is the president, then the modern equivalent to the queen must be the president's wife. If Bill Clinton is the Ahab of the modern apostasy, then Hillary Clinton must be the Jezebel of the same template. We will refer to this part of the paradigm as "the queen" or "first lady," both of the roles occupied by Jezebel.

> The princess and future queen will come to the throne from the elite of a cosmopolitan culture. She will leave that cosmopolitan culture to marry the future king. She will travel to a land, the culture of which will appear to her as conservative if not backward and insular. She will embody to that land cosmopolitan values and a new morality.

Jezebel left the cosmopolitan world of her homeland to join her husband in a decidedly anti-cosmopolitan culture. Unlike Bill Clinton, Hillary Rodham was born in a cosmopolitan city, Chicago. When she considered marrying Bill Clinton, she was working on the East Coast and was deemed to have a bright future in the Democratic Party. She left a cosmopolitan culture and moved to Arkansas, where she would marry Bill Clinton.

As was the Phoenician princess in Ahab's Israel, so was Hillary in Bill Clinton's Arkansas. Hillary Clinton was now the first lady of the state. As did Jezebel, she would represent cosmopolitan values in a conservative land.

We know that Jezebel held the culture of her adopted land in contempt. Whatever her personal views regarding her adopted land, many in the state distrusted her and saw her as holding values foreign to their culture and as concealing her own personal agenda. Such perceptions were part of the reason Bill Clinton was defeated after one term as governor of Arkansas.[1]

Of course America is bigger than Arkansas. But these perceptions have followed Hillary Clinton throughout her career and onto the national stage from governor's wife to first lady, senator, and presidential candidate.

> The new first lady will fully hold to her former and native identity and ways despite her marriage to the king.

In the paradigm the transplanted Phoenician princess tenaciously clings to her pre-Israelite identity. So after marrying Bill Clinton, Hillary Rodham, as first lady of Arkansas, refused to take his last name. She even refused to do so during his first term as governor of Arkansas. Only after he was defeated in his bid for reelection as governor did she take the name *Clinton* as her own. But the issue persisted and resurfaced in what later seemed to be Hillary Clinton's aversion to accepting the standard functions of first lady and what many believed to be her disparagement of the role of wife.[2]

> The union of the king and queen will be a political marriage, one that will function as an instrument for political purposes.

Historians are agreed that the union of Ahab and Jezebel was a political marriage, undoubtedly arranged by their fathers to strengthen the alliance of Israel and Phoenicia. Certainly the union of Bill and Hillary Clinton was not an arranged political marriage, nor are we to presume that it lacked the emotions we would expect to be present in any healthy marriage. But there always appeared to be political factors in the mix. As far back as the early 1970s, before their marriage, Hillary Clinton was telling others that one day Bill Clinton would become president of the United States.[3] Political purposes and considerations never seemed far from the relationship. Their union would ultimately become the most prominent political marriage of their age. More than any other union in the modern world the marriage of Bill and Hillary Clinton was seen, as was the union of Ahab and Jezebel, as a vessel for a political agenda.

> The queen's conflict or contempt will be focused on the conservative values of her land and particularly on the religious conservative values that stand in the way of her agenda. She will view them as restrictive and adversarial.

So Hillary Clinton's story has followed the paradigm of the ancient queen. She has continually come into conflict with the conservative and particularly religious conservative values held throughout America. These have continually stood in the way of her agenda. Her views on such values as expressed in her actions have indicated contempt.

> The first lady and queen will seek to change the nation to adapt to her ways and values. She will come to her position with an agenda, a mission. She will be an activist, an agent for societal and cultural change.

As was Jezebel, Hillary Clinton was never only a first lady or a politician. She was an activist. She had a mission and an agenda. She would seek to change American society and culture and when she could, society and culture throughout the world.

> The queen will see herself as an agent of enlightenment, bringing the liberalism of a new morality to her nation. She will wage war against traditional and biblical values and seek to overturn the deep-seated religious beliefs that still exist among many of its people.

As with Jezebel, Hillary Clinton would wage a war she believed was one of enlightenment. She would stand at the forefront of the culture wars, promoting the new morality against the traditional morality and biblical values that much of America held to. She would seek to overturn them.

> The queen's view regarding men and women and her
> own ambitions for political power will strike many as
> radical. She will constitute a new phenomenon. She
> will appear to be a queen hungry for her own political
> power. She will at times appear to dominate her hus-
> band and others. She will exude ambition for power.
> In both her views and actions she will serve as a cul-
> tural agent ultimately working against the traditional
> or natural distinctions of gender.

In modern times Jezebel has been embraced by some as an icon of feminism. So too feminism has always been a major part of Hillary Clinton's
ethos and agenda. As with Jezebel she was an unprecedented phenomenon—
a first lady seen as craving political power. In her views and ambitions she
would be a cultural agent working against the traditional distinctions of
gender.

King Ahab would campaign for societal change, but that campaign was first
and foremost Jezebel's cause. Ahab would convert that agenda into national
policy. But it was first and foremost *her* agenda. Ahab would campaign for
societal change. But Jezebel would embody it. Ahab would advance the new
morality. But Jezebel would personify it.

> Though the king will carry it out, the agenda will
> first and foremost belong to the queen. The king will
> call for societal change, but the queen will epitomize
> and embody it.

The fulfillment of this part of the paradigm is revealed in Hillary Clinton's own words:

"While Bill talked about social change, I embodied it."[4]

In the paradigm of Jezebel the queen is especially linked to the killing of
children on the altars of Baal.

> The queen will become the nation's chief advocate
> and ambassador for the practice in which parents
> offer up their children. She will hold, defend, and
> champion the act as a sacred right and a sacrament.

According to the paradigm of Jezebel, Hillary Clinton has likewise been especially linked to the act of killing children in abortion. If there is one thing she has consistently advocated for and battled over, it is this one specific act. In the paradigm of Jezebel it is above all the queen who in the nation's apostasy functions as the chief advocate for the killing of children. Accordingly, in the American apostasy, it is her antitype, Hillary Clinton, who has functioned as the nation's chief advocate for the killing of the unborn. As in the case of ancient Baal worship she has championed the practice as a sacred right, with the unchallengeable status of a sacrament.

> The queen will never be fully trusted by most of her subjects. Her motives and ambitions will always be suspect. And for those who remain faithful to the ways of God, the queen's impact on the nation will be seen as a dangerous one, not only in intensifying the war that divides its culture but in setting the nation at war with God.

One Bible commentary characterizes Jezebel as a mix of:

"suspect political authority and religious antipathy."[5]

As with her ancient counterpart, Hillary Clinton would never be fully trusted even by many of those who agreed with her agenda. In the eyes of many Americans, if not most, her motives and ambitions would always remain suspect. As with Jezebel, she was viewed as a polarizing figure.

In her war of culture Jezebel either had no idea or never took seriously the danger of her enterprise until it was too late. She was ultimately warring against the living God. So in the modern case those who have waged such a war either have had no idea or have never taken seriously the danger of doing so. But for those who knew the ways of God, the implications were ominous.

The ancient mystery has revealed the first two players. What now happens when the two come together on the nation's throne? The next facet of the paradigm will reveal it.

Chapter 6

KING and QUEEN

THE REIGN OF Ahab was unlike any that had preceded it. Not only was it driven by a radical agenda to transform the nation's culture, but for the first time it involved two regents.

Jezebel broke the norms and standards concerning an Israelite queen. She would not be content to be known as the king's wife or to play a supporting or complementary role. She would be a co-regent in her own right. So now Israel had two monarchs, each committed to waging war against the ways of God.

> "Now therefore, send and gather all Israel to me on Mount Carmel, the four hundred and fifty prophets of Baal, and the four hundred prophets of Asherah, who eat at Jezebel's table."[1]

Ahab and Jezebel were maintaining hundreds of pagan priests on the royal payroll. Where did they come from? Undoubtedly Jezebel had imported them from her homeland. They were key agents in her program of cultural transformation.

But the passage reveals something else. They "eat at Jezebel's table." Jezebel had established her own court. She had her own attendants, her own working staff, and her own base of power. The magnitude of the numbers could help explain how Jezebel could wield such power and influence over Ahab. She had established herself as a monarch in her own right in her husband's palace.

As for the dynamics of the two, unlike Ahab, who appears often conflicted and changeable, Jezebel comes off as iron-willed, harsh, implacable, tenacious, given to fury, and especially consumed with ambition—the harder of the two.

> "But there was no one like Ahab who sold himself to do wickedness in the sight of the LORD, because Jezebel his wife stirred him up."[2]

The passage makes it clear that it was Jezebel who influenced Ahab to depart from the Lord and lead the nation to do likewise. The Hebrew word translated as "stirred him" can also mean to entice, to persuade, to move, to prod, and to incite. And the picture we have of Jezebel throughout the account is exactly that, a woman continually influencing, inciting, persuading, enticing, and moving her husband into her agenda, into the worship and the advocacy of foreign gods. It was Jezebel who caused Ahab to build Baal a temple in the capital city. It was Jezebel who influenced Ahab to wage war against biblical faith and morality. And it was Jezebel who prevailed upon Ahab to be the first king in Israel to champion a religious system that included the practice of sacrificing children.

Jezebel would become the power behind the throne. She would use her husband's office to accomplish her program of societal change. She would rule through him and at times apart from him. Only Jezebel's incitement could explain how Ahab crossed the boundaries that no king of Israel had ever before crossed and championed the pagan practices that his own people would find, at least at first, shocking and abhorrent.

The Paradigm of the King and Queen

We now open up the paradigm of the two co-regents:

> The reign of the king and queen will be unlike any other the nation has ever before witnessed. The queen will not be content to be known as the king's wife or to play a traditional supporting role. She will be the nearest thing to a co-regent. Their reign will constitute the first time a king and queen represent a co-regency.

As with the reign of Ahab and Jezebel, the age of the Clintons was unlike any other America had ever seen. Hillary Clinton would not be content to be known as Bill Clinton's wife or to play a traditional supporting role. She would co-lead the country with her husband. Indeed, while campaigning for the presidency, Bill Clinton told the voters they would be getting two for the price of one.[3]

Hillary Clinton would break all precedents. She would be given the most powerful official position ever given to any first lady in any administration. She would work out of an office in the West Wing of the White House and would exercise unprecedented authority in major matters of national policy. As did Jezebel in the palace of Ahab, Hillary Clinton maintained her own people, her own staff, and her own power base. The area in which her staff worked was even given its own name: "Hillaryland."[4] From there she would work on her agenda for America. As the reign of Ahab and Jezebel was a co-regency, so the reign of Bill and Hillary Clinton was a co-presidency and was labeled as such at the time.

How much influence did she have over the president? The paradigm of Ahab and Jezebel says this:

> The first lady will influence, stir up, prod, incite, influence, persuade, and guide the king toward her agenda, an agenda that will stand in opposition to the ways of God.

As Jezebel guided Ahab's decisions, so the same dynamic had been observed in Bill Clinton's presidency. She had been called "the power behind the throne."[5] Those closest to the two reported that there was never a major decision made without her, and rarely, if ever, did they witness the president overruling her. And when there was a difference between them, rarely, if ever, did they see him prevail.[6] As with Ahab and Jezebel, the impact of this dynamic with regard to America cannot be overstated.

> The queen will influence the king to champion the practice of child sacrifice.

In the paradigm Jezebel moves Ahab to the worship of Baal and thus to champion child sacrifice. When Bill Clinton was considering signing executive orders that would strip away the safeguards preventing the advance of abortion around the world, he was advised against doing it. But Hillary Clinton had prodded him to go through with it anyway.[7] It was her plan to do it to send a signal to America and the world that the Clinton era had begun.

> The queen will seek to compel the people of the land to support the new morality and to take part in the practice of killing children.

Hillary Clinton's first and foremost project as first lady was to nationalize America's health care. The plan, known as "Hillarycare," would ultimately go down in flames.[8] Most people had no idea what it actually entailed, namely the establishment of abortion as a right to be funded ultimately by the American taxpayer. It would represent the compelling of the American people to take part in the sacrifice of children.

In the cult of Baal children were sacrificed to obtain increase and prosperity from the deity:

> The king and queen will be linked to the sacrifice of children for the purpose of obtaining material benefits from their deaths.

On June 10, 1993, Bill Clinton struck down the ban against using tissue from the bodies of unborn children for the purpose of experimentation.[9] In this too Clinton, like Ahab, was a pioneer. He was the first president in American history to authorize such practices. As in the worship of Baal, the culture would seek to obtain blessing and benefits from the death of children.

> The king and queen will champion the most horrific forms of child killing.

It is hard to fathom how Ahab and Jezebel, or for that matter anyone, could champion the killing of children in the most gruesome of ways on the altars of Baal. And yet in modern times we have perfected equally horrific forms of killing children. One of them was labeled "partial-birth abortion." It involved the partial delivery of a baby, where much of the baby's body is outside the mother's womb. The abortionist then kills the baby in a procedure that typically involves the sucking out of his brain and the collapsing of his skull.[10]

In the mid-1990s both houses of Congress banned the gruesome procedure. But after Congress passed the ban, Clinton overturned it with his veto. Congress would pass another ban. Clinton would veto that ban as well. Clinton was again the first president in American history to veto the banning of so gruesome an act. In this too he followed the paradigm of his ancient predecessor, Ahab.

When Ahab and Jezebel championed the cult of Baal, they were endorsing sexual immorality as exemplified by the practices of the male and female temple prostitutes of Canaanite worship.

> The king and queen will endorse a new value system that will embrace sexual immorality and the confusion of gender.

Bill Clinton was a pioneer in another realm. He would become the first president in American history to normalize and endorse the practice of homosexuality. Thus he was the leader who opened the door for the complete overturning of the values that had undergirded Western civilization since ancient times. He would ultimately clear the way for the overthrowing of biblical morality.

To transform Israel's culture, Ahab and Jezebel had to wage war against the eternal precepts and immutable ideals that had guided the nation since its inception. They would do this by redefining what had previously been known as sin. It was now to be held as sacred. This too was the war waged in the days of the Clintons. If there was any doubt, Bill Clinton made it brazenly clear when he became the first president to address an event dedicated to gay activism. He announced:

> "We are redefining in practical terms the immutable ideals that have guided us from the beginning."[11]

Clinton was speaking about nothing less than the overturning of thousands of years of Judeo-Christian civilization.

But Ahab and Jezebel went further. They were not content to normalize the rites of Baal and what God's Word had deemed to be sexual immorality. They would give it official sanction and seek to compel the people to celebrate it:

> The king and queen will give official sanction to that which the Word of God deemed immoral. They will then seek to compel the people to take part in its celebration.

Bill Clinton thus became the first president in American history to dedicate an entire month to the celebration of homosexuality. He issued a proclamation calling for all Americans to honor gay pride with ceremonies and activities of celebration.[12]

The ancient template reveals the public acts and agendas of the co-regency. But does it also contain a more personal revelation, a revelation concerning the two personalities and dispositions of the two regents? The case of Ahab and Jezebel produces this template:

> The queen's personality will appear much harsher than that of her husband. She will strike many as iron-willed, unyielding, and embittered. She will be the one more apt to react to their opponents with fury. And to many she will appear consumed with ambition for power.

The contrast between Ahab and Jezebel provides the paradigm for Bill and Hillary Clinton. Of the two it was she who appeared to most as the harder, the more iron-willed, the more unyielding, and the more given to fury. To many in her nation she seemed especially consumed with ambition for power.

There has long been an association in the public's mind between the Clintons and the Shakespearean tragedy *Macbeth*. The play, a cautionary tale on the blinding ambition for power, charts the rise and fall of Macbeth and his wife, Lady Macbeth. It has been the association of Hillary Clinton with Lady Macbeth that has proved especially potent in the public's perception.[13] What makes the association all the more striking is the fact that

Lady Macbeth has herself been long associated with another figure—the queen of the paradigm—Jezebel.

Jezebel herself has been called "the Lady Macbeth of Hebrew history."[14] One commentator writes, "Lady Macbeth is unequivocally tied to Jezebel, and their respective stories illustrate a combined warning to those who abuse God-given power."[15] The connection between Jezebel and Lady Macbeth is so strong that it even appears in Bible commentaries:

> "The marriage of Ahab with Jezebel was evidently the fatal turning-point in the life of a man physically brave, and possibly able as a ruler, but morally weak, impressible in turn both by good and by evil. The history shows again and again the contrast of character (which it is obvious to compare with the contrast between Shakespeare's Macbeth and Lady Macbeth), and the almost complete supremacy of the strong relentless nature of Jezebel."[16]

This is not to judge the association of the American first lady and the Shakespearean character as accurate, but the mere fact that in the public's mind the first lady was associated with an updated version of one particular ancient queen—Jezebel, the queen of the paradigm—is stunning. That such an association has been made without any awareness of the paradigm or any of the other connections is even more stunning.

What we are now about to see is an ancient mystery behind an event that transpired in the highest of places. The story surfaced for a moment in the media. But behind the story lay ancient connections and an ancient mystery. Those connections and that mystery are revealed by the paradigm. We will now uncover them as we open up the mystery of the goddess.

Chapter 7

The GODDESS

WHOM DID JEZEBEL worship? She worshipped Baal. Baal was the king of the Phoenician gods. Thus in Phoenician religion there were other gods to be worshipped. Foremost among them was the goddess Astarte, or Ashtart, wife of Baal. The Hebrews called her Ashtoreth, a name that communicated shame. If Baal was the supreme male god of the Phoenician pantheon, Astarte, or Ashtoreth, was the supreme goddess.

Jezebel had a special connection to this particular deity. Astarte was the goddess of whom Jezebel's father was high priest. So Jezebel would have grown up especially entrenched in the worship of this particular deity. Aside from bringing Baal to Israel, Jezebel would have undoubtedly also brought Astarte.

Who was Astarte? As Baal was Phoenicia's fertility god, Astarte was its fertility goddess. She was, on one hand, seductive, the goddess of sexuality and erotic passion, but on the other, the fierce goddess of war and destruction. In Arabic she was known as *Athtar*. In Babylon and Assyria she was called *Ishtar*. Later the Greeks would adopt her as *Aphrodite*, and the Romans, as *Venus*.

Not only would Jezebel, by virtue of her past, be especially bonded to Astarte, but she would even bear a resemblance to the deity. Astarte was queen. So too was Jezebel. Astarte was fierce. So too was Jezebel. Astarte waged war. So too did Jezebel. Astarte brought destruction. So too would Jezebel. The connection gives us revelation into Jezebel. Jezebel would have grown up worshipping the female principle and female power. And this particular female deity took on traditionally masculine functions. Thus Jezebel would grow up worshipping female power as applied to traditionally male roles and functions. Jezebel's life would be a manifestation of the deity she worshipped. She would strive for power and strive to take up traditionally masculine roles. And as with her goddess, she would be a destroyer.

The account in 1 Kings 18 speaks of four hundred prophets of Asherah whom Jezebel kept in her royal court. The word *Asherah* can refer to a Phoenician goddess closely linked to Astarte. The two were sister goddesses. And the two were often interchangeable. Further, the word *asherah* can refer to the groves where both goddesses were worshipped. *Asherah* can also refer to the idols that represented Astarte. And in the Septuagint, the ancient Greek translation of the Hebrew Bible, the word *asherah* is twice translated as Astarte.

When Jezebel brought the priests of Phoenicia to the royal court, she was continuing in what she had known and done from childhood. She was venerating the female principle. She was worshipping the goddess.

What do we know of that worship? We know it involved sexual licentiousness. It appears that Astarte was also known by the name *Kedashah*, the same word that refers to a temple prostitute.

What else would have been associated with the cult of the goddess? The killing of children. Astarte was the wife of Baal, and her worship was the female side of Baal worship. Thus throughout Scripture the two are mentioned together.

Further on in the Bible's account of Jezebel we are given another glimpse into the queen's religion. The Hebrew word *keshaf* is used to describe it. *Keshaf* can be translated as to whisper a spell, to enchant, to practice sorcery, witchcraft. By looking at what the Scriptures record of King Manasseh of Judah, who followed in the religious practices of Ahab, we are given even more insight into Jezebel's religion. The following passage gives us more detail:

One of the practices associated with pagan religion and undoubtedly with Jezebel's faith was the conjuring up of familiar spirits, the ministry of conjurers:

> The queen will bring into the palace those who practice talking to familiar spirits, the spirits of the dead.

Hillary Clinton's meetings with new age ministers in the White House were not just meetings—they were sessions. During these sessions the first lady would go into something of an altered state of consciousness. She would then speak as the departed. One of the departed given voice by the first lady was Eleanor Roosevelt.[5]

When the story leaked to the press that Hillary Clinton was holding séances in the White House, there was an immediate campaign of damage control. It was claimed that what took place during these sessions was simply a form of brainstorming[6]—only it wasn't.

Brainstorming is defined as holding a spontaneous group discussion to produce new ideas or answers. But Houston herself describes the practice she regularly promulgated in a book she released during that same period when she was conducting sessions with Hillary Clinton in the White House. She speaks of channeling the dead. On one hand, she would mention the dead as living in the subconscious of the living. On the other hand, she would write of the dead as having an objective reality. According to Houston, the one who contacts the dead:

> "...*feeds their spirits*....In turn *they invest* your dreams with numinous power."[7]

The practice of communing with the dead was a common feature of pagan religion, as in that of Jezebel. The Scriptures prohibit such practices as occult and evil.

> The queen's religion will involve priestesses and conjurers.

No amount of damage control could change the fact that what took place in the White House was a form of channeling. In this case the first lady herself became, in effect, a *channeler*, a medium, through which the spirit would speak.

Houston, who guided the first lady, functioned in the form of a conjurer. She had another role as well. On the cover of one of her books published at the time was a telling title:

"Jean Houston is a very *high priestess.*"[8]

The declaration was made by another new age guru, Marianne Williamson. Williamson, it turns out, happened to be one of the other leaders the president and first lady summoned to the initial gathering at Camp David to give counsel.[9]

> What takes place in the palace will be linked to communion with the gods.

Jezebel brought the priests of her religion into the royal court for the purpose of worshipping and communing with the gods. As for the sessions that took place in the White House, what were they actually all about?

In the same book released in that same period, Houston answers the question. She entitles one section "Dialoguing with the Neters."[10] What exactly are "the neters"? The word comes from ancient Egypt, from the word *neteru.* It is defined this way:

"The common word given by the Egyptians to God, and god[s], and spirits of every kind, and being[s] of all sorts, and kinds, and forms, which were supposed to possess any superhuman, supernatural power, was *neter.*"[11]

So behind even the departed spirit or one's subconscious is the neter, and the neter is a being, as in a god. Houston gives specific instructions for dealing with neters:

"Ask the questions and the neter or other self provides the answer. Or you may decide to engage two or more neters at the same time and let them talk with each other."[12]

Houston gets even more specific:

"Actively dialogue with *the gods and goddesses...*"[13]

And thus even the gods and goddesses of the ancient case have reappeared in the paradigm's modern replaying. And they've reappeared in connection in the highest house of the land and connected to the ancient queen's modern antitype.

And yet the fulfillment of the paradigm will get even more eerily specific:

> The queen will bring into her circle and into the royal
> palaces the priests of the pagan goddesses.

Earlier in this chapter I noted the great unlikelihood of there being a modern match between the highest echelons of American political life and the ancient pagan gods. But this is part of the paradigm. Could there also have been a specific match to the goddess?

When Houston came to the White House for her sessions with the first lady, she was wearing an object around her neck. It was a medallion. It was the figure of an ancient pagan goddess.[14]

And there was another connection. The book that Houston released at the time of her sessions in the White House focused specifically on a pagan goddess. The goddess was Isis. Houston didn't write the book as mere history but as an endorsement of goddess worship. This is what she writes:

"And yet, as you become aware of her, Isis may change for you in form and face and dress, for she is a goddess for all seasons, for all people.... With her other hand she reaches out to you and you extend yours to receive hers.

"Perhaps you feel now or can imagine that you feel a subtle current, a cloud brush of texture, or even the feel of a true hand in yours. Allow yourself to feel her hand in yours as tangible, real, and her presence as fully alive to you as possible. She is Queen Isis, your guide and friend, Friend to the Universe, Great Mother....And she exists in you and you in her.

"Feeling her presence grow more and more real to you....Let her lead you forward into her embrace. She embraces you like a mother, and you feel that you have come home at last in her arms....And now you have entered into the heart of Isis..."[15]

This is nothing less than the call to worship a pagan goddess. As in the paradigm, the queen brings into the royal court the ministers of the goddess.

And yet there's one more piece to the mystery. In her book on Isis, Houston relays the story of the ancient goddess. Isis wanders the earth searching for the body of her husband, Osiris. Finally she arrives on the shores of a foreign land. What land? Phoenicia—*the land of Jezebel.* There the queen of Phoenicia sends for the Egyptian goddess and brings her into the Phoenician palace. Who exactly is the queen? The queen is *Astarte*—the queen is the *goddess of Jezebel*.[16]

So the mystery comes full circle. The one who ministers to the first lady in the White House not only advocates the worship of the goddesses but specifically brings up the goddess of Phoenicia, the goddess of Israel's apostasy, and the goddess of Queen Jezebel—Astarte.

The mystery goes even deeper. In ancient times Isis was known as the "Queen of Heaven." Astarte was also known as the "Queen of Heaven." And in Egypt the two goddesses actually became one; *Isis became Astarte*.

Against all odds but in perfect accord with the paradigm of the ancient queen of Israel's apostasy, the first lady had brought into the nation's highest chambers priestesses, the priestesses of the goddess.

———

A new figure is about to enter the stage of the paradigm. But before we meet him, a question: Is it possible that even the years of a modern president, the time he would be given on the national stage, could have been determined and revealed in the mystery forged over two and a half thousand years before his birth?

Chapter 8

The DAYS of the KING

COULD THE PARADIGM reveal not only the events of the modern world but the timing of those events? Could it contain the exact length of time given to a modern leader—the number of years he would be given on the national stage?

There is of course a major difference between the reigns of ancient kings and the terms of modern leaders. The kings of the ancient world could reign for any amount of time. There were no set term limits—just the factor of death or overthrow. But in the case of modern democratic states the leader's time in power is set by the term limits established for his office. In the case of the American presidency the term limit is of course four years with the possibility of two terms and thus a maximum limit of eight years.

So it would thus seem that the varied and unlimited time periods of the ancient leaders could not correspond with the set, limited, and uniform terms of the modern leaders. On the other hand, in modern democracies most presidents remain on the national stage and in power for periods of time much longer than that of their presidential terms. Unlike the ancient case where a king assumes his office suddenly upon the death of the previous king, the rising of modern leaders is in most cases a gradual process taking place, again, over the course of several years. Thus whoever occupies the presidency will most likely have been in government and on the national stage several or many years before the start of his presidential term.

So could the two durations, that of the biblical monarch and that of the modern president, be connected? Or could the years of the ancient king actually determine the years of the corresponding modern president?

The King's Paradigm of Days

The first king in the paradigm is Ahab. The Ahab of the modern replaying is Bill Clinton. So when exactly did Bill Clinton emerge on the national stage? When did his time on the national stage begin? And is there a clear event that marked the beginning of his rise to the presidency?

There is. The clear defining event that marked the beginning of Clinton's time on the national stage and his rise to the presidency was his election as governor of Arkansas. At thirty-two years of age he was America's youngest governor. The governorship would be the platform from which he would rise in prominence on the national stage and from which he would launch his campaign for the presidency. He would go directly from the governor's mansion in Little Rock to the White House in Washington, DC.

Early on in his career he suffered a major setback when he was defeated at the polls after his first term as governor. Since at that time the gubernatorial elections were spaced just two years apart, he would begin planning his comeback almost immediately. In the same year of his defeat he was already working on regaining his office. The next election would bring him back into the governorship. He would remain governor of Arkansas through the 1980s, during which time he would continue to rise in prominence on the national stage.

In 1985 he was chosen to give the Democratic response to President Reagan's State of the Union address. In 1986 he became the chair of the National Governors Association. Though he considered running for president in 1987, he would decline, deciding that the time was not yet right.

On October 3, 1991, he announced his candidacy for the presidency. Though considered a long shot at the time and dogged by scandal, he won an upset victory to become the forty-second president of the United States. In 1996 he won a second term, which would last until the start of 2001. Thus

2001 would be the year marking not only the end of his presidency but the end of his time in government, public office, and power.

So how long was Bill Clinton's time on America's national stage? How many years was it from the start of his rise to the presidency to the end of his last term as president, from his first election as governor of Arkansas to the day he left the White House? Clinton was sworn into the governorship of Arkansas for the first time in January 1979. His political career came to an end in January 2001 with the inauguration of his successor. From January 1979 to January 2001 was a period of *twenty-two years*.

If Bill Clinton is the Ahab of the paradigm, then is it possible that the years of his prototype would hold the mystery to his own years? Clinton's time in power was determined by the election cycles of the Arkansas governorship and the American presidency. Ahab's time in power of course had no such cycle to determine its length. Nor was it a gradual rise. When King Omri died, Ahab was catapulted to the throne. He would remain on that throne until his death on the battlefield.

So what was the length of King Ahab's reign, the years between his father's death and his own? The answer is found in the Book of 1 Kings chapter 16. It's given in the very first appearance of his name:

> "Ahab the son of Omri reigned over Israel in Samaria *twenty-two years.*"[1]

It is an exact match. The time span of Bill Clinton is the same exact time span as revealed in the ancient paradigm of his forerunner, King Ahab. The years of the prototype and the years of the antitype are an exact match. The years of Ahab are the same as the years of Bill Clinton.

> The king who presides over the deepening of the nation's apostasy from God, who stands at the forefront of a culture war to the overturning of biblical standards, and who rules with his wife—his days in power, his time on the national stage—will be *twenty-two years.*

What happens if we look at a different measure—that of public office? Though it didn't constitute his entrance to the national stage, nor was it the platform for his rise to the presidency, Clinton had served a short time in public office before becoming governor. He had run unopposed for state attorney general of Arkansas. He assumed the office in 1977. It was his first time holding public office. He would go from there to the governorship.

It was the election of 1980 that saw him lose the governorship. It was the election of 1982 that saw him regain it. Thus he was out of public office from January 1981 to January 1983. He then continued in public office in the governorship and then the presidency until January 2001, when his days in public office came to an end. So how long was Bill Clinton actually in public office?

From his becoming attorney general to his defeat as governor, January 1977 to January 1981, he served four years. Then from January 1983 to January 1993, his subsequent time in the governorship, he served ten more years in public office. And finally from January 1993 to January 2001, his years in the presidency, were eight more years of public office. Four plus ten plus eight comes out to *twenty-two years*—again the same number as in the paradigm of Ahab.

Two figures—the ancient ruler of the paradigm and the modern ruler of its replaying, prototype and antitype, King Ahab and President Clinton. Their worlds could not have been more different. One presided over an ancient Middle Eastern monarchy, the other over a modern Western democracy and superpower. One came to his office through royal inheritance; the other, through the winning of elections.

The reign of the one was determined by the death of his father and then his own death on the battlefield. The reign of the other was determined by ambition, campaigns, losses, comebacks, political concerns and strategies, delays, the American electorate, foreign affairs, and the particular term limits of the American presidency.

And yet with all these countless factors and variables the days of the modern figure would follow the days of the ancient. The time parameters of King Ahab's reign would become the time parameters limiting and framing the years of Bill Clinton—the twenty-two years of the king.

We will now uncover the paradigm of a very different figure, a stranger, from beyond the borders of ancient Israel—an enemy. He will end up playing a pivotal role within the paradigm. And he will reveal the mystery behind one of the most critical figures of the modern age.

Chapter 9

The NEMESIS

T HE MARRIAGE OF Ahab and Jezebel cemented Israel's alliance with its northwestern neighbor Phoenicia and so provided a measure of peace between the two nations. But to the east it was a very different story. To the east of the Jordan River and extending as far north as the borders of the Assyrian Empire was the kingdom of Aram-Damascus. Reigning over Aram-Damascus was Ben-Hadad.

Ben-Hadad would serve as Ahab's nemesis and an ever-looming threat to Israel's security. He would pose a growing threat and danger to the nation's safety in the latter part of Ahab's reign. He would plot attacks, invasions, and incursions into the land. He would issue threats against Ahab and the kingdom. In the face of his threats Ahab would vacillate between weakness and sudden shows of strength. Throughout all this, as the Scripture records, God showed grace to Israel and its king by saving them from the full measure of destruction Ben-Hadad was capable of bringing.

During one of Ben-Hadad's attempts to bring devastation on the land, God delivered him into Ahab's hands. In view of the danger Ben-Hadad posed to Israel, it would have been expected that Ahab would have had his enemy put to death or at the very least had him permanently imprisoned. But Ahab did something totally unexpected. He released him. He let the man who posed the clearest and most present danger to Israel's safety go free.

It was no minor event. The decision would prove the turning point with regard to Ahab's reign. It was important enough for the Lord to send the king a word concerning it. After Ahab released Ben-Hadad, a prophet stood at the side of a road, waiting for the king to pass by to give him a prophetic word:

> "Then the prophet departed and waited for the king by the road, and disguised himself with a bandage over his eyes. Now as the king passed by, he cried out to the king and said, 'Your servant went out into the midst of the battle; and there, a man came over and brought a man to me, and said, "Guard this man; if by any means he is missing, your life shall be for his life, or else you shall pay a talent of silver." While your servant was busy here and there, he was gone.'
>
> "Then the king of Israel said to him, 'So shall your judgment be; you yourself have decided it.' And he hastened to take the bandage away from his eyes; and the king of Israel recognized him as one of the prophets.
>
> "Then he said to him, 'Thus says the LORD: "Because you have let slip out of your hand a man whom I appointed to utter destruction, therefore your life shall go for his life, and your people for his people."'"[1]

Ahab's decision to let Ben-Hadad go after God had delivered him into his hands would be fatal. It would lead to Ahab's judgment. For the first time the end of his reign and his life was decreed and prophesied. The decision to let Israel's nemesis go would spell disaster, not only for Ahab but for the nation itself. Ben-Hadad would go on to threaten and endanger the nation's security. And in future days he would invade the land and bring calamity.

The Paradigm of the Nemesis

Is it possible that even this facet of the paradigm has a parallel in the modern world? Could there be a figure in the modern world that corresponds to the paradigm of the nemesis, the invader? In other words, has the paradigm of Ben-Hadad manifested in our times?

Ben-Hadad II began his reign a number of years before that of Ahab. But it appears that only at the time of Ahab's reign did he become an active threat and danger to the nation of Israel. If President Clinton is the antitype of Ahab, then the paradigm would speak of another rising up during his presidency who would threaten the nation—the antitype of Ben-Hadad. Did the paradigm of Ben-Hadad manifest in our day? We will refer to this facet of the paradigm as "the nemesis."

> Parallel to the reign of the king, there will arise a man who will pose a threat and active danger to the nation—he will be the nemesis of the king and the nation.

Bill Clinton was sworn in as president of the United States in January 1993. If the paradigm of Ben-Hadad is to manifest in the modern world, then his antitype would arise during the Clinton presidency. Does any such person appear?

He does appear. In fact, he would manifest as an active danger to the world's peace less than thirty days before Clinton was sworn in as America's forty-second president. It happened on December 29, 1992. It was a terrorist attack. The man behind the attack was named Osama Bin Laden.

American soldiers were staying at the Gold Mohur Hotel in Aden, Yemen, on their way to take part in Operation Restore Hope in Somalia. Agents of the terrorist group al Qaeda detonated a bomb at the hotel designed to kill the soldiers. The bombing was unsuccessful, as the soldiers had already left the premises before the explosion. But the event is believed to be the first act of terrorism involving Osama Bin Laden.[2]

So the two, the Ben-Hadad of the paradigm and the Ahab of the paradigm, assumed their roles less than one month apart, the one as leader of the Western world and the other as its nemesis.

> He will become the nation's archenemy.

In the Clinton years Bin Laden's hatred for America and everything America represented would progressively intensify. In the middle of the Clinton years Bin Laden would issue a public declaration of war against the United States.[3] America was late in seeing the threat Bin Laden posed but would eventually come to see him as its principal enemy and threat—the nation's nemesis.

Ben-Hadad came from Aram-Damascus in the east of Israel and from the east waged war against it. He came from a Semitic people and thus was related to the Jewish people. He would have spoken a form of Aramaic, a Semitic tongue. And so in a Semitic tongue he issued his threats. Thus the paradigm:

> The nemesis will come from a land east of the nation with which he wars, from a Semitic land. He will be a Semite and will issue his threats against the king's land in a Semitic tongue.

As did Ben-Hadad, so Bin Laden came from the east and from the east waged his war against the nation of his hatred. Bin Laden was an Arab. Arabs are a Semitic people. Thus as was Ben-Hadad, Bin Laden was a Semite. Arabic is a Semitic tongue. Thus as did Ben-Hadad, Bin Laden would issue his threats and declarations of war in a Semitic tongue.

> The nemesis will continually plot, strategize, and verbally threaten destruction against the king's land.

As in the years of Ahab, Ben-Hadad issued threats of destruction against Israel, throughout the Clinton years Bin Laden issued threats and devised plots against America—even to the point of declaring war and threatening to bring destruction on its soil.

> The nemesis will not only threaten but will act. He will carry out several attacks against the king's nation and bring death and destruction.

Bin Laden not only would issue threats against America during the Clinton years but would execute attacks against America and American citizens around the world.

> The nemesis will become an increasing threat and a present and active danger specifically in the latter years of the king's reign.

As the danger of Ben-Hadad intensified in the latter years of Ahab's last years, so it was with the danger of Osama Bin Laden. It was in 1996, in the middle of the Clinton presidency, that Bin Laden issued his declaration of war against America. In 1997 he signed a fatwa, an Islamic legal document, authorizing and calling for the killing of North Americans and their allies and declaring it an Islamic duty.[4] In 1998 he masterminded the bombing of two American embassies in East Africa, resulting in the death of hundreds and the injury of thousands.[5] It was this attack that placed Bin Laden's name on the lips of the American public and on the FBI's most wanted list. He was now seen as a serious threat to the nation's security, and with good reason. He would soon begin planning an even greater and deadlier attack against the nation of his loathing.

> The name of the nemesis will be formed out of the joining of two Middle Eastern words. In Hebrew the word will consist of the letter *bet*, or *b*, followed by the letter *nun*, or *n*. This will form the sound and the name *Bn*.

The name of Israel's ancient nemesis, Ben-Hadad, was formed out of the joining of two Middle Eastern words. So too the name *Bin Laden* is formed out of the joining of two Middle Eastern words. In English the name *Ben-Hadad* consists of eight letters broken into two words. So too the name *Bin Laden* in English consists of eight letters broken into two words. The first word in the ancient name consists of three letters. The second consists of five. So too the first word in the name *Bin Laden* consists of three letters. And the second consists of five. The two names also share the same vowel-consonant pattern.

The first word in each man's name appears to be virtually identical: Ben and Bin. In fact, in North Africa the name known as Bin Laden is often rendered as Ben Laden. And in the Middle Eastern languages from which the names come, there is no real difference. *Bin* is simply the Arabic version of the Hebrew *Ben*. In the original Hebrew Scriptures, in which there are no written vowels, the word is simply the Hebrew letter *bet*, or *b*, followed by the Hebrew letter *nun*, or *n*. Thus it is rendered as *Bn*. In written Arabic it is the same; vowels are often omitted. Thus it is rendered the same—*Bn*.

It is hard to think of any person in the modern age known throughout the world by a name that shares these same properties with Israel's ancient nemesis Ben-Hadad—other than Osama Bin Laden.

> The first word of the nemesis's two-part name will in his native tongue bear the meaning of son.

In the Hebrew of the ancient account and in Aramaic, Ben-Hadad's native tongue, the word *Ben* means son. In Arabic, the native tongue of Bin Laden, the word *Bin* means the same—son.

In the paradigm the Lord delivers the nation's enemy into King Ahab's hands. Ahab now has the chance to end Ben-Hadad's evil and to preempt the calamity he would bring upon Israel in future days. But he lets him go.

> The king will have the nemesis in his hands and the chance to stop him. But he will instead let him go.

For this part of the paradigm to come true, Clinton would have to have Bin Laden delivered into his hands and the chance to stop or eliminate him but instead would let him go. Could this have happened?

On November 27, 2002, the 9/11 panel was established to investigate the events leading up to the attack of September 11. It was found that President Clinton had had the chance to apprehend or kill Bin Laden but had decided to pass on the opportunity. The panel found that Clinton or the Clinton administration was given this chance not once but nine times. Each time Clinton or someone under his authority either passed on the opportunity, or one way or another the chance was missed. Each time it resulted in Bin Laden slipping through their hands.[6]

This is not to judge the reasoning behind letting go of Bin Laden, but whatever the reason or reasons it constituted the replaying of the ancient paradigm of Ahab and Ben-Hadad, the letting go of the nemesis.

> The king's decision to let the nemesis go will in the following years bring calamity to the land in the form of a strike of destruction.

Ahab's decision to let Ben-Hadad go would bring calamity to the nation. One of these calamities would involve a strike on the king's land. The strike would involve the kingdom's principal city.

So too Clinton's decision to pass on the chance of ending the threat of Osama Bin Laden would end up bringing calamity to American shores. In future days Bin Laden would orchestrate a strike on American soil—the worst terrorist attack in American history. The attack would focus on America's principal cities.

Adding to the tragedy, Clinton had been warned by the director of the CIA's Counterterrorism Center that Bin Laden's terrorist organization, al Qaeda, was making preparations to attack America and that those preparations involved the training of his agents to hijack airplanes. The warning came at the same time that one of the key opportunities to kill Bin Laden opened up. Intelligence reports revealed that Bin Laden was staying at the governor's residence in Kandahar, Afghanistan. Clinton decided to pass.

Later, after the end of his presidency, Clinton would speak about his decision not to kill Bin Laden in order not to risk killing innocent people. Yet his decision was puzzling in view of his earlier order to bomb a pharmaceutical factory that also involved the risk of killing innocent people. "I nearly got him," said Clinton. "And I could have killed him."[7]

The timing of his statement was striking. He made it on September 10, 2001. Within hours after those words America was struck by al Qaeda agents in the attack that would kill nearly three thousand people under the direction of Osama Bin Laden. The convergence of Clinton's acknowledgment that he had decided to let Bin Laden go with the actual calamity that fell on American soil is especially eerie in light of the paradigm of Ahab and Ben-Hadad. It becomes all the more eerie in light of the word spoken by the prophet to Ahab after he let Ben-Hadad go:

> "Then he said to him, 'Thus says the LORD: "Because you have let slip out of your hand a man whom I appointed to utter destruction, therefore your life shall go for his life, *and your people for his people.*"'"[8]

The decision to let Ben-Hadad go would result in future calamity and death for the people of Israel. So too the decision to let Bin Laden go would result in calamity and death on American soil on a warm September day foreshadowed by the paradigm.

We have seen the role of Ahab and Jezebel in a nation's fall from God, but now we will move into another realm, the realm of a scandal, a hidden sin, a tale of greed, deception, and murder, all of which concern a vineyard and an act that would determine not only Ahab's future but that of his wife— and the nation.

Chapter 10

The VINEYARD

Most people have never heard of the name *Naboth*. Yet this one name would determine the future of Ahab, Jezebel, their dynasty, and their nation.

Ahab and Jezebel's great sin was their all-out war against God and His ways—their role in facilitating the spiritual downfall of their nation. But the case of Naboth was an entirely different matter. It had to do with a very different kind of sin, not national or cultural but personal. Naboth had to do with their greed, covetousness and lust for gain, deception, manipulation, false witness, theft, and murder. Naboth was the scandal of their lives.

Who was Naboth? Naboth was a man who lived in the shadow of Ahab and Jezebel's palace in Jezreel. He owned a vineyard:

> "And it came to pass after these things that Naboth the Jezreelite had a vineyard which was in Jezreel, next to the palace of Ahab king of Samaria. So Ahab spoke to Naboth, saying, 'Give me your vineyard, that I may have it for a vegetable garden, because it is near, next to my

house; and for it I will give you a vineyard better than it. Or, if it seems good to you, I will give you its worth in money.'"[1]

Though he was the richest man in Israel, Ahab wanted more. He saw a vineyard that belonged to another and wanted it for his own. So he offered Naboth another vineyard or a comparable sum of money. But it was against the law of God to sell the possession of one's ancestors. Naboth appears to have been a godly man. His response to the king echoes God's law:

> "But Naboth said to Ahab, 'The LORD forbid that I should give the inheritance of my fathers to you!' So Ahab went into his house sullen and displeased because of the word which Naboth the Jezreelite had spoken to him…"[2]

Again Ahab's tempestuous nature comes to the fore, and his behavior here is more fitting of a small child than a king. He lays down on his bed and refuses to eat. When Jezebel asks him what the problem is, he tells her of Naboth's refusal to sell the vineyard.

> "Then Jezebel his wife said to him, 'You now exercise authority over Israel!'"[3]

The queen's words have also been translated, "Are you the king of Israel?" For Jezebel the whole affair was beneath Ahab's dignity. Phoenician monarchs were, in effect, above the law and could do as they pleased. The monarchs of Israel, on the other hand, were just as subject to the law of God as their subjects. But Jezebel recognized no such law and no such sovereignty.

> "I will give you the vineyard of Naboth the Jezreelite."[4]

The queen's nature is exposed by her words. One can see her disdain, her impatience, her imperiousness, her domination of the king, and her refusal to accept any obstruction to her will, even if that obstruction came from the Word of God. To Jezebel, Ahab is too weak to do what a king should do, so she herself will now take charge.

> "And she wrote letters in Ahab's name, sealed them with his seal, and sent the letters to the elders and the nobles who were dwelling in the city with Naboth."[5]

Here we see the queen's tendency to use her husband's authority to advance her own plans. In this case her plan involves murder. She arranges for a gathering to take place in which Naboth is to be treated as an honored guest. There two men are to bear false witness against him. Naboth is then to be taken away and stoned to death.

> "Then they sent to Jezebel, saying, 'Naboth has been stoned and is dead.'"[6]

With Naboth's death Jezebel sees nothing left to hinder Ahab's taking possession of the dead man's vineyard.

> "And it came to pass, when Jezebel heard that Naboth had been stoned and was dead, that Jezebel said to Ahab, 'Arise, take possession of the vineyard of Naboth the Jezreelite, which he refused to give you for money; for Naboth is not alive, but dead.'"[7]

So Ahab heads out to Naboth's vineyard to take it as his own. There is nothing to stand in his way—except for God—and a prophet named Elijah.

> "Then the word of the LORD came to Elijah the Tishbite, saying, 'Arise, go down to meet Ahab king of Israel, who lives in Samaria. There he is, in the vineyard of Naboth, where he has gone down to take possession of it.'"[8]

There in the vineyard Elijah would give Ahab a prophecy, a word that would seal his end, the end of Jezebel, and the end of their dynasty.

The Paradigm of the Vineyard

If the paradigm of Ahab and Jezebel has manifested in the modern world, then could there as well be a manifestation of Naboth? And if so, what form would it take?

The answer to the first question is yes. The answer to the second is that it has more than one manifestation. Naboth will be an example wherein a single event in the ancient world will have more than one manifestation in the modern world—where different facets and attributes of that same ancient event will correspond to or produce different manifestations in the modern.

The paradigm of Naboth will produce more manifestations than can be revealed in one chapter. We begin with the first.

> The reign of the king and queen will not only be known for national apostasy but for their own personal scandals.

What happened to Naboth would cause Ahab and Jezebel's reign to be marked not only by national apostasy and departure from biblical standards but by scandal. So too the reign of Bill and Hillary Clinton would not only be known for their activism against traditional or biblical values but also for scandal. All through the Clinton years there were scandals, one after the other, and sometimes more than one at the same time. This is not to judge the matter of truth or wrongdoing involved in any one scandal, but the mere fact that the Clinton years were known for scandal and that both the president and first lady were involved in one or more of them is another match to the paradigm of Ahab and Jezebel.

> The king and queen will be haunted by scandal for years and to the end of their reign.

The scandal of Naboth as exposed by the prophet would haunt Ahab and Jezebel for the rest of their lives. The president and first lady were likewise haunted by scandal to the end of the Clinton years. Scandal followed them from the days of Clinton's governorship to their entrance into the White House and to their exit. Even up to the last day before the end of his presidency Clinton was still dealing with scandal.

> The king and queen's scandal will center on a piece of real estate property.

The scandal of Ahab and Jezebel involved a piece of land, real estate, the taking of Naboth's vineyard. So in the Clinton presidency one scandal haunted them for the longest period of time. It was called "Whitewater." What did it center on? A piece of real estate property. In biblical history it is hard to think of a royal couple linked to a scandal so focused on a single piece of real estate other than Ahab and Jezebel. And in American history it is hard to think of a president and first lady connected to a scandal focusing on a piece of real estate other than Bill and Hillary Clinton.

> The scandal will involve the acquisition of land executed by the king and queen.

In the late 1970s, at the beginning of his political career, Bill Clinton, along with his wife, Hillary, entered into a partnership to purchase land in the hope of personal profit. The partnership was called the Whitewater Development Corp.[9] Thus the scandal was focused on their acquisition of real estate property—the same fundamental elements involved in the ancient scandal of Ahab, Jezebel, and Naboth.

> The scandal will concern the issue of illegal activity surrounding the land and those who acquired it.

Ahab and Jezebel's acquisition of Naboth's vineyard was illegal. The Clinton's acquisition of Whitewater land would be surrounded almost from the start by questionable financial activity. Their chief partner would be sent to jail, along with his wife, who would be imprisoned for refusing to answer questions as to whether President Clinton lied in court concerning the affair. By its end fifteen people connected to the scandal had been convicted of federal crimes.[10] Though the Clintons were never convicted, their actions raised continual suspicions and triggered continual investigation. Words didn't appear to match reality, documents went missing, and suspicious activity continued to surround the affair for years. This is not to assign guilt to the Clintons. It is not about their guilt or innocence; it's about an ancient template. Ahab and Jezebel were continually haunted by a scandal centering on land, its acquisition, and the illegal nature of its acquisition. So too Ahab and Jezebel's modern antitypes found themselves in the midst of a scandal and an investigation that centered on a piece of real estate, the acquisition of land, and the question of illegal activity surrounding that land.

But there was another element to the scandal—Naboth himself and of course his death.

> The king and queen's scandal will be linked to a man's death.

In July 1993 Vince Foster, White House counsel to Bill Clinton, was found dead in Fort Marcy Park, Virginia. His association with the Clintons went back to the mid-1970s. He moved with them from Arkansas to

Washington, DC, and served as their attorney. His death became the subject of controversy, rumors, and suspicion throughout the Clinton presidency even though at the time it was ruled a suicide.[11] The death of Vince Foster became one more factor in the cloud of suspicion and scandal that hung over the Clinton White House. There were many who believed it to be murder. Foster's death even became the focus of a major government investigation.[12] This is again not to say that the rumors were based on truth, but in the realm of appearance there is again correspondence to the ancient scandal. As it was with Ahab and Jezebel, the scandals associated with Bill and Hillary Clinton would involve a man's death and the issue or question of murder.

> The man whose death is linked to the king and queen will also be connected to the plot of real estate acquired by the royal couple and to the scandal surrounding it.

More than anything Naboth is known for the land over which he was murdered in the scandal of Ahab and Jezebel. Therefore could there be any link between Vince Foster and Whitewater, the land of scandal? The answer is yes.

Vince Foster and Hillary Clinton worked together in Arkansas in the Rose Law Firm. The firm was involved in real estate transactions that would later be the focus of the Whitewater investigation. In fact, it was Foster who in 1992 represented the Clintons in their last Whitewater deal. He signed the papers selling the Clintons' remaining interest in the Whitewater Development Corp. to James McDougal, their former Whitewater partner. And it was Foster who was the keeper of the Whitewater papers up until the time of his death.[13]

Foster's death would add yet another layer of controversy to the scandal. Within hours of his passing, White House aides entered his office and removed legal records concerning the Whitewater affair. Behind the removal was Bernard Nussbaum, the chief White House counsel. Nussbaum gave the records to Maggie Williams, Hillary Clinton's chief of staff.[14] Later on Foster's death would become the focus of a federal investigation, along with the investigation of Whitewater. As in the case of Naboth, so in the federal investigation the royal real estate scandal would be linked to a man's death.

Later investigation would reveal that the scandals surrounding the Clinton administration would play a key role in Foster's death. He found himself overwhelmed by the pressure and what he saw as the damaging of his reputation.[15] As with Naboth, he found himself the focus of public accusation and the defaming of his reputation.

The plot of land that Ahab wanted for himself was a vineyard. A vineyard is, of course, a place of fruits. The name of the man who kept the vineyard was Naboth. What does Naboth mean? Naboth means fruits. Whether by coincidence or the design of God the name of the victim, Naboth, was connected to the plot of land at the center of the scandal, a vineyard—a place of fruits.

> The victim's name will be connected to the plot of land the king and queen have taken, the property that forms the focus of the scandal.

What was the land that the Clintons acquired, the center of the scandal? It was forest land. Through the Whitewater Development Corp. the Clintons purchased two hundred acres of forest along the White River in the Ozarks.[16] So the "vineyard" of the Whitewater scandal was a forest.

If the name of Naboth was linked to the land of the ancient scandal, is it possible that the name of the modern-day Naboth could likewise be connected to the land of the Whitewater scandal?

What does the name *Foster* mean? It can be rendered as:

"an official in charge of a forest."[17]

So a man called Foster was the keeper of the forest. And that is what Vince Foster would become—the legal guardian of the forest land of Whitewater. He would be connected to the land through his legal dealings, through his actual selling of the land, and through the federal investigations that would inquire into the connection between the two. And yet his very name connected him from the beginning. As the name of Naboth was in the ancient case connected to the vineyard, so the name of Foster in the modern case was connected to the forest. In medieval times the foster, or "keeper of the forest," served as the representative of the interests of the ruler of the land, or the royal personage who owned the forest. So Foster would be the legal caretaker of Whitewater for the president and first lady.

The connection between Naboth's vineyard and Whitewater goes further. We know from ancient records and biblical references that vineyards were places not only of vines but trees. Trees would provide more efficient and varied use of the vineyard's soil as well as framing to grow the vines. So a vineyard keeper would tend to trees—just as would the keeper of a forest. A vineyard was a place of both fruits and trees—fruits, as in the name *Naboth*, in the ancient case—and trees, as in the name *Foster*, in its modern replaying.

And yet there's more to this part of the paradigm. Likewise there would be more to the modern story—more secrets, more scandals, and more repercussions, all of which would be joined to the ancient vineyard.

The paradigm will now reveal a scandal that shook America and transfixed much of the world—but not only the scandal and its exposure—but the actual time of its exposure—the exact year it was to take place.

Chapter 11

The PROPHECY

T HE SCANDAL OF Naboth was so egregious that it would provoke God
to seal the judgment of Ahab, Jezebel, and their dynasty. By taking
away Naboth's ancestral land, they had broken the law of God. But
that wasn't the only law they broke. They had transgressed the Ten Commandments. As it was written:

> "Do not covet your neighbor's house. Do not covet your neighbor's wife,
> his male or female servant, his ox or donkey, or anything that belongs
> to your neighbor."[1]

The account begins with coveting. Ahab covets his neighbor's possession.
With Jezebel's entrance into the story things rapidly escalate. What began
with coveting ended with murder.

These were Jezebel's specific instructions to the elders of Naboth's village:

> "Proclaim a fast, and seat Naboth with high honor among the people;
> and seat two men, scoundrels, before him to bear witness against him,

saying, 'You have blasphemed God and the king.' Then take him out, and stone him, that he may die."[2]

The plan required two men to give false testimony against Naboth to accuse him of blasphemy. This constituted yet another breaking of the Ten Commandments:

"You shall not bear false witness against your neighbor."[3]

So the royal couple had broken another of the Ten Commandments. They caused false witness to be borne against Naboth, their neighbor.

Jezebel's plot requires that a man be stoned to death. Ironically she will use the charge of blasphemy as the pretense for accomplishing this:

"Then they took him outside the city and stoned him with stones, so that he died."[4]

And so the royal couple broke yet another of the Ten Commandments:

"You shall not murder."[5]

So in this one scheme Ahab and Jezebel had broken four of the Ten Commandments. And as king and queen it appeared as if they would get away with it. But in the act of taking possession, Ahab encountered the prophet Elijah, who came to give him a word from God:

"Thus says the LORD: 'Have you murdered and also taken possession?... In the place where dogs licked the blood of Naboth, dogs shall lick your blood, even yours.'"[6]

Ahab's release of Ben-Hadad had been followed by the first prophecy of his death. But the murder of Naboth would not only seal his judgment but determine its nature. What had been done to Naboth would be done to Ahab. But the prophecy and its judgment would go still further:

"I have found you, because you have sold yourself to do evil in the sight of the LORD: 'Behold, I will bring calamity on you. I will take away your posterity, and will cut off from Ahab every male in Israel, both bond and free. I will make your house like the house of Jeroboam the son of Nebat, and like the house of Baasha the son of Ahijah, because of the provocation with which you have provoked Me to anger, and made Israel sin.'"[7]

The judgment would be twofold. God would bring the reign of Ahab to an end. Ahab would be killed. But He would also bring to an end his dynasty and its evils.

It is clear from Elijah's words that the coming judgments would be a response not only to Naboth's murder but the answer to all the evils Ahab and Jezebel had brought upon Israel by leading the nation away from God:

> "…because of the provocation with which you have provoked Me to anger, and made Israel sin."[8]

The murder of Naboth was the final straw. But since the sins of Ahab's house had touched and involved the entire nation, the judgment would also bring shaking to the nation. And it would fall as well on the one who began it all. It was also in Naboth's vineyard that the queen's end was foretold.

> "And concerning Jezebel the LORD also spoke, saying, 'The dogs shall eat Jezebel by the wall of Jezreel.' The dogs shall eat whoever belongs to Ahab and dies in the city, and the birds of the air shall eat whoever dies in the field."[9]

God would bring the days of Ahab to an end and also the days of Jezebel. It is noteworthy that the judgments of the two are pronounced separately. It is also noteworthy that the focus of the rebuke and judgment is the king. Even though Ahab was incited by Jezebel, it is he who is ultimately held most responsible.

When Ahab hears the words of Elijah, he does something surprising:

> "So it was, when Ahab heard those words, that he tore his clothes and put sackcloth on his body, and fasted and lay in sackcloth, and went about mourning."[10]

The tearing of one's clothes, the putting on of sackcloth and ashes, and the refraining from eating are acts of sorrow, remorse, and repentance. It was another display of Ahab's divided nature. The Lord takes notice and extends a measure of mercy:

> "And the word of the LORD came to Elijah the Tishbite, saying, 'See how Ahab has humbled himself before Me? Because he has humbled himself before Me, I will not bring the calamity in his days. In the days of his son I will bring the calamity on his house.'"[11]

Thus there will be a stay on the judgment, a delay of repercussions—at least in part. The judgment will not fall all at once. The calamities will come at diverse times. Ahab's own end will come first and then that of his house and Jezebel.

So what took place at Naboth's vineyard would prove to be most critical and pivotal. It would expose the evil of Ahab and Jezebel, define their reign, and stand as a marker to foretell their end.

In Whitewater we saw the first manifestation on the modern world stage of the scandal that haunted the house of Ahab. Now we will see the rest. And in this we will discover another of the paradigm's dimensions, one that reveals not only the events of the modern world but the time they are to take place.

The Paradigm of the Prophecy

The template of Naboth, as shared in the previous chapter, provides an example of a single event of the paradigm with more than one manifestation on the modern world stage, where different facets of that single event are manifested separately. We saw one of those manifestations in the previous chapter, the scandal over a piece of property and its acquisition. But now we see another.

The scandal of Naboth involved greed, covetousness, concealment, the taking of what did not belong them, theft, false witness, deception, and murder, the breaking of God's most fundamental laws. It was followed by the exposure of their sins. It would define their reign and seal their legacy. It would take place in the latter part of King Ahab's reign.

Was there any such event, any such exposure, any such scandal in the reign of President Clinton?

> In the reign of the king and queen there will come a major exposing of personal sin. The exposure will take place in the latter part of the king's reign.

In 1998 a scandal broke forth that would indelibly mark the Clinton years. It would involve the exposure of the president's personal sins. It would be known as the Monica Lewinsky scandal. The exposing of the scandal took place in the latter part of his presidency. It would represent the converging together of the earlier scandals, as the investigation of the Whitewater affair, the death of Vince Foster, and other scandals converged on the Lewinsky affair. All the Naboths of the former years coalesced into one.

It would be the foremost scandal of the Clinton years. It would taint and color the rest of his years. It would mark and define his presidency.

> The scandal will expose sin, lust, and covetousness in the highest echelons of government—the king coveting and taking what didn't belong to him.

As the scandal of Naboth involved the king's covetousness and lust for what didn't belong to him, so too did the Lewinsky scandal with regard to Bill Clinton. The scandal centered on the president's adulterous affair with a White House intern, Monica Lewinsky. It involved sin, covetousness, and lust. It was carried out in the highest of places, the White House.

> The scandal will involve deception and the bearing of false witness.

The scandal of Naboth involved deception and the bearing of false witness. The Lewinsky scandal involved the president bearing false witness as he lied about the affair before the entire nation.[12] He would also bear false witness in courts of law as he gave misleading and deceptive answers.[13]

> The scandal will involve the breaking of the most fundamental laws of God, the transgression of the Ten Commandments.

In the scandal of Naboth, Ahab and Jezebel had coveted their neighbor's possessions, engineered the giving of false witness, committed murder, and stolen what didn't belong to them—the transgression of the Ten Commandments. In the Lewinsky scandal, the president coveted and took what didn't belong to him, committed adultery, and bore false witness—likewise involving the specific transgression of the Ten Commandments.

> The king will be confronted over his sins. They will be publicly exposed.

Ahab was confronted over his sins by the prophet Elijah. His actions would undoubtedly become known throughout Israel and were chronicled in the Scriptures as a matter of public record. The president would be confronted over his sins by the media, by the federal investigations, by the judicial system, by both Houses of Congress, and by the American people. His sins would be publicly exposed in all these realms even as their details would cause a degradation of popular culture.

> In the exposure of his sins and in the shadow of judgment the king will express sorrow, remorse, and repentance.

Though Ahab had hardened his heart and waged a long war against the ways of God, when his own personal sins were exposed, he responded with a surprising show of sorrow and repentance. So too Ahab's antitype, President Clinton, after the exposing of his sins and the failure of his denials, would respond with a show of sorrow and repentance.

Because of Ahab's repentance God granted a stay in the judgments decreed on his life, his house, and his nation. They would still come, but they would be delayed. And they would not fall all at once but over a period of time. The weight of the judgments would take place after the king's death. Thus many of the consequences of Ahab's reign would fall on the nation in the days of his successors.

> A stay will be granted on the decreed judgment. The consequences and repercussions of the king's actions, those of his personal sins and his leading of the nation away from God, will be deferred to a later time. The judgments, consequences, and repercussions will not fall at once but over an extended period of time. Most will fall after the end of the king's reign—in the reign of a subsequent king.

Is it possible that this dynamic could be seen in the Clinton years—a deferment of repercussions and consequences during those years to a later time?

What was it that happened to America after the end of the Clinton presidency? The nation would be shaken by two epic events. One of these was the global financial implosion of 2008. Could this have been one of the repercussions and consequences of what was actually sown in the days of the Clintons and then fell in the days of a subsequent president?

According to the *Columbia Journalism Review*, Clinton supported and signed into law more legislation deregulating the financial realm than any other president. He pushed the Democratic-controlled House of Representatives to pass the Gramm-Leach-Bliley Act. The act overturned key restraints of the Glass-Steagall law, which had barred investment banks from engaging in commercial banking activities and which had been in place since the Great Depression.[14]

Further, through the Commodity Futures Modernization Act, he deregulated derivatives. This act caused the very risky derivatives market to become what one writer described as a "laissez-faire Wild West."[15] Further, he signed into law the Riegle-Neal Interstate Banking and Branching Efficiency Act. This would lead to a wave of banking mergers and would eviscerate state regulation of the banking industry.[16]

Beyond that Clinton would change the laws concerning government-sponsored enterprises, loosening standards and controls, and would direct Fannie Mae and Freddie Mac to massively invest in sub-prime mortgages.[17]

Undoubtedly Clinton thought he was doing right in all these things and did not fathom the consequences his decisions would have. Nevertheless, the effect of any one of these things on the coming global financial implosion was major. But their combined effect was devastating. Thus the *Columbia Journalism Review* would conclude:

> "The bottom line is: Bill Clinton was responsible for more damaging financial deregulation—and thus, for the [2008] financial crisis—than any other president."[18]

Thus the overall dynamic of delayed consequences and deferred repercussions that marked the reign of Ahab with regard to Israel's history can likewise be seen in the presidency of Bill Clinton and the years that followed. The global financial collapse that struck America and the world in 2008 was a consequence deferred from the days of the Clinton administration.

But there was another epic global event and crisis that took place right after the end of the Clinton years. It was 9/11. Could the same dynamic of Ahab's paradigm apply as well to the worst terror attack in American history? Could what happened in New York City and Washington, DC, have been another deferred consequence of the Clinton years?

We have already witnessed the answer. It was during the Clinton years that Osama Bin Laden surfaced as a danger to America and the world. Clinton passed on the chance to kill Bin Laden just as Ahab had passed on the chance to kill Israel's nemesis invader Ben-Hadad. And as we have seen, Clinton would even admit that much just ten hours before the planes struck their targets.

> At the same time that the king is reproved for his
> sins, he will be given word concerning the coming
> calamity.

It was in Naboth's vineyard that King Ahab was given a word from
Elijah both reproving him for his sin and prophesying of future calamity.
In December 1998 President Clinton was reproved before the US Congress,
impeached on the charges of perjury and the obstruction of justice concerning the Monica Lewinsky scandal.[19] Could he also have been given a
word that same month on a future calamity?

It was that same month, December 1998, that Clinton was given a secret
memo from the CIA. It was entitled "Bin Laden Preparing to Hijack US
Aircraft and Other Attacks."[20] It was the most definitive warning yet given
of the calamity that would come to American shores. As with Ahab in
Naboth's vineyard, the king had received both a rebuke for his sins and the
foretelling of the future calamity.

The fall of King Ahab would bear an underlying connection to the tribe
of Levi, from the day of the scandal to the day of his judgment. Levi was
the third son of Israel's patriarch Jacob. His descendants were known as
the Levites and constituted one of the most prominent and important of the
nation's twelve tribes. Levi was the priestly tribe, the tribe of ministers. The
Levites were in charge of the Temple, the sacrifices, the holy days, the holy
vessels, and the worship of God. The Levites were the keepers of God's law.
They ministered its commandments and instructed the nation in its precepts. Thus the Old Testament law of Moses is known as the "Levitical law."

But when the northern kingdom broke away from the South, it rejected
the Levitical law and the Levitical priesthood. Its first king, Jeroboam,
replaced the Levites with priests of his own choosing. But Ahab, as in
so many other ways, took the apostasy to new depths. He, with Jezebel,
appointed for Israel a new priesthood, the priesthood of Baal.

Ahab's downfall began when he sought to take away Naboth's vineyard.
Naboth refused the king's wishes by stating that he could not give away his
father's possession. He was referring to the ordinance that made it illegal
to take land away from its original owners. The land had to remain in the
possession of its original owners or at a set time be returned to them. It
was one of the commandments of the Levitical law. So one commentator
observes:

> "Desiring to add to his pleasure-grounds at Jezreel the vineyard of his
> neighbor Naboth, he proposed to buy it or give land in exchange for it;

and when this was refused by Naboth in accordance with the *Levitical law*, (Leviticus 25:23) a false accusation of blasphemy was brought against him, and he was murdered, and Ahab took possession of the coveted fields."[21]

The principle first appeared in Leviticus, the book that derives its name from the tribe of Levi. Ahab's downfall, as one commentary notes, may have originated in his ignorance of the Levitical law caused by the northern kingdom's rejection of the Levites:

> Moreover, the law in Israel was intended to keep the ownership of farmland within a family.... Ahab may have been ignorant of this law since the Levitical priests had lost their positions in Israel.[22]

Thus Ahab's end was set in motion the moment he transgressed the Levitical law. But the Levitical connection would not end there. On the day of his judgment it would reappear. That judgment would take place in the battle of Ramoth Gilead. Ramoth Gilead was a city that Israel had lost to the kingdom of Aram. Ahab would be killed in his attempt to regain it. So the city was both the cause that led to Ahab's judgment and the ground on which it fell.

But Ramoth Gilead was not just any city of Israel—it was a *Levitical* city. It was given to the tribe of Levi. They were to inhabit it. So in his attempt to take a land that didn't belong to him, Ahab had transgressed the law of the Levites. And in his attempt to take the city of the Levites, he would meet his end. Or in other words, his downfall would begin as he broke the Levitical law and would end with his judgment in the city of the Levites. Thus his transgression, his scandal, his downfall, and his judgment were all linked to the tribe of Levi. And thus the paradigm:

> The king's scandal will begin with his transgressing the law of the Levites. So too the judgment of his sins will be linked to Israel's priestly tribe. Thus the king's fall, from his sin to the judgment of his sin, will be intrinsically bound to the tribe of Levi.

Could even this part of the paradigm manifest in the modern replaying? Could there somehow exist a link between Ahab's antitype, President Clinton, and the tribe of Levi? Could there be a link between the scandal that shook and stained his presidency and Israel's ancient priesthood?

The first connection is the nature of the scandal itself. It was not only that Clinton's scandal involved the breaking of universal ethics; it specifically involved the transgression of the Levitical law—the Ten Commandments comprising the beginning of the law. But there was more to the scandal that went back to ancient times.

In the years and centuries that passed since biblical times, the descendants of Levi, the Levites, would adopt last names to preserve their identity. These names came from the ancient Hebrew name *Levi*. From *Levi* came the Jewish last name *Levin*. From *Levin* came the last name *Levinsky*. And from *Levinsky* came another last name—*Lewinsky*. In other words, the scandal that brought judgment on Bill Clinton's presidency was linked to the tribe of Levi. The name *Lewinsky*, as in Monica Lewinsky, means nothing more or less than the tribe of Levi. Thus the president's scandal, the Lewinsky scandal, bore the name of the tribe of Levi. And thus it was linked to the ground on which Ahab was judged for the scandal of his kingship, Ramoth Gilead, the city of the Levites.

And it wasn't only a name. Monica Lewinsky not only bore the name of the Levites, but she *was one*. When one is born with such a name, it means that one is a descendant of the tribe of Levi. Monica Lewinsky was a Levite, of the same people who in ancient times upheld and carried out the law that King Ahab had broken, the law that had led to his downfall. She was of the same tribe that owned the city in which Ahab's judgment had fallen.

What King Ahab had done constituted the breaking and desecrating of the Levitical law. What President Clinton had done not only constituted the breaking of the Levitical law in coveting, false witness, and adultery; it involved the desecration of a Levite. As it was with Ahab in ancient times, so it was with his antitype in modern times. In this King Ahab and President Clinton were yet once again joined together. The scandal and downfall of each was marked and bound to the tribe of Levi.

When in Ahab's reign was he exposed for his sin? We know it took place in the latter part of his reign. And we know more than that. The Bible gives us the data needed to identify the exact year. The exposure of Ahab's sin took place in the nineteenth year of his reign. Thus the paradigm:

> The king's exposure will take place nineteen years after his accession.

What happens if we take nineteen years of the paradigm, from the time he began to reign to the time of his scandal and apply it to the Ahab of the modern era, Bill Clinton? What will happen?

We would have to begin with Clinton's accession as he assumes the office of governor in 1979. If we add the nineteen years of Ahab, it takes us to the year 1998. Is there anything significant about that year? There is. It is the very year that the Monica Lewinsky scandal, Clinton's Naboth, broke forth.

But what if we follow the paradigm into another level of detail? Clinton's days in power began when he took the oath of office as governor. When exactly did that take place? It took place in the month of January of 1979. Add the nineteen years of Ahab, and where does it take us? It takes us to January 1998. Did any significant event take place in that particular month? January 1998 is the exact month that the greatest scandal of the Clinton presidency broke out, that his sins were exposed.

Two rulers—one rules an ancient kingdom; the other, a modern nation. The scandal of the first surrounds a vineyard outside the royal palace; the scandal of the second surrounds the White House. And yet the two rulers are joined once again—even in their scandals. The scandal of the ancient king begins in the nineteenth year after his accession to power. The scandal of the modern president—through all the countless actions, events, details, and variables of politics, media, and state—begins at the same point, in the nineteenth year after his accession to power.

And yet there is even more to the mystery. We have watched the paradigm reveal the timing of events in the modern world. We will now enter another realm where the paradigm's revelation will become even more eerily exact.

Chapter 12

The END

T HE WORD GIVEN in Naboth's vineyard to King Ahab spoke of things yet to come. The first involved the end of his reign and life. When would these things take place?

Because of Ahab's display of sorrow the prophesied judgment is deferred, at least in part, specifically as touching the judgment of his dynasty. The king's judgment would come first and later that of his house. The account of that judgment would begin in the very first verse following the granting of the delay. Events would begin coalescing to fulfill the prophecy of the king's end, and it would be Ahab himself who would set them in motion:

> "And the king of Israel said to his servants, 'Do you know that Ramoth in Gilead is ours, but we hesitate to take it out of the hand of the king of Syria?' So he said to Jehoshaphat, 'Will you go with me to fight at Ramoth Gilead?'"[1]

After letting Ben-Hadad go free three years earlier, Ahab decides to war against him to regain the Israelite city of Ramoth Gilead. He enlists the help of Jehoshaphat, king of Judah:

> "So the king of Israel and Jehoshaphat the king of Judah went up to Ramoth Gilead. And the king of Israel said to Jehoshaphat, 'I will disguise myself and go into battle; but you put on your robes.' So the king of Israel disguised himself and went into battle."[2]

Ahab disguises himself with good reason:

> "Now the king of Syria had commanded the thirty-two captains of his chariots, saying, 'Fight with no one small or great, but only with the king of Israel.'"[3]

So Ben-Hadad instructs his commanders to focus the battle against just one person—Ahab. Apparently the disguise worked. The account contains no record of Ahab being discovered. Nevertheless God's judgment had been decreed. And so even in a disguise that no one could recognize, the prophecy would be fulfilled:

> "Now a certain man drew a bow at random, and struck the king of Israel between the joints of his armor. So he said to the driver of his chariot, 'Turn around and take me out of the battle, for I am wounded.' The battle increased that day; and the king was propped up in his chariot, facing the Syrians, and died at evening."[4]

Thus on the battlefield of Ramoth Gilead the reign of King Ahab comes at last to its end. He would be killed battling the man he had let go free, Ben-Hadad. And the Lord had warned him of this very thing, that his own life would go for the life of the one he had spared.

What happened on the battlefield of Ramoth Gilead had all been foretold by Elijah in Naboth's vineyard; even the random firing of the arrow was an implicit part of its fulfillment:

> "Thus says the LORD: 'In the place where dogs licked the blood of Naboth, dogs shall lick your blood, even yours.'"[5]

What appeared to be a series of random events would cause the prophecy to be fulfilled:

> "The blood ran out from the wound onto the floor of the chariot. Then, as the sun was going down, a shout went throughout the army, saying, 'Every man to his city, and every man to his own country!'

"So the king died, and was brought to Samaria. And they buried the king in Samaria. Then someone washed the chariot at a pool in Samaria, and the dogs licked up his blood while the harlots bathed, according to the word of the LORD which He had spoken."[6]

It all happened in accordance with "the word of the LORD which He had spoken." The account emphasizes the connection between the king's end and the exposure of his sins in the vineyard years before. The arrow of the battle answers the prophecy of the vineyard, and the blood of the king answers the blood of Naboth, his victim.

So the reign of King Ahab, the man who with Jezebel "did evil in the sight of the LORD, more than all who were before him," comes to a fitting and scandalous end with dogs licking up his blood by a pool of prostitutes.

The Paradigm of the End

To what would the paradigm of Ramoth Gilead point? We will now open the mystery of the king's end and the precise connection it bore to the king's scandal.

We must start where we left off, but now focusing on the paradigm of Ramoth Gilead:

> The king's scandal will continue to haunt him and bear consequence to the very end of his reign. The end of his reign will be marked by the scandal.

It is obvious that Ahab believed Elijah's prophecy to the point where it caused him to go into deep mourning. It had to have haunted him. And the prophecy would frame every subsequent event of his life until they all coalesced with the end of his reign.

In the modern case the scandal would likewise continue to haunt the president and bear consequences throughout his presidency. It would follow him to the end of his term. On the very last full day of his presidency, after having been found in contempt of court for giving intentionally false testimony, Clinton surrendered his Arkansas law license and admitted to bearing false witness under oath concerning the Lewinsky scandal as part of a deal to avoid being disbarred and indicted for perjury.[7] He was guilty. As the reign of King Ahab had ended in scandal, so too had the presidency of Bill Clinton.

The end was marked by scandal and still mired in the Lewinsky scandal, his Naboth.

The scandal of Naboth involved the exposing of the king's sin. In the modern scandal how did that exposure come?

It was winter 1998. The independent counsel Ken Starr was investigating the scandal surrounding the land purchased by the Clintons, the Whitewater affair. Starr was contacted by an employee of the Pentagon, Linda Tripp. Tripp informed Starr of the Lewinsky affair. The next day Tripp, working with the FBI, recorded a conversation with Lewinsky at a bar in Pentagon City.

Three days later, on the Friday of that week, Starr was granted permission by the attorney general to expand his investigation into the possibility of crimes by the White House, including obstruction of justice. The same day, FBI agents and US attorneys questioned Lewinsky in a hotel room. That same night Tripp's lawyers headed out to the Washington offices of *Newsweek* to deliver two tape recordings made of Tripp's conversations with Lewinsky. The editors of *Newsweek* decided to wait on the story.

That Saturday, President Clinton under oath denied having sexual relations with Lewinsky. Further, he stated that he couldn't remember if he was ever alone with her. That night the Internet site the Drudge Report posted a story on the web revealing that *Newsweek* had killed an article about a former White House intern having sex with the president. Internet journalism was a relatively new phenomenon, and though awareness of the story would begin to spread to the subscribers of the site, it took some time before it would be accepted by the mainstream media. The Washington bureaus of the major mainstream news organizations became aware of the story by the following Monday.[8]

But it was the next day, Tuesday, that the story that would forever mark the Clinton presidency broke to the nation and to the world. That night a stunned White House press secretary Mike McCurry informed the president that the *Washington Post* was going to break the story in its morning edition. That same night a multitude of cars and satellite trucks, television cameras, and reporters wearing night vision goggles converged on the house of Linda Tripp in hope of a story.

The *Washington Post*, along with the Washington bureau of the *Los Angeles Times*, was preparing to publish the story on the front page of the morning edition. And then it happened. At 10:30 p.m. they released the story on the Internet. At the same time, Jackie Judd of ABC News prepared to report the story on that night's broadcast of *Nightline*. But the program's host, Ted Koppel, decided against it. Judd decided to get the story out on ABC radio as well as on ABC's news website. That was it. The news had broken. The story became front-page headlines around the nation and around the world. It was now everywhere.[9]

Ahab's sins and scandal were exposed by a prophet in a vineyard. From that moment the king's fate was, in effect, sealed. From the exposing of his sin to the end of his reign it was only a matter of time—but how much time? How much time elapsed from the exposing of the scandal to the end of Ahab's reign? The answer is found in the very first verse after the vineyard account:

> "Now *three years* passed without war between Syria and Israel. Then it came to pass, in the third year, that Jehoshaphat the king of Judah went down to visit the king of Israel."[10]

There would be three years in between the exposing of the scandal and the end of Ahab's reign, three years in between the prophecy and its fulfillment. Thus the paradigm:

> From the moment of the exposure of the king's sin and scandal to the end of his reign *will be three years.*

Thus, according to the template, if we take the time of the exposing of the king's scandal and add three years, we come to the time of the king's end, the end of his reign. Or conversely, if we take the end of the king's reign and subtract three years, we will come to the time of the king's scandal.

What happens if we now apply the template to the modern case? The rule of Ahab's antitype, Bill Clinton, came to an end in the year 2001. If we now take that year and subtract the three years of King Ahab, where does it take us? It takes us to the year 1998. It is exactly as in the paradigm. 1998 is the year of the scandal. 1998 is the year the president's sins were exposed. From the president's scandal to the president's end is a period of three years, the three years of Ahab.

But could the paradigm's mystery go even farther?

In the ancient case we don't know the exact date of Ahab's end. But in the case of the modern Ahab we do. Clinton's twenty-two years of power came to an end in the winter of 2001 with the inauguration of his successor. The day was January 20.

Therefore January 20, 2001, is the specific date that would correspond in the paradigm with the end of Ahab's reign. So what happens now if we subtract three years from that date that marks the end of the Clinton years? Where will it take us?

It takes us to January 20, 1998. Is there anything significant about that date? January 20, 1998, was a Tuesday. January 20 was the day on which the presidential scandal broke to the world. January 20 was the day the news media surrounded the house of Linda Tripp. January 20 was the day that the president was informed that the *Washington Post* would run the article. January 20 was the day that the news of the scandal was released on the Internet. January 20 was the day of the exposure: the day of Naboth. It transpired exactly as in the template. In this the paradigm is revealing the timing of modern events down to their exact dates.

Conversely if we had at the time taken note of the day that the Clinton scandal was exposed and added the three years of Ahab, the paradigm would have taken us to January 20, 2001, the exact day that the Clinton presidency came to its end—the exact day that concluded the twenty-two years of the modern Ahab.

From the day of King Ahab's scandal, when Elijah exposed him in the vineyard of Naboth, to the day he was struck down on the battlefield of Ramoth Gilead, the day that ended his reign as king, was a period of three years. From the day of President Clinton's scandal, when the Monica Lewinsky affair broke to the world, to the day of the inauguration that brought the Clinton years to their end was a period of three years—to the year, the month, the week, to the exact day.

That a three-thousand-year-old template could lie behind or be determining the events of the modern world is a radical proposition. And yet, as we have seen, the paradigm of ancient Israel not only corresponds to events that transpired thousands of years after the paradigm was formed but reveals those events down to the exact days of their transpiring.

We are now about to see how the mystery foretold one of the most pivotal events of modern history and was so exact that if one had known the paradigm, one could have marked on a calendar the exact day it would take place—years before it happened.

Chapter 13

The DAY

WE WILL NOW open up one of the facets of the paradigm that involves an event that has changed the course of modern history. We will see how the ancient template did what no expert, no system, and no technology of the modern world was able to do—it foretold this critical event down to its exact timing, a phenomenon with mind-boggling ramifications.

To uncover what happened, we must return to the vineyard. It is there that one more revelation lies waiting. But the revelation will not lie in the words of Elijah but the actions of Ahab. When Ahab heard Elijah's prophecy of judgment,

> "…he tore his clothes and put sackcloth on his body, and fasted and lay
> in sackcloth, and went about mourning."[1]

The king was manifesting all the signs of repentance. As to what was in his heart, it's hard to be certain. It appears that he was experiencing genuine remorse in light of the judgment that was now being decreed for his sins. And yet judging by what happened afterwards, it appears that his repentance was not deep or real enough to produce any lasting change.

Nevertheless it was something. And as we have seen, the Lord took note and showed mercy:

> "Because he has humbled himself before Me, I will not bring the calamity in his days. In the days of his son I will bring the calamity on his house."[2]

So God would extend mercy. The judgments would still come but not in Ahab's lifetime—or rather none but the first, that of his own end, would come in his lifetime. The others would fall after the end of his kingship, in the reign of another. It is crucial here that we keep in mind the other prophecy given to Ahab after the release of Ben-Hadad:

> "Because you have let slip out of your hand a man whom I appointed to utter destruction, therefore your life shall go for his life, and your people for his people."[3]

There is more than one calamity contained in this prophecy as well, that of the king's end and that of a destruction that comes on his people. The implication is that the destruction that was to come upon Ben-Hadad would now come upon Ahab and his people. It can be further inferred that the destruction would involve Ben-Hadad. Ahab had allowed Ben-Hadad to go free. Therefore he would be free to inflict calamity on the nation in the days to come.

There would be future calamity. Do we have any other clues as to what it would involve? Elijah's vineyard prophecy contained the Hebrew word *ra*, which can be translated as evil, but also as adversity, trouble, calamity, harm, distress, hurt, sorrow, misery, and injury. All of these things would come upon the land and to the house of Ahab.

Putting together the two prophecies, this is what we have: The judgment on Ahab and his house would have more than one manifestation and would take place over an extended period of time. It would start with Ahab's end but after that would involve others. It would come in response to the king and queen's personal sins but also in response to their role in the nation's apostasy from God.

Since we have the benefit of knowing what happened next, we can identify yet another element of the prophecy and thus of the paradigm. The calamity would at one point involve outsiders, those from beyond the nation's borders, the nation's enemies. It would involve the nation's arch-enemy, Ben-Hadad.

In the last mystery we witnessed two events of modern history pinpointed by the ancient paradigm down to the exact days they were to take place. The starting point for that pinpointing, or countdown, was the day of the exposing, the day when the king's sins were revealed. The modern events followed the template of Ahab's exposure in the vineyard of Naboth. But what took place in that vineyard involved more than that exposure. It also involved the king's response to that exposure—his repentance. Each of these things would play an equal part in determining the time the future calamities would fall.

Thus it will be these two facets of the paradigm—the exposure of the king's sin and the king's repentance for his sins in the wake of that exposure—that will open a mystery concerning one of the most critical events of modern history.

The Paradigm of the Day

We now uncover the paradigm's other mystery—the king's repentance. Could this facet of the ancient account have manifested as well in the modern scenario? And if so, how? It could only be found in the president's response to the exposure of his sins, the revealing of the scandal. So what was his response?

In the days after the news of the scandal, Clinton publicly and repeatedly denied he had had a sexual relationship with Lewinsky. It was during those days that he would utter one of the most famous statements of his presidency: "I did not have sexual relations with that woman..."[4] The first lady also was part of the denial as she uttered one of the most famous statements of her public career, charging that it was all a falsehood fabricated by a "vast right-wing conspiracy."[5] The president held to his denial for seven months.

But then on August 17, after giving testimony before a grand jury where under oath he was forced to admit his relationship with Lewinsky, Clinton went on television to admit to the American people that everything he had been saying about the affair up to that point was false. He had indeed carried on a sexual affair with Lewinsky and had done so in the White House. He said this:

> "This afternoon in this room, from this chair, I testified before the Office of Independent Counsel and the grand jury. I answered their questions truthfully, including questions about my private life, questions no American citizen would ever want to answer. Still, I must take complete responsibility for all my actions, both public and private."[6]

So was this the repentance of the king? It was an admission, but it was not repentance. It was done out of necessity. Once Clinton had confessed to the affair before the grand jury, he had no other choice. It was as much a political defense as anything else. The president then mentioned his January deposition:

> "While my answers were legally accurate…"[7]

Only they weren't. It was another false statement. Later on, in a deal to avoid perjury charges, he would acknowledge that he had, in fact, borne false witness under oath. Then in a show of anger he began to attack the investigation that had brought the scandal to light:

> "The fact that these questions were being asked in a politically inspired lawsuit…This has gone on too long…It's nobody's business but ours…It is time to stop the pursuit of personal destruction and the prying into private lives…"[8]

It was an act of political necessity. It was not repentance. Unlike Ahab's response to the exposing of his sins, there was no evidence of any real sorrow or remorse for what he had done. The speech was much criticized, and even Clinton himself would later admit that it was not repentant, as it should have been. But in the ancient case, even if it was not long-lasting, the king had shown the signs of what appeared to be humility and true repentance—thus the paradigm:

> After being exposed for his sins, the king will display sorrow, remorse, humility, and repentance before God and man.

If this, then, is the paradigm, did such a thing ever take place? Was there any comparable act of repentance on the part of the Ahab of modern times, as there was on the part of the Ahab of ancient times? The paradigm would indicate that there would be. And there was.

It would happen at the annual White House prayer breakfast in the East Room before a gathering of over one hundred ministers. The president said this:

> "I agree with those who have said that in my first statement after I testified I was not contrite enough. I don't think there is a fancy way to say that I have sinned. It is important to me that everybody who has been hurt know that the sorrow I feel is genuine….I have asked all for

their forgiveness. But I believe that to be forgiven, more than sorrow is required—at least two more things. First, genuine repentance—a determination to change and to repair breaches of my own making. I have repented....And if my repentance is genuine and sustained, and if I can maintain both a broken spirit and a strong heart, then good can come of this for our country....I ask that God give me a clean heart..."[9]

This was the president's act of repentance. He even identified it as such. And though one can never fully know another's heart, his words could hardly have been more repentant or contrite. He expressed sorrow over his sins, the need for forgiveness, and the requirement of lasting change. One would be hard-pressed to think of any other president in American history who had made such an explicit, unreserved, and public demonstration of repentance. It was a central part of Ahab's paradigm. And the one president who fulfilled it happened to be the one who was Ahab's antitype. The Ahab of modern times had now done the same as the Ahab of ancient times.

We now have the puzzle piece we need: the repentance of the king.

We must therefore now ask the question "How long was it after Ahab's act of repentance that the first calamity of Elijah's prophecy came upon the nation?" It would have to be the same period of time as in the last mystery. The answer is revealed immediately after the account of Ahab's repentance:

> "'See how Ahab has humbled himself before Me?' Because he has humbled himself before Me'...Now *three years* passed without war between Syria and Israel. Then it came to pass, in the third year..."[10]

The Scripture links the king's repentance with a period of three years. It would be three years after Ahab's repentance over the scandal, the calamity would fall.

> Three years after the king repents over his sins after the exposing of his scandal—the calamity will fall.

To follow the paradigm, we must mark the day of the king's repentance, in the modern case the day President Clinton publicly repented at the White House prayer breakfast. In the paradigm the day of repentance is separated from the day of calamity by a space of three years. Thus starting with the day of the president's repentance, we must add three years and see where it brings us.

In accordance with the paradigm, could the day it brings us to be significant? So then to what day does the ancient paradigm bring us?

It brings us to *September 11, 2001.*

The day of the president's repentance was September 11, 1998. Three years later the calamity fell. The greatest terrorist attack in American history, 9/11, fell exactly three years from the day of the king's repentance.[11]

And it was not only the day—the president made his confession on the *morning* of September 11, 1998. So too the coming calamity would fall on the *morning* of September 11, 2001.

The White House event in which the confession took place officially began at 8:30 a.m. The time would pinpoint the hour that the calamity would commence. It would all begin three years later to the hour, as the first plane crashed into the North Tower of the World Trade Center on September 11, 2001, at 8:46 a.m.

The president spoke in between 9 and 10 a.m. Three years later that same hour would comprise the peak of the calamity—the hour that would see the striking of the South Tower, the striking of the Pentagon, and the collapse of the South Tower.

The calamity would end with the collapse of the North Tower. It would happen at 10:29 a.m.—three years to the hour—to the moment. The White House event officially ended at 10:30 a.m. Three years from that end brings us to 10:30 a.m. September 11, 2001.

September 11, the day that would shake America and the world and alter the course of modern history, took place according to the exact time parameters given in the ancient paradigm.

In the ancient case Ahab appears to have repented at the same time his sins were exposed. But in the modern case the president didn't repent until several months after his sins were exposed. So in the modern case the king's exposure and the king's repentance were separated by over seven months—234 days. Thus when we add the three years of the paradigm to the two events of the modern case, we end up with two other dates: The first is January 20, 2001, the day that marks the end of the Clinton years. The second is September 11, 2001, the day that marks the greatest American calamity of modern times. These pivotal events are thus ordered and separated by the same 234 days that separate the king's exposure and the king's confession three years earlier.

In the paradigm both of these events are linked to what took place on the day of the battle at Ramoth Gilead three years after the vineyard prophecy. It was the day that the king's reign came to an end. But it was also a day of calamity for Israel on several counts, a day of a military defeat, a day of bloodshed, and a day of lives lost. Thus the paradigm:

> Three years after the king's repentance will come a day of bloodshed and the loss of life—a day of national calamity.

So three years to the day after the president's repentance came September 11, 2001, a day of bloodshed and the loss of life—a day of national calamity.

What else was Ramoth Gilead? It was the day that marked the return of the nation's archenemy, Ben-Hadad. It was the day of his resurfacing as a clear and present danger to the nation. It was the day of his victory, the day he struck a deadly blow against the nation. It was the day of the nemesis.

> Three years after the king's repentance will come the day when the nation's invader and nemesis reemerges. It will be the day that the danger he has posed in previous years will come back to strike the nation with a traumatic and deadly blow. Three years after the day of the king's repentance will come the day of the nemesis.

Three years after Clinton's repentance in the East Room of the White House came the day of the nemesis, the day of Osama Bin Laden. It was the day he struck America with a traumatic and deadly blow.

Ben-Hadad would direct his army in the war of Ramoth Gilead against King Ahab. But there's no record of Ben-Hadad actually fighting in the battle or personally carrying out the fatal blow. But he directed it. He masterminded its strategy.

> The nemesis will not carry out the fatal blow himself but will set it as a goal and direct its carrying out. He will order his men into the battle. He will mastermind its strategy.

So too Bin Laden would not personally carry out the terrorist attack of September 11, but he would direct it. He would come up with the plot. He would set it in motion. He would oversee its execution. He would be its ultimate mastermind.

Other elements of the template would also come into play. Ben-Hadad, in the days after Elijah's prophecy, would not only strike blows against Israel's army but would invade Israel's land and lay siege to Samaria, which was both the nation's capital and chief city.

> The nemesis will not only attack that which belongs to the kingdom; he will invade its land and strike its capital and chief city.

So Bin Laden would not only attack American interests around the world, but as he had threatened and promised to do, he would bring his war to American shores. In the case of Ben-Hadad, Samaria was both the nation's chief city and its capital. In the modern case these attributes would be borne by two different American cities—New York City and Washington, DC. So on September 11, 2001, both cities would be the targets and suffer the wrath of Bin Laden.

There were other elements as well. The word *ra* used in Elijah's prophecy to speak not only of the ending of Ahab's reign but of the calamities that would come after the end of his reign would also apply to what came upon America after the end of Clinton's reign. September 11 would be a day of ra, of trouble, calamity, harm, distress, injury, sorrow, and misery.

The calamities of Elijah's prophecy possessed a national, as well as personal, dimension. Even though Ahab was most responsible in leading Israel against the ways of God, in causing Israel to sin, still the nation had followed him into apostasy. And the coming calamities would cause the entire nation to be shaken. So too 9/11 would cause America to be shaken. And it would come at a time when the nation's departure from God was accelerating. Indeed the nation's first response in the wake of the calamity was to invoke the name of God, to gather in prayer, to flock to the nation's houses of worship, and to ask for God's blessings. But the "return" was short-lived and without repentance or any altering of the nation's course. Thus as the shock wore off, the nation resumed its downward course of national apostasy.

When Israel's hedge of protection was broken and the nation's enemies struck the land, it was a wake-up call, a sign of correction, a warning, an alarm, even the first signs of national judgment. As for 9/11, it was not only part of the paradigm but part as well of an ancient mystery of warning and judgment. It is that which *The Harbinger* reveals and that which will be touched on in a later chapter.

September 11 saw the breaching of the strongest system of national defense and security ever put in place by any nation and the thwarting of the most sophisticated system of national intelligence ever devised. Every department and apparatus of state was taken by surprise. On that serene morning of September 11, no one knew it was coming. And yet the paradigm had already pinpointed the time it would take place. A biblical template forged in a Middle Eastern land over two and a half thousand years earlier had fixed the timing of the calamity down to the year, the month, and the week it would take place— even giving its exact date.

Long before the date would become seared into the world's consciousness, long before the agents of al Qaeda had ever heard of the date, and long before even Osama Bin Laden could conceive of the date, the date was there set by the parameters of the ancient template. If one had known the paradigm and had seen the first match between the exposure and the end of the Clinton years, one could have then marked September 11 as the date set for calamity. One might have even surmised the nature of what would take place on that day. For the paradigm had fixed September 11, 2001, not only as the day of national calamity but as the day of the return of the nemesis, Osama Bin Laden.

Long before the morning that caught the greatest powers in the world unaware, the paradigm had determined it.

We have come to the end of King Ahab's reign and to the end of the Clinton presidency. What came next in American history was a very different era. Does the paradigm continue? And will it continue to give us revelation into the events of our times?

The answer is absolutely yes.

Chapter 14

The SHADOW QUEEN

THE KING WAS dead, slain in his chariot, his lifeless body carried back to Samaria to be interred in the capital city. As to what happened next, the commonly held picture is that Jezebel's end would soon follow. But what actually did happen was quite different.

Jezebel's position and power had always been dependent on Ahab. He was the nation's native-born king. She was the outsider. With his death the basis of her power was taken away. Her former position could not be sustained. But Jezebel was too driven and too ambitious to fade into obscurity, to leave the national stage, or to move far from the center of power. From what is revealed further on in the account, it becomes evident that Jezebel continued to play a substantial role in Israel's government.

So while Ahab's reign comes to an end, Jezebel goes on. She would survive the end of her husband's reign and continue to walk the halls of power as an active agent and one of the most prominent figures in Israel's government. She would dwell within the nation's capital and within its royal palaces. She would no longer possess the same position and authority she had possessed in her husband's reign. She would no longer preside as co-regent, as reigning queen, or even as first lady of the kingdom. But she would continue to operate and dwell in the highest places and to affect the nation's government. She could not command from above, as she once did, but she could influence those who did.

She now had to reinvent herself in her new position with an identity independent from that of her husband. She would leverage her husband's authority to establish her own. She would build a new base of power among the court and among the people. Her supporters would consist of those most strongly in favor of the new morality, those most opposed to the traditional, or biblical, morality, and those most enmeshed in the worship of Baal. That would mean her strongest supporters would come from those most involved with or in favor of the practice of child sacrifice.

There had of course been other former reigning queens who had outlasted the reigns of their husbands. Typically they would have then been given an honorary status. But Jezebel's nature and history, together with her ambitions, would not allow her to be content with any such honorary or ceremonial status. Rather she would seek to continue to function as a prominent political player in the center of power.

The controversy that surrounded her as reigning queen would follow her into her new role as former queen. While the nation's other former first ladies would have been seen in mostly nonpolitical and nonthreatening terms, Jezebel would remain a polarizing figure, fiercely political, hailed by some, hated by others, a former queen with followers on one hand and, on the other, enemies.

Though in her new position she would have to act in a more restrained or subtle manner, she would always be known for what she had done while on the throne when there was little to restrain her will. There would undoubtedly be many in Israel who would never fully trust her intentions. Those who sought to hold true to the ways of God would see in her a danger, a person driven above all by power and at enmity with God. And no matter how long she had reigned on Israel's throne and no matter how much she had appropriated the trappings of her adopted kingdom, she would remain to many the Phoenician zealot who disdained the traditional values of the kingdom over which she presided and who warred against the biblical foundation on which that kingdom had been established.

Indeed, we have no evidence that Jezebel in her more restrained role had in any way softened the radical views she had implemented while on the throne. Nor does it appear that her zeal for the worship of Baal and all that came with it had in any way diminished. All the more, those who stood against her agenda would have feared what would take place if Jezebel was ever able to act again without restraint—namely that she would use the throne to launch an all-out war against God and His ways.

So for now Jezebel would continue to walk the nation's halls of power and dwell in its highest chambers as the nation's most conspicuous former and shadow queen.

The Paradigm of the Shadow Queen

> The king's reign comes to an end. The paradigm now shifts its focus to the queen. She will go on alone.

In January 2001 Bill Clinton came to his political end. The Clinton administration, the Clinton reign, and the Clinton years were over. The paradigm will now shift to his wife, Hillary Clinton.

Though in the modern scenario the man still lived and was there to advise his wife, as king, as ruler of the land, he was no more. Ahab met his end, but Jezebel would go on. Thus, according to the paradigm, after Bill Clinton's reign as ruler of the land came to its end, Hillary Clinton would continue. She would now begin her solo quest for power.

> With the end of the king's reign the queen's primary source of political power will be removed. But she will be too ambitious to fade away, to leave the national stage, or to move far from the center of power.

As Jezebel at the end of her husband's reign was left without her primary source of power, so Hillary Clinton at the end of her husband's presidency was left without her primary source of political power. But as with Jezebel, she was too ambitious to fade away or depart from the national stage. She would seek national power. And she would plan to stay close to the nation's center, its center of power. Thus she would pursue the office of US senator. In this she would be able to both remain on the national stage and stay close to the center of the American government.

> After the end of her husband's reign the queen will no longer possess the same position and authority she had possessed as co-regent. Nor will she retain her status as queen or first lady of the land. Yet she will still dwell in the nation's halls of power and sit in its highest chambers.

As Jezebel no longer possessed the same position and authority she had possessed during Ahab's reign yet continued to dwell in the palaces, chambers, and halls of the monarchy, so too her antitype, Hillary Clinton, bereft of the authority she had known in the days of her husband's reign, would continue to walk America's halls of power, dwell in its house of Congress, and sit in its highest chambers.

> The queen will continue on as an active agent and prominent figure in the nation's government and will exert influence on those in power.

So the former American first lady would continue as an active agent in the nation's government as a US senator. Her history and her persona would combine to make her one of the most prominent members of the American government. And she would still bear influence on the nation's leaders.

> The queen will dwell in the nation's capital.

After her days as reigning queen Jezebel would still dwell in the royal palaces of Israel and in Samaria, the nation's capital city. So her modern antitype, the former first lady, as senator, would likewise dwell in the nation's capital city, Washington, DC.

> The queen will now reinvent herself within the parameters of a new position and role, an identity independent from that of her husband.

So at the end of Bill Clinton's presidency Hillary Clinton would reinvent herself with the parameters of a new position and a new political identity independent from that of her husband. It was no longer Hillary Clinton, first lady, but Hillary Clinton, leader in her own right.

> The queen will use her husband's authority to build her own base of power. Her core supporters will come from those factions most strongly in favor of the new and cosmopolitan morality and most strongly opposed to traditional and biblical morality.

So Hillary Clinton began building her own power base. Her most zealous supporters were those of a liberal orientation, a cosmopolitan outlook, most in favor of the new morality they would view as progressive, and most strongly opposed to traditional and biblical morality. She would choose to run for office in New York, as the electorate there constituted one of the most liberal and cosmopolitan of electorates and least connected to traditional or biblical values. Thus she would likely find more success there than in other places.

> The queen's strongest supporters will be those who champion the practice of child sacrifice.

Jezebel's strongest supporters would be the worshippers of Baal, those who practiced or were in favor of child sacrifice. So the strongest supporters of her modern antitype, Hillary Clinton, would be those who practiced or were in favor of the practice of killing the unborn. So those most radically in favor of abortion would rally behind her.

> She will be unlike other former first ladies of the land not only in her striving to acquire her own political power but in being a polarizing figure, fiercely political, loved by some, hated by others, with followers on one hand and enemies on the other.

There had never been a former queen in Israel like Jezebel. And there had never been a former first lady in America like Hillary Clinton. Never in the nation's history had a former first lady vied for her own political and elected power. Clinton was intensely political and in the eyes of many, threatening. She was a polarizing figure with passionate followers and passionate enemies.

> Her motives, her agenda, and her ambitions will be mistrusted by many. And many people of faith will fear what would happen if she was once again to gain the power to act without restraint.

Throughout Hillary Clinton's years in the Senate the suspicion of many was that her office in Congress was only a stepping-stone in her pursuit of the presidency. And many people of faith feared what would happen to religious freedom if that pursuit was ever realized.

> Even in her more restrained role as former first lady of the land the queen will still hold to the same radical views she held to from the beginning, including her passion for the practice of child sacrifice.

The evidence we have indicates that Jezebel never turned from her worship of Baal and thus of her advocacy for child sacrifice. So too Hillary Clinton's passionate championing of abortion would continue after the end of her husband's reign. The extreme nature of that continued championing would be evidenced in March 2003 when she took to the Senate floor to defend the gruesome practice of partial-birth abortion, the same gruesome act her husband had defended as president.[1] If there had ever been one consistently and passionately championed issue throughout Hillary Clinton's career, it was that of abortion.

This next facet of the paradigm might appear to be a necessary corollary, but it is worthy of note:

> The queen will assume her new position of power twenty-two years after the king first assumed his.

Jezebel's new role and position of power began twenty-two years after Ahab began his reign as king. Hillary Clinton's life was destined to change at the end of the Clinton presidency. But had she gone back into private life, as had been the norm for a former first lady, the correspondence to the paradigm would have ended there. On the other hand, had she begun her solo political career at a later time, there may have been a parallel in nature but not in timing.

But instead, she arranged to run for the Senate well before the end of the Clinton administration. So as the Clinton presidency approached its last days, she went immediately from first lady in the White House to her career as a prominent governmental personage in the nation's highest halls of power—as had her predecessor, Jezebel. And it all took place at the twenty-two-year mark of her husband's time in power, just as it had in the paradigm of Jezebel. And as it happened in January 2001, it was twenty-two years to the month.

In 2007 the expectations of many were realized when Hillary Clinton announced her run for the presidency. It was the first time she had ever publicly announced her intention to do what most people believed had been her intention all along. The date was January 20.[2]

The date should sound familiar. January 20 was the day that marked the end of the Clinton presidency, that which in the paradigm corresponds to King Ahab's death in his chariot at Ramoth Gilead.

Hillary Clinton may have chosen the day in confidence of becoming the next president, as it marks the day of American presidential inaugurations. But whatever her motives, the date she chose was doubly striking. January 20 is also the date that marks the greatest scandal of the Clinton years. It was the day the Lewinsky scandal broke forth, the day the king's sin was exposed. Further, January 20 began the three-year countdown, the three years of Ahab, from the exposure in the vineyard to the end of his reign on the battlefield, or from the presidential scandal to the end of the Clinton presidency.

But contrary to her expectations and the expectations of many, her quest for the nation's highest seat of power would fail. But this too was already there, contained within the paradigm:

> In the reigns of the two kings following her husband the former queen will not be able to take the throne for herself.

So in the days following the end of Bill Clinton's reign, in the days of his two successors, Hillary Clinton would not take the American presidency.

What then will happen to the throne? The revelation of the paradigm is this:

> The throne will not go to the queen but to another—
> to a man of a younger age.

Who was he? He will now appear in the paradigm.

Chapter 15

The HEIR

T
HE ACCOUNT OF Ahab and Jezebel soon turns its focus to a new
character.

His name was *Joram*. He was Ahab and Jezebel's son. For the
remainder of the account it will be his reign that will form the backdrop.

Joram was the second-born son of Ahab's house. The first, Ahaziah,
would end up little more than a footnote, as his time in power was cut short
inside the space of two years. Most of the events prophesied concerning the
house of Ahab would take place in Joram's reign. As Ahab was confronted
for his wrongdoing by the prophet Elijah, Joram would be confronted for
his wrongdoing by Elijah's disciple, Elisha.

As the son of Ahab and Jezebel, Joram was raised in a house of sin
and apostasy. From Jezebel he would have been instructed in the ways of
paganism. From Ahab he would have been given an example of gross apostasy. And yet just as Ahab had maintained an awareness of God, to waver
back and forth, it appears that Joram maintained the same awareness, even
if he lived in defiance of God's ways.

In the likeness of his father, Joram might occasionally utter the name of God and even heed a word of godly counsel. But for the most part, as in the likeness of his father, he would live at best as one whose knowledge of God was without root or depth and at worst as one engaged in an active war against Him.

And yet it appears that Joram's nature and personality were very different from his father's. While Ahab was expressive and given to dramatic fluctuations of emotion, Joram appears to have been of a much cooler temperament. Whereas Ahab could go from great sin to great sorrow and repentance, it is hard to picture Joram ever allowing himself to show public remorse or to display any penitence.

If Ahab could act with recklessness, Joram appears decidedly cautious. It was apparently this caution that caused him, after witnessing the fall of judgment on his father and the land, to remove as a safeguard the pillar from the Temple of Baal. But even this appears to have been the outward act of trying to hedge his position rather than any act of sincere conviction. We have no evidence that Joram ever stopped or even opposed the worship of Baal. Rather it continued throughout his reign. The pagan Temple of Baal still stood in the midst of the capital city throughout Joram's reign. Further, he continued in the ways of idolatry, which meant that the nation's descent into moral relativism, carnality, sexual immorality, and the overturning of absolute values would continue unabated.

He was not the brash pioneer of his father, Ahab. Nor was he the fierce zealot of his mother, Jezebel. His parents had broken the ground, but Joram had continued the apostasy. So even though Joram's temperament appears more measured than that of his parents, he would in many ways continue to advance what they had begun. And so the nation would continue its descent.

The Paradigm of the Heir

In the template of Joram the key figure will be known as "the heir" to distinguish him from Ahab, who will continue to be referred to as "the king."

> In the time of the paradigm, in the days after the end of the king's reign, it will not be the queen who reigns on the throne—but a man considerably younger—the heir.

Though Hillary Clinton began as the overwhelming favorite to win the Democratic nomination in 2008, by a turn of events that surprised most observers, the nomination went to another—Barack Obama. He was considerably younger than Clinton, on the edge of another generation.

> The heir will represent the continuation of the king and queen's legacy.

In all the issues of critical import to the apostasy and the paradigm Barack Obama followed in the course inaugurated by the Clintons. Politically, culturally, and ideologically he was their heir.

Obama's political career began with his election to the Illinois State Senate. The year was 1996. The year marked the center point of the Clinton years. The same election that brought Bill Clinton back to the White House brought Barack Obama to his first public office. Obama's political birth took place in the heart of the Clinton years, a fitting time for the birth of an heir.

> The heir will in many ways take up where the king had left off. What the king had attempted to do the heir will seek to bring to fruition. What the king had initiated the heir will seek to complete.

Obama took up where Bill Clinton had left off. Policies that Clinton had pioneered Obama advanced. Programs and legislation that Clinton attempted to pass Obama reintroduced. Executive orders that Clinton had signed but had later been reversed, Obama reversed their reversal. He was the antitype of Joram, the heir to the antitype of King Ahab.

> The heir will be the third king of the paradigm, the second in line to sit on the throne after the end of the king's reign.

As Joram was the second in line to sit on the throne after the reign of Ahab, so Obama would be second in line to sit in the seat of the presidency after the end of the Clinton years.

As for Ahaziah, with a reign of less than two years, not only does it become a footnote in the royal account, but it becomes impossible to apply apart from a president resigning or dying in office two years or less from the moment of his inauguration. But beyond that the paradigm is one of apostasy. Its clear focus is the spiritual descent of the nation and the rulers who lead the nation in that descent. Whatever one thinks of the presidency of George W. Bush, with regard to the issues of apostasy the Bush presidency was a break in the progression that had begun in the Clinton years. Rather than championing such issues, he sought to stem or reverse them. The same dynamic is seen in the harbingers. Virtually every leader connected to the biblical harbingers of judgment that appeared on American soil belonged to the Democratic Party. It is not a value judgment. It is simply the outworking of the events, the unfolding of the mystery. Every leader in *The Harbinger* who uttered the ancient pronouncement of judgment upon America was a Democratic politician. So too in the paradigm the template of apostasy follows a chain of Democratic leaders until it reaches a dramatic turn of events.

This is not to say that all the stands of one political party are biblical or that all the stands of the other are not. Nor is it to say that all those affiliated with one party support unbiblical positions. Nor is it to say that there is anything intrinsic to the Democratic Party that necessitates a connection to unbiblical or anti-biblical positions. In the 1950s even its most liberal presidential candidate, Adlai Stevenson, in accepting the presidential nomination told the convention, "We must reclaim these great Christian and humane ideas." But since then the Democratic Party has undergone its own metamorphosis to become the party that has campaigned for the killing of the unborn and waged a war against biblical values. Thus on the key issues linked to Israel's downfall, the central issues of the paradigm, it has allied itself against Scripture and the ways of God. It has become the party that has championed the American apostasy.

And so as the paradigm's primary focus is the apostasy, its spotlight will be on those leaders, institutions, and powers that embody or advance that apostasy. Beyond that the ancient paradigm specifically follows the house of Ahab and after Ahab's end focuses on the two major players of that house, Jezebel and Joram. Thus in its modern replaying it will follow the house of Clinton and its legacy and will focus on two principal players, Hillary Clinton and Barack Obama. Through these two figures the modern replaying will move in a continuous progression.

And though not every detail of the ancient template must manifest, the presidency of George Bush will actually cause other of the paradigm's details to align with events of the modern world. It will serve as a placeholder to cause Obama's reign as president to align with the order of Joram's reign as the third king of the paradigm.

> The heir will at times make outward displays of piety and observance but by his actions and inaction will lead the nation in defiance of God.

Joram removed Baal's pillar but allowed the Temple of Baal and his worship to continue to thrive. So Obama would display the same pattern. When running for the presidency, he stated that as a Christian and with God "in the mix" he could not be in favor of gay marriage but opposed it. He maintained this stand for the first few years of his presidency. But it was later revealed by one of Obama's close advisors that the president's words were false and in reality he was not opposed to gay marriage but had been in favor of it from early on.[1] Thus he made an outward display of biblical morality and invoked the name of God in his denial. He acknowledged by his admission that a Christian could not be for the breaking of the biblical standard of marriage as a union of man and woman. He then proceeded to do everything in his power to break that biblical standard and cause it to be struck down.

> The heir will continue the king's policies of altering the standards and measures of morality. He will likewise be an agent for the weakening of absolutes and the overturning of biblical values.

So Obama would continue advancing Clinton's policy of "redefining...the immutable ideals that have guided us from the beginning."[2] Whether in matters of marriage, the sanctity of life, sexuality, faith, Christianity, the nature of male and female, or religious liberty, Obama would continually oppose biblical standards and values and the underlying moral presuppositions of Western civilization that had been in place for millennia.

> The heir will continue in the king's policies concerning sexual morality and the confusion of gender.

As the worship of Baal and other forms of idolatry continued under Joram's reign, so too would the accompanying displays of sexual immorality, including the rites of the kadeshim and the confusion of gender. So Obama would continue in the policies initiated by the Clintons concerning sexual morality, homosexuality, and gender. He would function as a tireless agent of the new and anti-biblical morality that the Clintons had begun to normalize. In the days of Obama they would become established.

> Under the heir the practice of sacrificing children will continue throughout the land.

As Baal worship continued to be practiced under Joram, so too did the practice of sacrificing children. So too Obama would come to the presidency holding the same beliefs concerning abortion as held by the Clintons. In the Illinois Senate he had even fought against a bill that sought to protect a baby *born alive* from being left to die. Many viewed it as infanticide. Even extreme pro-abortion legislators had voted in favor of such protections. This would place him at the most extreme end of the spectrum on the issue of abortion. He would bring these views into the White House and use the presidency to champion the practice.

> The heir will serve as another link in the chain of the nation's apostasy from God. Under his reign it will be further alienated from the biblical foundation on which it was founded.

Obama would campaign for the presidency on a slogan of "Change." And indeed he would act as an agent of change. But the most far-reaching changes he would bring would be in the social, moral, and even spiritual realms. And they would all be in the direction of moving America away from its biblical foundation.

In a speech given during his first presidential campaign Obama would broach the subject of faith. He would come out against religious conservatives. And he would make a statement that would haunt him in the days to come. He said this:

"Whatever we once were, we're no longer a Christian nation..."[3]

The fact that he then threw in the words "at least, not just"[4] when he realized what he had said in view of the fact that the written text had read "just a Christian nation" made the slip all the more striking. It would come to be seen as part of a pattern. That which Obama would present publicly on matters of faith and that which would then often come out unintentionally or in private or in subsequent actions or when speaking freely to like-minded audiences were often in stark conflict. He was nevertheless the first major candidate in the nation's history to publicly make such a declaration or any declaration even remotely along such lines.

However true it was that America was no longer a Christian nation when Obama first made that statement in his first campaign for the presidency, it would become far more true by the end of his presidency. Indeed, Obama would leave America less Christian than he found it—culturally, morally, and statistically.

———————

Not only would America become a less Christian nation; it would become increasingly an anti-Christian nation. How that connects to the paradigm and the reign of Barack Obama we will now see.

Chapter 16

The HOSTILE KINGDOM

THE CAPITAL CITY was under siege. Appalled by the misery and degradation caused by the siege, Joram becomes enraged. His rage finds a scapegoat:

> "Now it happened, when the king heard the words of the woman, that he tore his clothes... Then he said, 'God do so to me and more also, if the head of Elisha the son of Shaphat remains on him today!'"[1]

Though Elisha was not responsible for the nation's troubles, the king makes him the focus of his anger. But the prophet wasn't the only scapegoat:

> "But Elisha was sitting in his house, and the elders were sitting with him. And the king sent a man ahead of him.... And while he was still talking with them, there was the messenger, coming down to him; and then the king said, 'Surely this calamity is from the LORD; why should I wait for the LORD any longer?'"[2]

The king not only blamed the nation's trouble on the prophet—he blamed God Himself. It wasn't the first time. It was a pattern. The king had a history of blaming God for his problems as in the midst of his battle against the kingdom of Moab:

> "But the king of Israel said to him, 'No, for the LORD has called these three kings together to deliver them into the hand of Moab.'"[3]

One commentary explains it this way:

> "He had, however, a poor idea of the God of Israel, thinking of Him as a malevolent deity. Thus when the allied armies marching against Moab were suffering from a serious lack of water, he thought that it was God who was thus deliberately delivering them into the hands of the Moabites (2 Kings 3:13). Again, when the country was suffering from famine, at a time when the capital was besieged by the Arameans, he thought that these evils, too, had come from God, in whom one trusted in vain and from whom no good could be expected…"[4]

The Lord had shown patience and grace, not only to the nation of Israel but to Joram himself. More than once He had used Elisha to save him from danger. And yet Joram now sends a man to hunt Elisha down and execute him. But the problem was deeper than Joram's relationship with Elisha. It was rooted in his view of God.

We see in Joram a man whose view of God, and thus his view of everything else, is in conflict with the Scriptures and with the prophets of his day. He could invoke the Lord's name, but when it came down to the Word and ways of God, it was ultimately alien to him. The account reveals that he worshipped God in the form of an idol—in other words, a god the Israelites had made, a god of subjectivity. He could be comfortable with that, but not with the living God of the Bible and not with His ways. And as for those who held true to the ways of God, the king found them to be at best an enigma and at worst an obstacle. As seen in his attempt to take Elisha's life, he was not above persecuting the righteous. In the king's words and actions toward God, the ways of God, and those who followed the ways of God, there was a distinct and marked hostility.

The Paradigm of the Hostile Kingdom

> Though the heir may invoke the name of God, the ways of God will ultimately be alien to him. He will not be comfortable with those ways nor with those who uphold them. He will see such people as an enigma and obstacle to his agenda. His words and actions will reveal a distinct and marked hostility to the things of God.

So too Obama could at times invoke the name of God, but when it came to dealing with the Word of God or any true implication of that Word, he rarely seemed comfortable. Indeed, he rarely seemed comfortable dealing with matters of faith at all. And he appeared even less comfortable dealing with those who followed God's Word. In his days in the White House he separated himself from those who upheld biblical values while joining himself to those who most opposed those values. He would on more than one occasion allude to people of faith as problems, obstacles, or even enemies. Behind closed doors at a fund-raiser in San Francisco, Obama said this of small-town America:

> "And it's not surprising then they get bitter, they cling to guns or religion or antipathy toward people who aren't like them..."[5]

The statement caused a political uproar. But it was most revealing in providing a behind-closed-doors glimpse into Obama's true thoughts and worldview concerning God and those who follow Him.

His worldview would lead him to help bring about one of the most critical redefinings of values and overturnings of biblical standards in modern history. Midway through his presidency Obama announced that the position he had opposed while running for president, the position he said a Christian could not embrace, he would now embrace.[6] And he would not only embrace it; he would endorse it. He would champion the redefining of the historic and biblical definition of marriage. He began pressuring government bodies to overturn the historic definition of marriage. His efforts would succeed and would culminate in the Supreme Court's striking down of marriage as it had been throughout human history.[7] What Bill Clinton had begun Obama had completed. He had been instrumental in moving America even more decisively away from its biblical foundation.

> As the apostasy continues, the culture will not only accept what it has known to be wrong and what the Word of God has declared to be sin—but will celebrate and hallow it.

On the day that marriage as defined by God's Word was struck down, Obama ordered the White House to be illuminated in the colors of the rainbow to celebrate the act.[8] As in the days of Ahab and Joram the highest house in the land had been turned into a vessel of apostasy.

We began this chapter with a glimpse into King Joram's marked hostility to God and His people. We will now see the repercussions of it replaying in modern times.

> To the same degree that a civilization calls what is evil good, it will call what is good evil. To the same degree that it hallows the profane, it will profane the holy. And to the same degree it legitimizes unrighteousness, it will delegitimize the righteous.

This is the underside of the falling away. As the culture accepts what it had once known to be sin, it will begin to reject what it had once seen as righteousness. It will cease to reverence it. It will then only tolerate it and then marginalize it, then vilify it, then criminalize it, and then persecute it. So in the falling away of Western civilization from God and from its biblical faith we would expect to witness this phenomenon—a movement to persecution. This would involve the progressive marginalization of Christians and of those holding to biblical values. And this is exactly what we have witnessed beginning in American and Western civilization.

In any period of accelerating apostasy we would expect a corresponding acceleration in the marginalization of believers. And so we find it. The Clinton years that produced so many firsts in the American apostasy also produced a law that targeted those who protested the killing of children at abortion clinics.[9] The law was written so broadly that it led to the phenomenon of Christians being arrested and sent to prison for protesting what they saw as murder, or for giving counsel, or for simply praying.

But it was during the Obama years that the marginalization of Christians became especially pronounced. Part of this was the consequence of the culture's overall departure from God. But part, as in the paradigm, was a consequence of the nation's ruler, as in the template of Joram. Joram saw God as his opponent. But he also saw God's servant, Elisha, as his opponent. So it wasn't only that Obama in his policies warred against the Word of God; it was that he specifically vilified those who upheld the Word of God. When speaking to an audience of advocates for homosexuality, he spoke of those who could not go along with their agenda:

> "I don't have to tell you, there are those who don't want to just stand in our way, but want to turn the clock back..."[10]

The ones the president referred to as "those" included every person who upheld the Word of God. According to the president, they were standing in "our way." In one sentence he had marginalized and cut off all those who followed the Bible, as in evangelical Christians, from the mainstream of his America. Those who follow the Bible were not just cut off—they were obstacles, hindrances, opponents, threats, and enemies.

Likewise, when Obama became the first sitting American president to address the nation's largest practitioner of abortion, Planned Parenthood, he spoke of pro-life leaders as enemies, if not villains. His closing words of "God bless you" to the abortion organization left several commentators wondering which God it was who blesses those who kill and dismember unborn children.[11] There was one. His name was Baal.

The following is a record of some of the acts of hostility toward God, His ways, and His people that took place under the Obama administration.[12] Note that what took place in the American military provides an even more revealing picture, as military society is more subject to the influence and orders of government than is the general population. Further note this is just a sampling and one that only covers the first few of the Obama years:

- In January of 2009, the month Obama began his presidency, the same month he wiped away the safeguards put in place to protect the unborn,[13] his nominee for deputy secretary of state declared that Americans would be required to pay for abortions.[14] In February of that same year, Obama announced his plan to nullify conscience protection for health workers, meaning that they could now be forced to participate in acts that violated their faith—as in the killing of the unborn.[15]

- In March, Obama gave fifty million dollars to UNFPA, the UN agency that worked with population control officials in China who practice forced abortion.[16] The same month, his administration excluded pro-life groups from attending a White House–sponsored health care gathering.[17] In April the Obama administration ordered that a monogram representing the name of Jesus at a religious university be covered up while the president delivered a speech there.[18]

- In May officials from the Obama administration accused those who were pro-life of being violent and using racism in carrying out "criminal" acts.[19] The same month, the president refused to host services in the White House for the federally established National Day of Prayer.[20] In September a woman who declared that society should "not tolerate" any "private beliefs," including any private religious beliefs that might negatively impact homosexual rights, was appointed by the Obama administration to head the Equal Employment Opportunity Commission.[21]

- In July 2010 the Obama administration used federal funds to force the nation of Kenya to change its constitution to embrace abortion.[22] In August, under orders from the Obama administration, funding for 176 abstinence education programs was slashed.[23] In September the Obama administration told researchers to disregard a judicial decision striking down federal funding for embryonic stem cell research.[24]

- In October, Obama began omitting the word *Creator* in his quoting of the Declaration of Independence. The omission could not be considered accidental, as he would repeat the omission on no fewer than seven occasions.[25]

- In January 2011 the Obama administration refused to allow a cross from a World War I memorial to be re-erected in the Mojave Desert, as decreed by federal law.[26] For over two years Obama had allowed the post of religious freedom ambassador, a position established to work against religious persecution around the world, to remain vacant. He finally filled the post in February, but only after being heavily pressured by the public and Congress.[27] That same month, Obama ordered the Justice Department to cease defending the Defense of Marriage Act.[28]

- In April, Obama pushed for the passage of a nondiscrimination law that for the first time in American history contained no protection for religious groups.[29] In August the Obama administration released new health care regulations nullifying religious conscience protections for medical workers with regard to abortion.[30] In September the Army informed the Walter Reed National Military Medical Center that no religious items (as in Bibles) would be allowed in hospital visits.[31] That same month, the Air Force chief of staff banned commanders from informing airmen of the religious services available to them.[32] In December 2011 the administration attacked the religious beliefs of other nations on the grounds that they constituted an obstacle with regard to homosexuality.[33]

- In January 2012 the administration declared that churches had no First Amendment protection in hiring their ministers.[34] In February the Air Force removed the word *God* from its Rapid Capabilities Office patch.[35] In April the Air Force stopped ensuring that Bibles would be available in its lodgings.[36] In May the Obama administration opposed the protection of conscience for military chaplains who could not violate their faith by performing same-sex marriages.[37] In June the administration ordered that US military service emblems no longer be allowed to appear on military Bibles.[38]

- In January 2013 Obama declared his opposition to the inclusion of a protection for the right of conscience for military chaplains in the National Defense Authorization Act.[39] In February the administration announced that religious rights of conscience would not be recognized or protected under the Affordable Care Act.[40] In April the US Agency for International Development began training homosexual activists to overturn traditional and biblical values around the world, targeting first those nations with cultures strongly rooted in Catholicism.[41] That same month, the Air Force put together a "religious tolerance" policy without consulting any religious groups but seeking advice only from a militant atheist organization. The organization's leader described religious personnel as "human monsters" and "spiritual rapists" and stated that soldiers who spread their faith were guilty of treason and should receive punishment.[42] It was discovered that same month that soldiers in training were being taught that those who subscribe to evangelical Christianity and Catholicism were dangerous religious extremists and were to be associated with al Qaeda.[43]

- In May the Pentagon announced that if a member of the Air Force should share his or her faith with another member and it results in anyone feeling uncomfortable, then the one who shared his or her faith could be court-martialed.[44] The same month, the Obama administration ordered employers to offer abortion-causing drugs to their employees, contradicting the orders given by several federal courts to protect the right of conscience.[45] That same month, the administration strongly objected to a Defense Authorization amendment protecting the religious rights of soldiers and chaplains.[46]

- In July an Air Force sergeant who questioned a same-sex marriage ceremony performed at the Air Force Academy chapel was reprimanded and told that if he disagreed, he would need to leave the military. Later he was informed that he would be retired at the end of the year.[47] In October in a counterintelligence briefing at Fort Hood military leaders instructed soldiers that evangelical Christians were a threat to the nation.[48]

This again is only a sampling and only touches the first few years of Obama's presidency. It doesn't include such acts of judicial hostility as the arrest and imprisonment of a Christian county clerk for being unable to place her name on a same-sex marriage license—and the White House approval of her arrest.[49] The acts of hostility would continue to the very end of Obama's presidency. In his last months in office he would threaten to veto a defense bill because it contained religious protections.[50] Earlier that year an Air Force veteran who had been invited to give a speech at a retirement ceremony at Travis Air Force Base was physically apprehended in the middle of his speech by several men wearing army fatigues. They shoved and dragged him out of the ceremony. He was assaulted because he had mentioned the word *God*.[51]

With four months left to go in his presidency, Obama's Commission on Civil Rights released a report that called *religious liberty* and *religious freedom* "code words for discrimination, intolerance, racism, sexism, homophobia, Islamophobia, Christian supremacy or any form of intolerance."[52] Several analysts voiced the concern that by issuing such a report, the administration was paving the way for the ultimate elimination of religious liberty and future persecution of Christians. Two thousand years earlier it was the hostility of the state against Christians and its attempt to use force to compel them to act against their faith and conscience that led to the spilling of blood in Roman stadiums. Many became concerned that a similar pattern was beginning to unfold in modern-day Western civilization.

It is impossible to view such a record and evade the conclusion of a deep-rooted hostility against biblical faith. But the paradigm we are dealing with is that of Joram, a man whose words and actions reveal this very thing.

———————

But Joram was not alone in the royal palace. There was another.

Chapter 17

HEIR and QUEEN

JORAM DIDN'T RULE alone. He was king. But there was another residing with him in the royal palace, a figure of great influence, known throughout the kingdom and feared throughout the land—Jezebel.

She was a continual presence in Israel's political life not only after the end of Ahab's reign; she was so for *years* after the end of his reign. Most of those years focused on Joram's reign. She would have retained a place of prominence in his court not only as the former queen and first lady of the land but as queen mother. The king was her junior.

Her former position at the pinnacle of Israel's government combined with her many years in that position would have given her considerable status and influence. She had reigned at Ahab's side as his co-regent, and she knew well how to employ the machinery of state to accomplish one's purposes. As she was very much involved in the running of the nation's government in the days of her husband's reign, she would have undoubtedly sought similar influence in the days of her son's reign.

We know that Jezebel had incited Ahab to act and had guided his policies. Thus she was adept at using her influence to guide the king and affect and even determine his policies. This ability would serve her well in her new position as queen mother, where her primary power would lie in her ability to influence and sway the king. Even though she was no longer queen, the fact the king was her son would undoubtedly be a strong factor in her ability to continue influencing the government of the kingdom.

And then of course Jezebel was a particularly strong-willed queen with an unbending personality. At Ahab's side she had broken the bounds of what was expected of her position. We have no reason to believe that any of these characteristics ceased or diminished in her new position as queen mother.

Then there are the actions of King Joram himself. Though he was not as pioneering in apostasy as were his parents, he still followed in their course of defiance. His view of the God of Israel as an opponent would be consistent with his mother's view. Then there is the evidence of King Joram's own actions.

One can see Jezebel's influence in the words and actions of King Joram. When Joram treated Elisha as his enemy to the point of seeking his death, he was following in the footsteps of Jezebel, who saw Elijah as her enemy and sought his death. When he spoke of the God of Israel as his opponent, his view was consistent with that of his mother.

We know from what is revealed later on in the account that Jezebel's influence and impact on the kingdom was still considerable. We know also that she stayed in close proximity to the king, as they appear together later on in the account in the royal palace of Jezreel. Of Jezebel's role and influence in her post-Ahab years the commentaries say this:

> "After Ahab's death, Jezebel held power over her son..."[1]

> "It seems that after the death of her husband, Jezebel maintained considerable ascendancy over her son Jehoram [Joram]..."[2]

> "Even after Ahab's death, Jezebel still exercised much influence in Israel...her sons...ruled as successive kings and promoted her religious policies..."[3]

So Joram did not ascend the throne alone but with Jezebel, his mother, at his side. She was the one with greater experience in the highest echelons of power. She would be his counsel, advising him on affairs of state, foreign relations, domestic policies, and matters of religion. She would also at times undoubtedly sway and incite him to action. The two would preside over the nation's government, the younger man in the spotlight wielding the kingdom's ultimate authority, and the older woman, his counsel, wielding influence in the shadows of his throne.

As much as she was able, she would undoubtedly advocate for Baal and the gods of Phoenicia. Though her formal power had been diminished from what it was in the days of her husband's reign, her informal power, her ability to influence king and kingdom, would have remained considerable. Her role as queen mother, combined with her past as one who had once ruled the kingdom with an iron hand, would have made her an intimidating figure. Even from behind the throne she would have undoubtedly retained an outsized influence. She was, after all, Jezebel.

The Paradigm of the Heir and Queen

In all of American history there had never been a scenario that would have matched this template of the paradigm. If it was to be fulfilled, it would have to be fulfilled in the days of the modern antitypes of Joram and Jezebel.

Jezebel had gone on after the end of her husband's reign. She had continued to stay close to power and dwell in the nation's halls of government. So Hillary Clinton had gone on after the end of her husband's presidency. She had pursued her own political career, remained on the national stage, and dwelt in the capital city. But the paradigm goes further. Jezebel didn't just dwell in the capital city or in the high places of government; she dwelt *within the royal palace itself.* Thus the paradigm:

> Not only will the former queen and first lady reside in the nation's capital city; she will dwell in the royal palace, in the house of the king.

The modern American equivalent to the king's house or palace is the White House, the president's dwelling. The paradigm speaks of the former first lady dwelling in the palace of her husband's successor, active in the nation's governing. So for this part of the ancient template to be fulfilled, a former first lady would have to move and operate within the White House after the end of her husband's presidency. She would have to in some way be part of another president's staff or cabinet.

Never in American history had a first lady returned to the White House to become part of another president's cabinet. Yet this is what the paradigm reveals. Though it had never before happened, if it was to be fulfilled, its fulfillment would have to take place in the days of Joram's antitype, Barack Obama.

Within a week of his election to the presidency in November 2008 Obama contacted Hillary Clinton to ask her to become his secretary of state.[4] The fighting between the Obama and Clinton camps during the campaign was so fierce that few people imagined that such a thing was possible. But according to the paradigm, the former first lady would again dwell in the White House. So Clinton accepted and in early January was confirmed as secretary of state. What had never before happened in American history had now happened, the heir and the former first lady were now dwelling together in the palace according to the paradigm.

> The heir will begin his reign in the palace with the former queen as part of his court.

Joram began his reign as king with Jezebel at his side as part of his royal court. So Barack Obama began his presidency with former first lady Hillary Clinton as part of his cabinet. It is noteworthy that Obama's election represented the first return of a Democratic president to the White House since the end of the Clinton presidency. Thus it was the first possible moment that the paradigm could have been fulfilled, as she could have only returned to the White House under an administration of her own party. So the first moment it was possible, she was back in the king's palace.

> The former first lady will dwell in the king's palace not only as former first lady or as a member of the royal household or to function in a ceremonial role— but to play an active part in governing and influencing the reign of the new leader.

So Hillary Clinton returned to the White House not as former first lady and not in a ceremonial position but as an active agent in the new president's administration.

> The former queen will serve as counselor, a senior advisor to influence the new leader.

Jezebel would undoubtedly serve Joram as counselor and advisor, just as she had served as counselor and advisor to her husband in earlier days. She would likewise seek to influence the new king in the realm of public policy. So Clinton in her role as secretary of state would serve not only as Obama's representative but as his counselor in the realm of public policy.

Joram and Jezebel's days in the royal palace produce this paradigm:

> In the nation's highest house will dwell two major figures of power—the younger and more public of the two, the heir now reigning as king on the throne—and the older, the former first lady, a carryover from a previous reign, ambitious for power yet constrained by her position, and dwelling in the heir's shadow.

The combination of Clinton and Obama formed what was in many ways an unlikely duo and unprecedented—two major figures of power, the younger and more visible of the two, Obama, the president—and the older of the two, the former first lady, the remnant of the Clinton years, still ambitious for political power and for the presidency yet constrained by her position as a cabinet member to dwell in the current president's shadow.

As Jezebel's zeal for Baal would not have diminished in her days with Joram, she would have undoubtedly continued to advocate for Phoenician religious practice, including the offering up of children. Bill Clinton's presidency had begun with the signing of executive orders to expand abortion around the world. Barack Obama's presidency began exactly the same way, with the signing of the same orders. The two signings took place sixteen years apart. But there was one common denominator between them—one person remained the same and in the White House during both administrations—the one person for whom abortion was the crowning issue—Hillary Clinton. So it was in the reigns of Ahab and Joram, the most prominent common denominator between them was Jezebel.

Jezebel would have advised Joram not only on domestic issues but on foreign policy, on relations between Israel and her native Phoenicia, between Israel and Aram-Damascus, the land of her husband's archenemy, Ben-Hadad, and between Israel and other lands. If Jezebel could have spread the worship of Baal with its child sacrifices and sexual immoralities into other nations, she would have done so. It is unlikely that she or Joram had the power to do so—but Hillary Clinton and Barack Obama did.

> The former queen, by the heir's side, will still continue in her ways and beliefs and thus will still champion the new morality and the practice of child sacrifice. She will still oppose and seek the overturning of biblical morality and values.

Hillary Clinton, along with Obama, would use American foreign policy as an instrument to bring about social and moral change in other nations. They would make the new morality an objective of foreign policy. They would seek to pressure and force other nations with traditional or biblical views on moral issues such as abortion and homosexuality to change their views and policies. Clinton would make American foreign policy an apparatus of feminism. She and Obama would seek to expand abortion throughout the world. Millions of American dollars would pour into campaigns aimed at expanding the practice of abortion in poor nations.

And as Jezebel warred against traditional religious faith, so Secretary of State Clinton would now lecture the world on the subject. She would portray traditional religious belief as an obstacle, an opposing force to be overturned so that the values and policies she and Obama were seeking to advance could be imposed throughout the world.

Had Jezebel herself become the American secretary of state in the early twenty-first century, we could imagine her implementing just such an agenda.

But there was still a matter of unfinished business—Osama Bin Laden. He had still eluded capture. Could the paradigm contain even what would happen regarding America's nemesis? The answer is, amazingly, yes.

Chapter 18

The ASSASSIN

THE NATION'S NEMESIS was still at large. Ben-Hadad, king of Syria, or Aram-Damascus, had done more than threaten the kingdom of Israel—he had more than once brought tragedy to its borders, national calamity, invasion, the siege of its chief city. He posed a continual threat to Israel's security and well-being. King Ahab had made the mistake of letting him go. He would live to regret it, as Ben-Hadad would again bring calamity to the nation.

But the days of Ahab's reign were now over. Ben-Hadad had outlasted them. And he was still as great a danger to the nation's security as he had been in earlier days. But the recompense for his bloodshed was coming. The time of his end was drawing near.

> "Then Elisha went to Damascus, and Ben-Hadad king of Syria was sick; and it was told him, saying, 'The man of God has come here.' And the king said to Hazael, 'Take a present in your hand, and go to meet the man of God, and inquire of the LORD by him, saying, "Shall I recover from this disease?"'"[1]

So Elisha went to the land of Ben-Hadad, the nation's archenemy—and his own. Ben-Hadad had previously sent his soldiers into Israel to capture the prophet. The Scriptures don't reveal the reason for Elisha's visit, but the outcome of that visit reveals the sovereign purpose behind it.

The account introduces a new figure, Hazael. Hazael was a member of Ben-Hadad's inner court. His name is first mentioned much earlier, when God told the prophet Elijah to anoint Hazael king of Syria. We don't know if Elijah ever fulfilled the command given him. But now Elisha is going to meet Hazael and, in effect, do the same thing.

> "So Hazael went to meet him and took a present with him, of every good thing of Damascus, forty camel-loads; and he came and stood before him, and said, 'Your son Ben-Hadad king of Syria has sent me to you, saying, "Shall I recover from this disease?"'
>
> "And Elisha said to him, 'Go, say to him, "You shall certainly recover." However the LORD has shown me that he will really die.'"[2]

The prophet's response has lent itself to differing interpretations. One is that he was saying that Ben-Hadad's disease would not in itself be fatal. He would recover from his illness except that something more dangerous was awaiting him. Another is that the word was strategic, a matter of disinformation sent to an evil king that he not be aware of his end.

> "Then he set his countenance in a stare until he was ashamed; and the man of God wept. And Hazael said, 'Why is my lord weeping?'
>
> "He answered, 'Because I know the evil that you will do to the children of Israel.... The LORD has shown me that you will become king over Syria.'"[3]

The prophet, in tears, reveals to Hazael that he will become the new king of Syria in place of Ben-Hadad.

> "Then he departed from Elisha, and came to his master, who said to him, 'What did Elisha say to you?' And he answered, 'He told me you would surely recover.'"[4]

There are different views as well concerning Hazael. Some commentators believe that he had already entertained plans of seizing the throne from his master. Others believe it was Elisha's prophecy that placed the idea in his mind. We have no record of Elisha telling Hazael how the prophecy would be fulfilled. But the utterance of the prophecy was enough. Ben-Hadad was to die. Hazael was to become king of Syria. The meeting of the prophet and messenger would prove to be a most critical encounter. It would set in motion a series of events that would alter ancient history:

> "But it happened on the next day that he took a thick cloth and dipped it in water, and spread it over his face so that he died; and Hazael reigned in his place."[5]

Hazael took matters into his own hands and became his master's assassin. He would become the new ruler of Aram-Damascus. Though he was undoubtedly an evil and unscrupulous man, the event was the fulfillment of long-waiting prophecy and a long-coming judgment. Ben-Hadad's days of menacing Israel were finally over. The nation's nemesis was dead.

The Paradigm of the Assassin

The assassination of the leader of Aram-Damascus would seem an obscure footnote of ancient history. But this particular footnote belongs to the paradigm. Could even this obscure facet of the ancient template lie, as with the others, behind some of the most dramatic events of our times?

If the Ben-Hadad of the paradigm's modern replaying is Osama Bin Laden, and if the paradigm contains the death of Ben-Hadad, then could it also contain and foretell the death of Osama Bin Laden?

We will open the paradigm of the assassination, the death of the nemesis, and see where it leads us. To begin, we must reset the stage.

In the reign of King Ahab a nemesis arises against Israel, who will continually threaten the nation's security and invade it. The first of his two-part name will carry the sound *Bn* and means son. Ahab will have the chance to eliminate the nation's nemesis but will let him go. The nemesis will end up bringing calamity to the nation. He will at one point launch an attack that will strike its capital and chief city.

This is the paradigm of Ben-Hadad, the nemesis. It corresponds with the nemesis of our times, the man who arose in the reign of Bill Clinton, who continually threatened America, whose two-part name begins with the sound *Bn* and means son—Osama Bin Laden.

> Three years after the king's confession of his sin the nemesis will bring calamity upon the nation.

As we have seen, calamity would come to America on September 11, 2001, and behind it was the nation's arch nemesis, Osama Bin Laden. It would come according to the paradigm, three years after the president's confession, to the day.

But what happened *after* 9/11?

As soon as it was determined that Bin Laden was the mastermind of the attack, he became the most wanted man on earth. And thus began the most extensive and costly manhunt in world history. A reward of twenty-five million dollars was offered for his capture. Al Qaeda agents were rounded up and interrogated in secret prisons around the world. Intelligence agencies spent countless hours listening in on telephone calls and analyzing e-mails and satellite images.

Early rumors were that Bin Laden had been killed or gravely injured or was suffering from kidney failure or had died of natural causes. It soon became obvious that if Bin Laden wasn't already dead, he had completely eluded all efforts to detect his whereabouts. All the investigative efforts of American intelligence agencies and of intelligence agencies throughout the world had produced no tangible results.

By 2005, within the CIA it was widely believed that all leads in the hunt for Bin Laden had grown cold. National security and intelligence officials believed that Bin Laden was living in the remote mountainous region in between Afghanistan and Pakistan. This commonly held assumption proved to be false. Bin Laden turned out to be living in a compound in the midst of a populated area in Pakistan. He was hiding in plain sight. It was by a series of quirks, guesses, leads, and turns of events at the right time after years of exhaustive pursuit that the most massive manhunt in history would finally close in on its object.[6]

The events leading up to the death of Ben-Hadad would begin with Elisha, a citizen of Israel, the same kingdom against which Ben-Hadad had warred and invaded. It would be his words given in secret to Hazael and concerning Ben-Hadad's death that would set in motion the assassination.

> The events leading up to the death of the nemesis will originate from the same nation that the nemesis had warred against and invaded.

The events that would lead to the death of Osama Bin Laden would originate from the same nation the terrorist had threatened, warred against, and invaded on 9/11—America. The plans that would lead up to the assassination would first be conceived in secret in US intelligence headquarters.

In the ancient account the judgment is initiated by supernatural means. Elisha speaks of things he can only know by divine agency. Further it is Elisha's prophetic knowledge that works against Ben-Hadad in his attempts to bring destruction to Israel. At one point Ben-Hadad becomes alarmed that the words and plans he has spoken in secret are being made known to his enemies:

> "Therefore the heart of the king of Syria was greatly troubled by this thing; and he called his servants and said to them, 'Will you not show me which of us is for the king of Israel?'
>
> "And one of his servants said, 'None, my lord, O king; but Elisha, the prophet who is in Israel, tells the king of Israel the words that you speak in your bedroom.'"[7]

Elisha, by his prophetic gifting, knows what is being spoken in Ben-Hadad's bedroom. And it will be the operation of Elisha's prophetic gift that will bring about Ben-Hadad's end.

Bin Laden's end of course would not come about by prophetic gifts. But it would come about, nevertheless, more than anything by means of intelligence, by the acquisition of knowledge that would have otherwise remained secret. As Ben-Hadad was concerned over his words and actions becoming known to his enemies, so too would be Bin Laden. For that reason he would avoid any use of cell phone and Internet communication.

But the breakthrough would come when through covert surveillance US intelligence was able to trace his whereabouts to a compound in Abbottabad, Pakistan. It would lead those searching for Bin Laden to his living quarters—even to his bedroom.

In view of all this it is worth noting the meaning of Hazael's name. The nemesis will be killed by one whose name means God has seen.

Hazael is introduced in the biblical account as the one sent by Ben-Hadad to bear the king's message and bring the king's goods:

> "Take a present in your hand, and go to meet the man of God, and inquire of the LORD by him, saying, 'Shall I recover from this disease?'"[8]

The word that describes one who is sent to bear a message and goods is *courier*. One commentary describes Hazael's entrance into the biblical account this way:

> "Ben-Hadad does not issue an arrest order as on a previous occasion, but tenders a quite different kind of supplication…Ben-Hadad seeks a word from Elisha in the midst of his illness…*The courier of the king's message* is Hazael, making his first formal appearance in the story."[9]

Who is Hazael? He is Ben-Hadad's courier. He is sent to meet Elisha as courier because Ben-Hadad is unable to leave his quarters. He is then sent back to Ben-Hadad as courier to relay the prophet's words. But it will be Hazael's function as courier that will lead to Ben-Hadad's death. The paradigm of the courier:

> The nemesis, unable to leave his quarters, will use a courier to send forth and receive messages and items. But in the end it will be his courier who will be the vessel and key in bringing about his assassination.

In the paradigm it is the courier of the nemesis who is the key instrument in bringing about the assassination. In the hunt for Bin Laden interrogations of al Qaeda operatives turned up stories of a man especially trusted and used by Bin Laden—Bin Laden's *courier*. Gradually intelligence agents were able to uncover the courier's family name. They then began intercepting communications between the courier's family and anyone in Pakistan.

In the summer of 2010 Pakistani operatives of the CIA wrote down the license plate of a white Suzuki driving the streets near Peshawar, Pakistan. The car was being driven by Bin Laden's courier. They began tracking him throughout central Pakistan. Finally he led them to a heavily fortified complex in the city of Abbottabad. After years of fruitless searching, the courier had led them to Bin Laden's compound.[10]

Though he certainly never gave his consent to the death of his master— nevertheless it was the courier who became the primary key and vessel in the killing of Osama Bin Laden. As in the paradigm it is the courier who ends up bringing about the assassination of the nemesis.

In the paradigm Ben-Hadad, when speaking of Elisha, the man who will initiate the events that will bring about his death, speaks of his own *bedroom*. Thus the bedroom will be central in the paradigm of the assassination.

When Hazael approaches to take his life, Ben-Hadad is lying in bed, presumably asleep:

> When his assassination draws near, the nemesis will be lying in his bed.

On May 1, 2011, a fleet of helicopters carrying a commando team of Navy SEALs took off from their base in Jalalabad, Afghanistan, and raced across the Pakistani border toward the compound in Abbottabad. In Pakistan it was just past midnight. The helicopters swooped down on their target, and the Navy SEALs stormed the compound. A firefight broke out. Several of Bin Laden's people were killed as the commandos made their way up to the third floor, where they found the object of their mission—Bin Laden.

When the helicopters descended on the compound, Bin Laden was in his bedroom. As in the paradigm, when his assassination drew near, the nemesis was in his bedroom, lying on his bed.

Hazael entered Ben-Hadad's bedchamber with the intent of killing him. We don't know if Ben-Hadad resisted or not, but he was apparently in a weakened and defenseless position.

> The assassin will enter the nemesis's sleeping quarters. There the nation's archenemy will be killed in his own bedroom.

The first Navy SEAL to spot Bin Laden would find him peering out from the bedroom. He would be shot and shot again. He would die in a pool of blood in front of his bed. As in the paradigm, the assassin enters the sleeping quarters of the nation's archenemy, and there his target is killed.[11] The nemesis dies in his own bedroom.

———

What about timing? Could the timing of the assassination in the ancient paradigm reveal or have determined the timing of the assassination of Osama Bin Laden? What does the paradigm say?

The assassination of Ben-Hadad would not take place in the reign of Ahab. Nor would it take place in the reign of the king who followed him.

> The nemesis will not be assassinated in the reign of the first king of the paradigm, the one with whom the nemesis first warred. Nor will he be assassinated in the reign of his successor.

What about Bin Laden? In the 1990s, when he was increasing as a threat to American security, the Clinton administration had an interest in capturing or assassinating him but for varied reasons did not. The Clinton administration was followed by the Bush administration. Less than a year into its term came 9/11. From then on, the capture or assassination of Bin Laden was among the highest priorities of American foreign policy. Yet even the greatest manhunt in world history and the resources of the world's only superpower failed to come up with any tangible results in the years of the Bush presidency. This all followed in complete accord with the parameters of the paradigm. The nemesis would not be killed in the reign of the first king of the paradigm or in that of his successor.

Ben-Hadad would be assassinated in the reign of the third king, the second after Ahab's end. He would be killed in the reign of the heir, Joram.

> The assassination of the nemesis will take place in the reign of the third king.

If the paradigm assigns the assassination of the nemesis to the third reign of the template, thus to the third presidency, or the second presidency after the end of the Clinton administration—then it means that the assassination of Osama Bin Laden will take place in the presidency of Barack Obama. And so it did.

When Ben-Hadad was assassinated in his bedroom in Aram-Damascus, back in Israel, in the royal palace, King Joram sat on the throne. He would have undoubtedly rejoiced in hearing the news of his enemy's death. But he wouldn't have been alone. In the royal palace as well would have been the former first lady of the land, Jezebel. She too would have rejoiced in hearing of Ben-Hadad's assassination, as he had been the deadly thorn in the side of her husband's reign.

> At the time when the nemesis is killed, the third king, the heir, will be residing in the royal palace with the former first lady. Both will rejoice in the news of his assassination.

So at the time of Bin Laden's killing, Obama was in the White House, along with the former first lady Hillary Clinton. Both rejoiced when they heard Bin Laden had been killed.

Could there be even more contained in the paradigm concerning these events? Could it pinpoint even further the time when Bin Laden would be assassinated?

While the Scriptures do not provide exact time parameters concerning the events surrounding the death of Ben-Hadad, there is enough information from ancient history for the timing of the assassination to be determined. Hazael began his reign as king in 842 BC. Thus 842 BC is the year Ben-Hadad's reign came to an end—the year he was killed by Hazael.

tion within the parameters of the paradigm:

> The nemesis will be assassinated ten years after the end of the king's reign (the king against whom he first warred, the king who had the chance to arrest or kill him but didn't).

> The assassination will take place thirteen years after the king's sin is exposed, thirteen years after the scandal, and thirteen years after the king's repentance.

> The assassination of the nemesis will take place ten years after the day of bloodshed and calamity—ten years after his victory, when he dealt a deadly blow against the nation.

Let's take each of these and see where it leads us.

Ten years after the end of the king's reign: The first king of the paradigm and the one with whom Ben-Hadad first warred is Ahab. Ahab's modern antitype is Bill Clinton. So according to the paradigm, the death of the nemesis, Osama Bin Laden, will take place ten years after the end of Clinton's presidency. The end of Clinton's presidency came in 2001. Ten years after that end takes us to the year 2011.

Thirteen years after the exposing of the king's sin and scandal: The exposing of the president's sin and scandal took place in the year 1998. Thirteen years after the exposure takes us to the year 2011.

The paradigm points to the year 2011 for the assassination of the nemesis. *Osama Bin Laden was assassinated in the year 2011.*

Then there is the connection to September 11, 2001:

Thus according to the paradigm, Osama Bin Laden would be assassinated ten years after the calamity he inflicted on America—9/11. Thus, even with the greatest manhunt in history and with all the resources of American and global intelligence, according to the paradigm, Bin Laden would not be killed in the years immediately following 9/11. His death was appointed for the tenth year after the calamity he brought to American soil—2011.

When Bin Laden's courier led intelligence operatives to the compound in Abbottabad, and when the CIA then concluded that Bin Laden was inside that compound, it constituted the key event and critical breakthrough in the ten-year manhunt. From the moment of that discovery Bin Laden's death was sealed. When did it happen? It took place in September 2010. September 2010 also marked the turning point in the countdown, the start of the tenth year, the year in which the nemesis was to be killed.

Though he couldn't have known it, nor could his victims, from the moment Bin Laden carried out his plan to inflict calamity on America on September 11, 2001, he had sealed his fate. According to the paradigm, the nemesis would have ten years to live after that day. Then, in the tenth year, he would be assassinated in his bedroom.

We are now about to enter the final drama in which we will see all the elements of the paradigm come together and the fulfillment of everything that was prophesied.

Chapter 19

The WAR of THRONES

A SHOWDOWN WAS COMING. There were two nations in one. The first was represented by Joram, Jezebel, the house of Ahab, the worshippers of Baal, and the majority who simply went along with the apostasy. The second was represented by the prophets and those who had remained true to God and His Word. They were the minority, committed to following the ways of righteousness despite every pressure to the contrary. They were praying for a national return to God, a revival.

But the longer the house of Ahab was allowed to remain in power, the greater its ability to wipe away biblical faith and the greater its chance of doing so. Commentaries describe the gravity of the situation this way:

> "…Baal-worship would have been riveted upon the northern, perhaps even upon the southern, kingdom."[1]

> "Unchecked, this movement would surely have entirely stamped out biblical religion in the northern kingdom."[2]

The influence of the house of Ahab had now spanned decades. By virtue of time and inertia its ways were becoming more and more ingrained in government, custom, culture, and faith. Its impact was even spreading to the southern kingdom of Judah, where it would at one point threaten the very survival of King David's dynasty. For the people of God the situation seemed hopeless. The house of Ahab was entrenched on the throne. There was no way out.

But a prophecy had been given, Elijah's word to Ahab in the vineyard of Naboth. Jezebel had to have known of it. Whether she ever told Joram we don't know. The word foretold the overturning and vanquishing of Ahab's dynasty. It would involve the son of Ahab, the house of Ahab, and his wife, Jezebel.

When would it happen? According to Elijah's word, it would take place after Ahab's death, in the reign of his son. That son could only be Joram. The prophecy mentions Jezebel specifically by name. Thus Jezebel would still be present and a prominent force on the national stage at the time of the prophecy's fulfillment. So the overturning of thrones was appointed to take place at the end of Joram's reign.

Two forces, two worldviews, two courses, two futures, and two civilizations were about to come head-to-head and clash.

A showdown was coming.

The Paradigm of the War of Thrones

> There will be two nations in one—the one committed to or accepting of the new morality, the nation's descent of apostasy, and the overthrow of biblical morality. The other will be resolved to hold true to God and His ways, to resist the apostasy, and to pray for a national return to God. In the days of the heir the government and culture will be in the hands of the first.

During the Obama years American culture became especially polarized. There were two Americas—one largely committed to or accepting of an anti-biblical morality and the overturning of biblical values, and the other

By the end of the Obama years those who held to God's ways saw the state of American culture as increasingly hopeless. They had witnessed what appeared to be never-ending war against biblical values and an unrelenting encroachment against religious freedom. And now it seemed to be heading past the point of no return.

If in the coming election another came to the presidency committed to following in the path of Barack Obama, the apostasy would be sealed into permanency. The appointment of Supreme Court judges by such a president would further consign the nation to a course of apostasy far beyond the presidential election. And it looked as if everything in the nation's political realm, cultural realm, and spiritual realm was leading up to the same outcome.

> As the reign of the heir approaches its end, events will coalesce to bring about a dramatic clash of forces, directions, worldviews, agendas, cultures, and values.

In the case of Joram the end of his reign would witness a showdown of forces and worldviews. The resulting conflict would bring disaster upon the royal house. In the modern case a president's term in office always concludes with a conflict of agendas inherent in a presidential election. At the same time, elections do not always bring about a dramatic showdown of cultures and values. But the presidential election that took place at the end of the Obama years most certainly did. It would see a dramatic clashing of worldviews, and it would turn out to be one of the most dramatic and unprecedented elections in American history. So it was at the close of the Obama years that the conflict of cultures, worldviews, and values that had increasingly polarized the nation erupted onto the national stage.

> ...th the heir and the former first lady will be promi-

take place.

So both antitypes, that of Joram and that of Jezebel, Obama and Hillary Clinton, became focal points in the conflict of cultures, values, and parties that saturated the election of 2016. The former first lady would launch her second run for the presidency in April 2015.

Jezebel's conviction and agenda concerning the nation of Israel had always been that its deep-seated religious beliefs had to be changed. Why? So that the worship of Baal could expand. She had tried to change those deep-seated religious beliefs through edicts, cultural importation, and persecution. We have no evidence that her convictions and agenda ever changed concerning this objective.

> The former first lady's conviction and agenda will be that deep-seated religious beliefs must be changed.

The launching of Clinton's run for the presidency was made through a video commercial. The first major speech of her campaign came later that month. It happened at the 2015 Women in the World Summit in New York City. It was more than the first major speech of her campaign. It was per-haps the most revealing speech she had ever given as it contained perhaps the most revealing statement she had ever uttered in public. She said this:

> "…deep-seated cultural codes, *religious beliefs,* and structural biases *have to be changed.*"[3]

Never in American history had any major candidate for president ever uttered such radical words. Never had any president or major governmental leader uttered such radical words. There was no way around its ramifications. She was not only publicly declaring her conflict with religious belief; she was actually calling for its overthrow. Such a statement presumes an authority over that of God's Word. For a major candidate to publicly issue such a declaration at the very start of a presidential campaign was an omen of just how high the stakes would be in that election and in the war of values that would lie at its heart.

In the paradigm of Jezebel, at its very center, is the queen's attempt to change the deep-seated religious beliefs of her adopted land in order to expand the cult of Baal. Intrinsic to that cult was the offering up of children. So in order to expand this practice, she not only had to overturn the biblical prohibition against false gods and idols; she had to overturn the biblical precept concerning the sanctity of human life. So when Hillary Clinton called for the changing of deep-seated religious beliefs, what was the purpose of her call? The context was very clear. Religious beliefs had to be changed so that abortion could expand, thus meaning the death of more unborn children. For Clinton, as for Jezebel, belief in the sanctity of human life from the moment of its conception, as upheld in Scripture, was a hindrance that had to be eradicated. Thus the call to sweep away such religious belief so that the practice of sacrificing children could expand unabated had to be the most *Jezebellian* statement ever made in American presidential history. And the fact that it just happened to have been uttered by Jezebel's modern antitype was as stunning as the statement itself.

Jezebel's antipathy to religious faith and the consequences of that antipathy are described in this commentary:

> "From the course of her proceedings, it would appear that she grew to hate the Jewish system of law and religion on account of what must have seemed to her its intolerance and its anti-social tendencies. She hence sought to put it down by all the means she could command..."[4]

It was this same deep-seated antipathy to biblical faith and values that was evidenced in Clinton's run for the presidency. It would constitute the most brazenly anti-life campaign ever waged by a major candidate in American presidential history.

The strongest champions of the former queen and

Jezebel's strongest support would come from the priests of Baal and Ashtoreth, the practitioners and advocates of child sacrifice. So who were the greatest, strongest, staunchest advocates and supporters of Hillary Clinton's campaign? They were those who advocated abortion on demand. In fact, the largest abortion organizations in America pumped massive amounts of money into the Clinton campaign in the attempt to put her into the White House. The intensity of their support caused the nation's largest abortion organization to break all historic precedent and for the first time in its history endorse a presidential candidate while she was still in the primary stage.[5] That's how crucial they saw her to their cause. They all shared the common belief that if Hillary Clinton became president, she would wipe away virtually every restriction and safeguard put in place concerning abortion.

The Democratic National Convention of 2016, which nominated Clinton for the presidency, became the most brazenly anti-biblical convention in the history of the Democratic Party. No longer was the killing of the unborn cloaked in such euphemistic and indirect terminology as "reproductive health" or a "woman's choice." Now it was brazenly displayed in the open. Now it was celebrated.

The convention even featured as guest speaker the president of Planned Parenthood, who was also given the honor of being seated next to former President Bill Clinton, a gesture that showed just how highly esteemed and sacred the practice of child killing had now become. But she wasn't alone. To further celebrate the cause, the president of the National Abortion Rights Action League also addressed the convention. As she spoke of her own abortion, the crowd erupted into cheers. One writer called the convention "a celebration of the destruction of unborn life."[6]

In Jezebel's paradigm the worship of the Phoenician god and his child offerings were not only encouraged but compelled.

> The queen will not only encourage the practice that involves the sacrifice of children; she will seek to compel the nation's participation in it.

The convention that nominated Hillary Clinton for president put forth a platform that crossed a line that had never before been breached. It called for the repeal of every governmental protection against abortion so that abortion could now be performed in virtually every circumstance and on demand. It called for the striking down of the Helms Amendment, in place since 1973 to guard against the financing of abortions through foreign assistance funds. Further it called for the striking down of the Hyde Amendment, in place since 1976 to guard against the financing of abortions through federal Medicaid funding. It has been estimated that this one amendment alone saved hundreds of thousands of lives.[7]

The striking down of those protections would have meant that every tax-paying American, and thus every Christian and individual who saw the killing of an unborn child as a gravely immoral act would now be forced to fund and thus to take part in the act. Had Clinton won and that agenda been enacted, those who enabled that victory by their voting would have had a part in the blood of the innocent.

For the remainder of the campaign Clinton would brazenly champion the most extreme positions concerning abortion, including the advocacy of late-term and partial-birth abortion. She would even compare pro-life positions to the stands of "terrorist groups."[8] Her campaign would declare that there was *no more important issue* than defending abortion.[9] There was no way around it; the practice of killing unborn children was to her the cause above all causes.

As the election approached its final stretch, poll after poll after poll foretold that Clinton would win a decisive and substantial victory. Many of God's people began preparing for a future in which they would live as a persecuted minority within their nation. It all appeared hopeless.

And then something happened. It would shock the White House. It would shock the media. It would shock the Democrats. It would even shock the Republicans. It would shock the world.

And yet it was all there, from ancient times, contained in the mystery of the paradigm.

We now open up that mystery, as the paradigm unveils a new player on its stage, a most controversial figure—the warrior.

Chapter 20

The WARRIOR

THE PARADIGM WILL now take a dramatic turn. With the appearance of a single figure everything will change. His rise on the national stage will come suddenly and unexpectedly. It will throw the kingdom into chaos. And yet it was all foretold many years before his rise, the word given in the middle of a desert wilderness.

It was on Mount Sinai where the prophet Elijah had taken refuge after having his life threatened by Queen Jezebel that the name of Jehu, son of Nimshi, was first mentioned. The prophet was told to anoint Jehu as king over Israel. We don't know if Elijah fulfilled the command. But years later his successor, Elisha, would see to it that his master's mission was completed:

> "And Elisha the prophet called one of the sons of the prophets, and said to him, 'Get yourself ready, take this flask of oil in your hand, and go to Ramoth Gilead. Now when you arrive at that place, look there for Jehu the son of Jehoshaphat, the son of Nimshi, and go in and make him rise up from among his associates, and take him to an inner room. Then take the flask of oil, and pour it on his head, and say, "Thus says

the LORD: 'I have anointed you king over Israel.'" Then open the door
and flee, and do not delay.'"[1]

The act was revolutionary. A new king was being anointed while the
present king still sat on his throne. The present king was Joram. Jehu had
been anointed to succeed him. The anointing had taken place in Ramoth
Gilead, the same place where Ahab had met his end. That had been the first
part of the judgment. The second part, the end of Ahab's dynasty, had been
delayed. But its time had come.

> "So the young man, the servant of the prophet, went to Ramoth Gilead.
> And when he arrived, there were the captains of the army sitting; and
> he said, 'I have a message for you, Commander.'
> "Jehu said, 'For which one of us?'
> "And he said, 'For you, Commander.'"[2]

The servant found Jehu in a military encampment. He had been engaged
in battle for Ramoth Gilead under orders of King Joram:

> "Then he arose and went into the house. And he poured the oil on
> his head, and said to him, 'Thus says the LORD God of Israel: "I have
> anointed you king over the people of the LORD, over Israel. You shall
> strike down the house of Ahab your master, that I may avenge the
> blood of My servants the prophets, and the blood of all the servants
> of the LORD, at the hand of Jezebel. For the whole house of Ahab shall
> perish..."'"[3]

The servant anointed Jehu as king of Israel to succeed Joram and gave him
a prophecy. The prophecy foretold the end of Ahab's dynasty. The words
were similar to those given to Ahab himself by Elijah in Naboth's vineyard. But now the prophecy was being spoken to the one who would bring
it to fulfillment. With Jehu's anointing the die was cast. The overturning
and end of Ahab's house was now set in motion. Through this one unlikely
figure, a man who would rise to the nation's center stage with absolutely no
political experience and no political power, the history of the nation would
turn. Who was he?

Unlike those who dwelt in the royal house, those whose authority he
would rise to challenge, Jehu had no royal blood or lineage that would give
him any right to the throne. Nor was he a politician. He was an outsider, a
most unlikely ruler.

He was not a gentle man. He was rough and coarse. He had been known
as a leader but a leader whose authority rested entirely outside the realm

of politics or civil government. He was a warrior, a military commander, a fighter, confrontational, contentious, and combative. He could be ruthless and brutal.

It is clear from the account that Jehu did not exemplify many, if not any, of the qualities one might have expected of a godly man. It is doubtful that up to the time the prophet anointed him, Jehu had lived anything resembling a godly life. He could be boastful and given to self-promotion. He could be reckless and at times appear to be out of control. He could act impulsively, rashly, and in apparent disregard of the consequences of his actions.

On the other hand, he would speak of having zeal for God. He would follow the words of the prophet and go beyond them. And while he could move on an impulse, he could also act strategically, in tactical calculation, for the purpose of fulfilling his mission. He had next to no idea how to run a government or a kingdom. But he had complete confidence in himself that he could do it. In short, Jehu was a man of great extremes and a multitude of contradictions. He was unlike any other leader of his time. He defied analysis and destroyed conventions.

He was persistent, tenacious, and determined. He could show great daring and boldness. He could set massive events in motion. He could and would shake up the status quo of his day. He was a destabilizer. He was an agent of chaos. He would destroy. He would overthrow. He would tear down. He would turn everything around him upside down.

And yet he was a vessel, not in spite of these things but because of them. He had been appointed for an hour when evil was entrenched and empowered in virtually every realm of government and culture and was now threatening to eradicate the ways of God. He had risen at the very moment that the nation's apostasy appeared on the verge of becoming irrevocably sealed and when for God's people all seemed hopeless. He would bring shaking to a system of evil and a government of darkness.

Though there were undoubtedly mixed motives involved in his rising, and though he may have never fully grasped the significance of his role in the larger scheme of things, he was nevertheless a chosen vessel, an agent of change, a sword of judgment, an unlikely instrument anointed to hold back the sealing of the apostasy, to provide God's people with a space in time, and to overthrow a kingdom that warred against the ways of God.

The Paradigm of the Warrior

The paradigm now reveals a dramatic turn of events, an upheaval, an uprising on the political stage of ancient Israel. Thus we would likewise expect to see a dramatic turn of events and great upheaval take place on the modern political stage.

We now open up the paradigm of Jehu. He will be referred to as "the warrior."

In the last days of King Joram's reign Jehu began his rise to power. At the time of his anointing he had no political experience. His rise came suddenly and took Israel and its leaders by surprise.

> As the reign of the heir draws near to its end, a new and unlikely figure will begin his rise to power. He will come onto the national stage with no political experience. His rise will be sudden and unexpected. It will take the nation and its leaders by surprise.

For the manifestations of the paradigm to continue, it would mean that as the Obama years approach their end, an unlikely figure will appear on the nation's political stage. The sudden rise of this figure will take the government and nation by surprise.

In the ancient case it was the rise of this unlikely person that would bring the end of the king's reign. In the modern case of presidencies the end comes at its preordained time. Thus the rise to power of this figure in the modern case will not cause but coincide with the ending of the Obama presidency. Did any such unlikely figure with no political experience begin his rise to power at this time?

The answer is an unequivocal yes. Donald Trump was most likely the most unlikely of figures in the history of the American presidency. His rise to political power began on June 16, 2015, when he announced his candidacy for the presidency, as the Obama era began its closing chapter. Even more surprising than his announcement was his subsequent success and ascendancy. It would take America and America's leaders by surprise.

> He will be a controversial figure. He will act as a destabilizing agent. He will appear as a threat to the nation's status quo.

As Jehu was a man of controversy, so too was Donald Trump. To the governmental status quo, the political status quo, and the cultural status quo he was a threat—a destabilizing force.

> Coming from outside the realm of politics and government, he will enter the national stage as an outsider.

As Jehu was not a member of the royal house or of the ruling class, neither was Donald Trump a member of the government. He was not a politician. He campaigned for the presidency as an outsider to Washington and as an outsider to politics altogether.

> He will not be a gentle man or a diplomat. He will be rough and coarse.

As Jehu was not a gentle man but harsh, so too there was nothing gentle about Donald Trump. His communication was often blunt, his ways, abrasive, and his temperament, turbulent.

> Before the time of his rising, he will have already been known as a leader but of a nonpolitical and nongovernmental realm.

As Jehu was a known leader but of a different realm from that of Joram, so before his rise to political power Donald Trump was known as a leader but not of the political realm. As did Jehu, so Trump commanded authority but had no part in governing the nation's citizens.

> He will be a warrior, a fighter, a man of battles, confrontational, contentious, and combative. And at times he will be brutal.

Jehu was first and foremost a man of war, a fighter. So too his modern antitype, Donald Trump, was a fighter, a man of countless battles. It is worth noting that one of the most important experiences of his life was being sent as a youth to military school. His biographies mark his years at the New York Military Academy as formative and critical to the rest of his life. It was there that he learned how to compete and to win.

Trump was confrontational, contentious, and combative. And like Jehu, in the achieving of his goals he could at times be brutal. Of the ancient commander one commentary says this:

> "Jehu was a military man whose life was so dedicated to strategy and conquest that, unlike David, he couldn't bring faith and the glory of God into his battles…"[4]

Likewise Trump would often speak of life in terms of battle, winning and losing, victory or defeat. He was dedicated to success, conquest, and triumph.

> His past will not have exemplified the qualities one would have expected of a godly man. He will be given to boastfulness and self-promotion. He will be ruthless in dealing with his enemies and will not be averse to using deception to outsmart them. He will believe the ends justify the means.

It is clear from his subsequent ways and actions as recorded in the biblical account that Jehu had not lived his life as a man of God. So too it is clear in the case of Donald Trump that the life he had lived did not exemplify Christian virtues, nor did his actions exemplify that which would be expected of a godly man. And as Jehu is recorded boasting in the midst of his rise to power, so too Donald Trump would become known for boasting and self-promotion. One commentary speaks of Jehu taking "joy in outsmarting his enemies."[5] Such words could as well have been written of Donald Trump. And as with Jehu it would appear that in matters of war and conquest Trump believed that the ends would justify the means.

> And yet he will speak of God and of his zeal to accomplish the will of God. And he will at times heed the words of godly counsel.

As Jehu would speak of God, so too would Donald Trump, and he would speak of God publicly. He would declare his zeal to accomplish God's will as he sought to assure men and women of faith of the sincerity of his convictions. He would as well receive godly counsel and at times follow it.

> His natural temperament will play a part in his rise to power. He will show great tenacity, determination, boldness, and daring. He will exude confidence, being fully assured of his victory and of his ability to govern, despite his lack of experience. He will be skilled in setting massive events in motion.

As Jehu's temperament was an intrinsic part of his rise to power, so too Trump's temperament was central to his success. As did Jehu, Trump showed boldness, daring, and tenacity. And as with Jehu, he was brimming with confidence, fully convinced that, despite having no experience in government, he would be more than able to lead the nation.

> He will shake the status quo, upend convention, and defy analysis. He will break down and overthrow. He will throw the nation's political realm and its status quo into a state of chaos.

As Jehu was a destabilizer, so Trump's mere presence in the presidential arena would cause destabilization. He would defy analysis and convention. He would, as Jehu did, break down, dismantle, and overthrow. He would throw the American political realm and status quo into a state of chaos. He would even be called the "chaos candidate."[6]

> And yet beyond anything he is or is not, there will be a higher purpose in play. His rising will take place at the same moment that the nation's apostasy appears to be on the verge of being sealed into permanency and threatens to eradicate the ways of God. He will in spite of himself become an instrument to hold back the day of that sealing. He will be a sword to bring judgment, a plow to overturn and bring upheaval, and a hammer to smash apart.

Trump, like his ancient predecessor, was in spite of his flaws a vessel for the accomplishing of purposes beyond his own understanding. This begs the question "Can God use those who have not served, followed, or known Him for the outworking of His purposes?" He can. And in the case of Jehu, he did. So too Trump rose to power at a time when the nation's apostasy stood on the verge of attaining total supremacy, of being sealed into permanency, and of threatening to abolish the ways of God on every front.

There were undoubtedly other and mixed motives behind Trump's ascent. Nevertheless he was used to hold back at least for a time the encroaching forces of an anti-biblical, anti-God, and anti-Christian onslaught. He would pledge himself to the defense of religious liberty and to the sanctity of life.

> The warrior will be anointed to succeed the heir as king over the land.

The prophetic word given to Jehu was this: "Thus says the LORD God of Israel: 'I have anointed you king over the people of the LORD, over Israel.'"[7] So Jehu was called not only to battle but to the throne. He was anointed to succeed Joram as king.

Thus, according to the paradigm, the unlikely and controversial warrior was destined to become the new ruler of the land. Therefore in the modern case the template would ordain that Donald Trump would become the next president of the United States. As Jehu succeeded Joram, so Donald Trump would succeed Barack Obama.

> The warrior will be anointed to contend against the former queen and her agenda.

Jehu's conquest over Joram is implicit in the prophetic word given him to become king. But there was no mention in the prophecy of Joram. On the other hand, Jezebel's name would appear more than once. Jehu must ultimately come head-to-head against the former first lady and queen, Jezebel.

Thus according to the paradigm, the rough, brash, and contentious commander will come head-to-head with the former first lady. Thus the template would speak of Donald Trump and Hillary Clinton confronting each other face-to-face. And that is exactly what would take place.

The clash of values, cultures, and agendas will take place in the context of a presidential race. Thus it is eerily striking that the ancient mystery will now reveal an actual race—a literal race that will literally head for the nation's throne.

Chapter 21

The RACE

A FTER ANOINTING JEHU to strike down the house of Ahab, the prophet flees the camp. Those observing the encounter inquire of Jehu into its meaning:

"Then Jehu came out to the servants of his master, and one said to him, 'Is all well? Why did this madman come to you?'

"And he said to them, 'You know the man and his babble.'

"And they said, 'A lie! Tell us now.'

"So he said, 'Thus and thus he spoke to me, saying, "Thus says the LORD: 'I have anointed you king over Israel.'"'

"Then each man hastened to take his garment and put it under him on the top of the steps; and they blew trumpets, saying, 'Jehu is king!'"[1]

Hearing the prophecy, the troops proclaim Jehu king of Israel to succeed Joram.

> "So Jehu the son of Jehoshaphat, the son of Nimshi, conspired against
> Joram. (Now Joram had been defending Ramoth Gilead, he and all
> Israel, against Hazael king of Syria...)"[2]

Jehu now turns his attention to the overthrow of Joram. Joram had been
wounded on the battlefield at Ramoth Gilead, just as his father, Ahab, had
been wounded at the same site years earlier. He returned to the city of Jezreel to recover from his injuries.

> "So Jehu rode in a chariot and went to Jezreel, for Joram was laid up
> there..."[3]

Jehu mounts his chariot and with his men riding alongside him begins a
race to the throne. His first objective is to attack the king. After that he will
focus on Jezebel.

The account gives the impression that everything happened in rapid
succession. Jehu takes off in his chariot in a lightning-paced campaign
to reach the city of Jezreel. There is little time for him to come up with
any well-thought-out or detailed strategy. He acts on impulse. He appears
to be improvising as he goes. And yet at the same time he is a military
commander. He is well acquainted with strategizing. And in this case his
strategy is speed. He intends to reach Jezreel before word of his insurrection can get there. To that end he takes steps to ensure the secrecy of his
plan. The most powerful weapon of his campaign will be that of speed and
surprise. If he can keep his opponents off guard, he can win.

And so Jehu enters the center stage of Israel's history suddenly, abruptly,
out of nowhere, and without warning. He will surprise the king, who will
have no clue as to what is taking place. Jehu's rise will come as a total shock
to his opponents and the powers that be.

In the city of Jezreel, the watchman catches sight of Jehu's approach:

> "So the watchman reported, saying, 'He went up to them and is not
> coming back; and the driving is like the driving of Jehu the son of
> Nimshi, for he drives furiously!'"[4]

The watchman's description is fascinating. Apparently Jehu's chariot
driving was so distinctive it would identify him even from a distance. The
translation describes his driving as "furiously." The definition of *furiously*
is full of fury, rage, extreme anger, violent passion. The word thus would not
only describe Jehu's driving but also his temperament.

But in the original lies something even more striking. The Hebrew word
used to describe Jehu's driving is *shigaon*. It literally means mad, insane,

and crazy. In other words, Jehu normally drove his chariot crazily, insanely, and like a madman. It matches the picture we have of his nature—rash, impulsive, unrestrained, wild. One commentary puts it this way:

> "As his temper is hasty and fierce, so is his march."[5]

Jehu must have at times appeared to be a man out of control, even reckless. Another commentary puts it this way:

> "He came with such speed not merely because he had an errand to do,
> but because he was urged on by a headlong disposition, which had won
> him the name of a reckless driver, even among the watchmen."[6]

However much it may also apply to his nature, *shigaon* is the key Hebrew word given in the Bible to describe Jehu's race to the throne. And yet despite the mad and furious nature of his race it would end up bringing him to his set goal. And that goal would mark the fulfillment of Elijah's prophecy to King Ahab in the vineyard of Naboth.

The Paradigm of the Race

Now we open up the paradigm of the race.

> Before the warrior comes to power, the messenger of God will anoint him and speak over him a prophetic word.

Jehu's rise to power was set in motion by an anointing and the giving of a prophetic word. It was an unlikely event. Jehu was a man of bloodshed and far from godliness. But the act performed over him was holy.

So in the rise of Donald Trump to power could there have been any such act performed over him? The answer is yes. Though it may not have seemed likely at the start, he may have been the most prayed over and prophesied over presidential candidate in history. Throughout his campaign Christian leaders not only prayed for him and over him but also gave to him prophetic words. His inauguration would feature more prayers than any other in memory. In the case of Jehu the prophet's word and anointing did not constitute a blanket endorsement of all that Jehu had done or would do.

Rather it was a mark to signify that he would be used for a prophetic purpose. So too it was in the case of Donald Trump.

"So Jehu the son of Jehoshaphat, the son of Nimshi, conspired against Joram."[7]

> The warrior will turn his attention to the mounting of an attack against the leader of the land, the heir.

As soon as the prophet anointed him, Jehu set his focus on the house of Ahab and the present head of that house, King Joram. Even before Trump announced his candidacy, he had begun mounting attacks against Barack Obama. Once the announcement was made, the attacks increased. They would continue up to the election. Trump's campaign was first an attack on the reign of Obama.

"So Jehu rode in a chariot and went to Jezreel, for Joram was laid up there . . . "[8]

> The warrior will begin a race to the throne to assume the highest office in the land.

Jehu mounted his chariot and raced to the king's palace. The paradigm presents the warrior taking up a literal race to gain the highest office of the land. So Donald Trump would begin a race to the White House, the American throne, to become the new leader of the land. Behind it all was the paradigm of the ancient warrior's race to the royal palace.

> The warrior will enter the national stage abruptly, without warning, suddenly, and seemingly out of nowhere. He will rely more on impulse than strategy. He will make the most of his ability to surprise and shock. Catching his opponents off guard will be key to his success.

Both warriors, Jehu and his antitype, Donald Trump, appear on their nation's stage suddenly as if coming out of nowhere. And as Jehu's race to the throne seemed driven more by impulse than any carefully thought-out plan, so too Trump's race to the White House appeared likewise driven by impulse more than anything else. As did Jehu, Trump continually caught his opponents by surprise and off guard. His campaign produced continual shocks, the greatest of all coming at the end—the shock of his victory, a surprise that not only caught his opponents off guard but even many of his staunchest supporters.

> " . . . the driving is like the driving of Jehu the son of Nimshi, for he drives furiously!"[9]

> The warrior will lead his race to obtain the highest office of the land in a way that will appear to be *crazy*.

The Hebrew word used to describe Jehu's race to the throne also best describes Trump's race for the presidency—mad, insane, and crazy. The following is a sampling of how various translations render the biblical description of Jehu's campaign:

> "The one who drives the lead chariot drives like Jehu son of Nimshi; he drives *recklessly*."[10]

> " . . . the pace of him who is coming is like the pace of Jehu, the son of Nimshi, for he comes *impetuously*."[11]

> " . . . he drives like Nimshi's son Jehu drives—*irrationally!*"[12]

> " . . . It must be Jehu son of Nimshi, for he's driving *like a madman*."[13]

> "The troop's leader is driving *like a lunatic*, like Jehu . . . "[14]

> "The driving is like that of Jehu son of Nimshi—he drives *like a maniac*."[15]

> " . . . the driving [is] like the driving of Jehu son of Nimshi, for *with madness* he driveth."[16]

Of all the presidential campaigns led by a major party in American history, the one campaign that would most accurately match all of these descriptions is without question the campaign of Donald Trump, the man who just happens to be the modern antitype of the man of whom those were written.

Implicit in the paradigm is the image of a man who could appear to be out of control. One commentary on Jehu's race puts it this way:

"The reference to Jehu's reckless chariot driving (2 Kings 9:20) perhaps suggests that he has a reputation for reckless behavior and could be dangerous to the messenger."[17]

Jehu has been commended by Bible commentators as a man of action, decisiveness, and resolve. But he is also described as a man of rashness, impulsiveness, and at times recklessness. All these same things were spoken of his antitype, Donald Trump, especially in Trump's race to the White House.

> And yet despite the unorthodox and the wild nature of his campaign the warrior will end up arriving at the place of his destination—the palace.

As Jehu's campaign brought him to the palace, so perhaps the most amazing thing about Donald Trump's campaign was that given its nature it ended up bringing him to his destination, the White House. It not only caught his opponents off guard, it caught the entire nation off guard—and the world. From the media to the pollsters to the pundits to the leaders of both political parties to the people on the street, everyone seemed at a loss to explain it. It defied virtually every attempt at forecasting and then explaining. It was, in the words of most observers, "crazy." And yet it was all there in the paradigm, which in a nutshell said this:

> At the close of the reign of the third king of the paradigm will appear the warrior who will launch his race to the nation's throne. Though he himself will be among the least likely of candidates and though his race to the throne will be characterized by craziness, irrationality, and recklessness, it will against all odds bring him to the throne.

Before Jehu could become king, he had to first pay a visit to the ground on which a prophecy had been given years earlier. And it would be his going to that ground that would cause the prophecy to be fulfilled.

Chapter 22

The OVERTHROW

BEFORE JEHU COULD enter Samaria to take the throne, he had to first go to the place where it all began—the city of Jezreel. In Jezreel was Naboth's vineyard. There Ahab and Jezebel had committed murder, and there Elijah had given the prophecy of the judgment that would fall on both of them and upon their dynasty. So now Jehu had to go to Jezreel because it was time for the blood that was shed there to be avenged and the prophecy spoken to be fulfilled.

> "Now Joram had been defending Ramoth Gilead, he and all Israel, against Hazael king of Syria. But King Joram had returned to Jezreel to recover from the wounds which the Syrians had inflicted on him when he fought with Hazael king of Syria."[1]

Jezreel was Jehu's first destination. The prophecy had foretold the end of Ahab's dynasty and decreed that it would take place in the reign of Ahab's son. Joram was Ahab's son. Jehu's first war was against Joram. He would go to Jezreel to bring an end to the reign of Joram and to succeed him as king of Israel. That Joram happened to be at Jezreel at the time of Jehu's arrival would appear to be a chance event. The king had chosen the city as the place to recuperate from a battle wound he had just suffered at Ramoth Gilead. Nevertheless, it was all part of a long-waiting prophecy.

> "Now a watchman stood on the tower in Jezreel, and he saw the company of Jehu as he came, and said, 'I see a company of men.'"[2]

As Jehu approaches the city, Joram sets out in his chariot with his royal guest, King Ahaziah of Judah, to meet Jehu. None of them had planned it, but the place where they would all meet up turned out to be the property of Naboth, the man whose blood marked the land. As the king approached the commander, he asked, "Is it peace, Jehu?" Jehu replied,

> "What peace, as long as the harlotries of your mother Jezebel and her witchcraft are so many?"[3]

Even though he had just inquired if his commander had come in peace, he had not expected the answer he received. And he had foolishly gone out from his palace unprepared.

> "Then Joram turned around and fled, and said to Ahaziah, 'Treachery, Ahaziah!'"[4]

Jehu now assumed the role of avenger, the agent of judgment. He drew back his bow with all his might and shot his arrow at Joram. The arrow struck Joram between his arms and through his heart. Joram collapsed into his chariot. He died just as did his father, struck by an arrow in his chariot.

Joram had been shown mercy. Time and time again he had been delivered from his enemies by the hand of God and the word of Elisha. Yet he remained hostile to the Lord and to his prophet, even to the point of attempting his murder. But the time of grace was over. And the mercy that God had given to Ahab's house by delaying its judgment had run its course. Joram, the last son of Ahab who would ever sit on the throne, was dead.

> "Then Jehu said to Bidkar his captain, 'Pick him up, and throw him into the tract of the field of Naboth the Jezreelite . . . '"[5]

Not only did he die the death of his father, but his body was thrown into the field of the man his father and mother had murdered years before—Naboth.

It is here in the account that the prophetic nature of the event is emphasized as a surprising piece of information is revealed. Jehu turns to his captain, Bidkar:

" . . . remember, when you and I were riding together behind Ahab his father, that the LORD laid this burden upon him: 'Surely I saw yesterday the blood of Naboth and the blood of his sons,' says the LORD, 'and I will repay you in this plot,' says the LORD. Now therefore, take and throw him on the plot of ground, according to the word of the LORD."[6]

Jehu is repeating the words of the prophecy given by Elijah now on the day of their fulfillment. What it reveals is that Jehu was there in Jezreel with Ahab on the day that Elijah prophesied the king's judgment. Jehu was speaking of an event that had taken place many years earlier. Yet he had never forgotten. Thus he knew that Ahab and his house were destined to be judged. But on the day he first heard the prophecy, he never could have fathomed that he himself would be the instrument by which that judgment would come.

The passage reveals something else. Jehu had not only served Joram; he had served Ahab. He had apparently held a high and honored position in Ahab's army. Thus he was a servant of Ahab and Jezebel. And thus he was, in effect, a soldier of Baal, an agent of evil. He had fought on behalf of a house and kingdom of evil. But now he had changed. Now he would fight against that kingdom and the cause he had once defended and championed. Now he would be the instrument of its destruction.

With Joram's death Jehu would become king of Israel. And his reign would mark the fall of the house of Ahab.

The Paradigm of the Overthrow

> The warrior will ultimately come face-to-face with the former first lady. But he will first come against the heir. He will mount up an attack against his kingship. The first part of his campaign will be an insurrection against the heir's kingship and reign.

As Jehu would first come against Joram and then Jezebel, so the Jehu of the modern replaying, Donald Trump, would first come against the presidency of Barack Obama and then the former first lady Hillary Clinton. The first part of Trump's campaign was largely an uprising against the status quo of American politics. The leader of that status quo was Barack Obama.

Jehu attacked Joram. So Jehu's antitype, Donald Trump, would attack Joram's antitype, Obama.

> The warrior will catch the heir off guard. The heir will never expect the warrior to successfully execute an insurrection. He will find himself stunned and unprepared on the day of the warrior's victory.

Joram was unprepared for Jehu's insurrection and his coming to the palace. So Obama never expected Trump's campaign to be successful. Trump caught him off guard. On the day of Trump's victory Obama was unprepared and stunned.

> The rise of the warrior will mark the defeat of the heir and the ending of his reign.

The rise of Jehu would mark the defeat of the heir and the ending of his reign. So the rise of Donald Trump would mark a defeat for Obama and would be linked of course to the ending of his presidency.

Joram's end was haunted by the specter of Ahab and Jezebel. Ahab's days were long over, but Jezebel was still an active force on the national stage. The shadow of both still loomed large over the nation. Joram's reign would end on the field of Naboth, the ground that marked the sin of Ahab and Jezebel. So it was not only Joram's sins but the sins of his predecessors that would bring about his undoing.

> The heir's undoing will be connected to the former king and former first lady.

The defeat of Obama's agenda was not of course connected to the field of a Middle Eastern farmer, but as with Joram it was connected to a former king and queen. The campaign of 2016 involved the ghost of the Clinton years. It marked specifically the return of Bill and Hillary Clinton, only in reversed roles. As in the case of Joram the end of Obama's presidency was overcome by the shadow of his predecessors.

> The warrior will invoke the scandal and sin of the former king.

When Jehu arrived in Jezreel, he reminded those present of the sin King Ahab had committed concerning Naboth. He recalled Elijah's exposing of the sin and pronouncing of judgment.

What about the modern case? We have already seen the Naboth of the modern Ahab, the scandal that stained and haunted the Clinton presidency. For this part of the paradigm to be fulfilled, Donald Trump would have to invoke the personal sins of Bill Clinton, which would mean most prominently the Lewinsky scandal. And it happened. In the midst of the campaign Trump would do just that. He would invoke the sin and scandal of the Clinton years, the Lewinsky affair.

> The warrior will have known the former king, having been, in earlier days, on the king's side and one of his personal acquaintances. He will have supported and defended him in times past. But in the days of the heir he will set himself in opposition to the king's house.

The account reveals Jehu's past relationship and service to Ahab. He was his servant, his assistant, one of his chief aides. As such he would have supported and defended the king. But in the days of Joram, Jehu would turn against the government and the house he had once served.

So the paradigm would present the warrior and the former king as having once been acquaintances and allies. Was this the case? It was. Donald Trump and Bill Clinton had originally been friends. At the time of the Lewinsky scandal Trump even spoke in support of Clinton. But as Jehu turned against the house of Ahab in the days of Joram, so in the days of Obama Trump set himself in clear opposition to the Democratic establishment and the house of Clinton.

The ramifications of Jehu's service to Ahab are far-reaching. Jehu would not only have been a solider in an evil kingdom, he would have advanced the agenda of Ahab and Jezebel. Thus he would have been, in effect, a servant of Baal worship. He would have, in one form or another, upheld the practice of child sacrifice. He would have been an agent of the apostasy. Thus the paradigm:

> Before his rise to power the warrior will have been on the opposite side of the war. He will have advanced the course of the nation's apostasy. He will have supported the sacrifice of children. But he will change. And at the time of his rising on the nation's political stage he will oppose the evils he had once championed.

As Jehu was originally an advocate of Baal, so too Trump in the days before his rise was not known for being on the side of morality or of God. Rather, to many he epitomized worldliness and immorality. As Jehu in the days of Ahab would have defended and advanced the rites of Baal, the killing of the unborn, so too Trump in times past not only did not oppose the killing of the unborn—he supported it.

During the reign of the Clintons, Trump declared himself to be not only pro-abortion but "very" pro-abortion.[7] But as Jehu changed his course, so too did Trump. At the time of his rising to power he would oppose the killing of the unborn he had once championed. And as did Jehu, he would become a most unlikely champion of God's ways and people.

On the day of the victory that would enable him to succeed Joram as king, Jehu was not in the nation's capital city but in its chief northeastern city, Jezreel. So on the day of Trump's victory, his triumph at the polls that would enable him to succeed Obama as president, Trump was not in the capital city but in the nation's chief northeastern city, New York.

When Joram asked Jehu if he had come in peace, Jehu responded by asking how there could be peace when Jezebel was still committing evil. Thus Jehu's war against Joram was a war against Jezebel, and his war against Jezebel was a war against Joram. So too in Trump's battle for the presidency, he was waging two wars, one against Obama, and the other against Hillary Clinton. In fighting Obama, he was fighting Clinton, and in fighting Clinton, he was fighting Obama. Clinton was the one with whom he battled to win the presidency, but Obama was the one whose reign and agenda he would end to reign in his place.

> The end of the heir's reign will not see a friendly transition to a successor to continue his agenda, but a hostile transition to a successor who will have risen up against his agenda to overturn it.

Joram's reign would end with a hostile transition to the one who had risen up against it. In the case of Joram's antitype, Obama, the end of his reign would likewise not see a transition to another who would continue his agenda. But as it was at the end of Joram's reign, there would be a hostile transition as Obama would yield the presidency to one who would seek to overturn his agenda.

> The heir will be followed on the throne by one not belonging to the royal house, one who has never governed but has served as a commander—a warrior king.

Joram's reign would not be followed by a member of the royal house but by one who had never before governed. So too Obama would not be followed by his chosen successor, Hillary Clinton, but by a successor not of his house and who had never before governed.

In January 2017 Trump stood on the western terrace of the Capitol Building to become the forty-fifth president of the United States as Obama looked on. As Trump raised his right hand to assume the office of the presidency, Obama's reign came to an end. Though the only bloodshed involved was political, the reign of the heir would be sealed as the reign of his prototype in the paradigm had been sealed over two and a half thousand years earlier—by the rise of the warrior.

But there was more to Elijah's prophecy. And it has yet to be fulfilled. And there was another who happened to be in Jezreel as well on the day that Jehu arrived there. Two would now be left to contend for the throne. Now they would stand face-to-face. Only one will be left standing.

Chapter 23

The DOWNFALL

KING JORAM WAS dead, slain on the field of Naboth. But there was
another in Jezreel who still posed a threat to Jehu and the people
of God—Jezebel. It had all begun with Jezebel. It was she who had
incited Ahab to go against the ways of God. It was she who had first championed the worship of Baal and the gods of Phoenicia in Israel. And it was
she who had initiated the war against God's people. And now events had
conspired to bring them both to Jezreel on the same day.

Jehu's reply to Joram's question as to whether he had come in peace
focused not on the king but on the former first lady:

> "What peace, as long as the harlotries of your mother Jezebel and her
> witchcraft are so many?"[1]

Thus Jehu's fight was not ultimately against Joram but Jezebel. He had to
first wage war against Joram as the reigning king. He could not war against
Jezebel without first overcoming the monarch. By defeating Joram, he could
defeat Jezebel.

With Joram out of the way, the house of Ahab has just lost its last monarch. Its only viable hope lay with Jezebel. She was its standard bearer, the only one who had been there from the beginning, and the only person from the house of Ahab still living who had actually ruled the nation. Thus Jezebel would now be Jehu's main opponent. If he was going to overturn the corruption and evil of Ahab's house, he had to defeat Jezebel. Though no queen had ever before ruled the land of Israel on her own authority, the possibility of Jezebel seizing the throne for herself was very real. It was not at all unlikely that given the chance, she would have done exactly that.

So now with Joram's death there were two main contenders for the throne remaining, each one fierce and ambitious—Jehu, the warrior, rough, controversial, unpredictable, impulsive, at times ruthless, and always fighting—and Jezebel, the polarizing and controversial former first lady, now significantly older than in the days of her husband's reign, even a grandmother but still greatly feared, still at war with the ways of God, still potentially brutal, and to the people of God still as dangerous as ever.

They would represent diametrically opposed values and warring visions for the nation's future. Jehu would speak of the Lord and claim to be fighting for God and His people. Jezebel saw deep-seated religious beliefs as an obstacle to her agenda and a threat to be conquered. Jehu would speak of God and against Jezebel's sins, her corruption, and her enmity to God's ways. When he spoke of her "harlotries" and "witchcraft," he was referring to her participation in and advocacy of the pagan rites and worship of Baal and the gods of Phoenicia. This would have included idolatry, ritualized acts of immorality, and the offering of children. It was still taking place even in the highest of places in the days of Joram.

So now in the city of Jezreel the two adversaries had finally come face-to-face.

> "Now when Jehu had come to Jezreel, Jezebel heard of it; and she
> put paint on her eyes and adorned her head, and looked through a
> window."[2]

Hearing of Jehu's coming, Jezebel paints her eyes with makeup and adorns her head, most likely with a royal crown. It seems a strange act. Some interpret it as if she was trying to seduce Jehu. More likely it was an act of defiance. She adorns herself as a queen and looks down in disdain on the warrior. When she sees him, she calls out,

> "Is it peace, Zimri, murderer of your master?"[3]

By that she was likening him to the chariot commander Zimri who in a previous generation had murdered Israel's King Elah and yet had lasted only seven days before he himself was murdered. Jezebel addresses Jehu with pure contempt. Jehu is not deterred. He doesn't respond but calls for her judgment.

> "And he looked up at the window, and said, 'Who is on my side? Who?' So two or three eunuchs looked out at him. Then he said, 'Throw her down.' So they threw her down, and some of her blood spattered on the wall and on the horses; and he trampled her underfoot."[4]

Jezebel falls to her death. It was a dramatic and violent end and a brutal act on the part of Jehu. But Jezebel too had shed much blood and had lived a decidedly brutal life. The evil she had done to others had now returned in her day of judgment.

Jehu goes inside the palace to eat. There he experiences a softening of heart and concludes he should treat Jezebel's remains with dignity. He instructs his servants:

> "Go now, see to this accursed woman, and bury her, for she was a king's daughter."[5]

His servants return with the report that her remains are nearly all gone. It is then that he remembers the word given by Elijah to Ahab in Jezreel, the same place—Jezebel's body would be devoured by the dogs. The prophecy was now fulfilled and in the same place where Jezebel had shed Naboth's blood. The one who had brought so much calamity and bloodshed to Israel was now gone. As one commentary sums up her life,

> "She had introduced Baal; slain the Lord's prophets; contrived the murder of Naboth; excited her husband first, and then her sons, to do wickedly . . . . Three reigns her reign had lasted, but now, at length, her day was come to fall, and meet with the due reward of her deeds."[6]

Jezebel had managed to stay in the center of Israel's political stage through the reign of three kings. But now, finally, at the end of the third king, came her judgment and downfall.

It was an unlikely victory. It was an unlikely revolt. Most political revolutions are carefully plotted out over time. But this one came out of the blue and with virtually no planning. Yet it succeeded. Had Jezebel escaped, there would have always been the chance that Joram's legacy and that of Ahab's house would be revived. But with Jezebel's defeat it was over. And though Jehu's mission and warfare were not yet completed, with Jezebel's end there was no one left of any comparable stature to stand against his ascent to the throne. And though he had not yet ascended to that throne, he was now for all intents and purposes Israel's acting king.

The Paradigm of the Downfall

> The warrior who had first directed his attacks against the heir will now redirect them against the former queen and first lady.

After attacking Joram, Jehu directs his warfare against Jezebel. So Trump would at first direct the focus of his attacks on Barack Obama and the status quo. But as his campaign wore on, his attacks would become increasingly focused on the former first lady.

> With the end of the heir's reign it will come down to two fierce contenders for the throne—the warrior and the former first lady.

As in the ancient case, so in the modern, the war of thrones will come down to two fierce and ambitious figures: Donald Trump and the former first lady Hillary Clinton. As was Jehu, so Trump was the rough, controversial, impulsive, and often ruthless fighter. And as was Jezebel, so Clinton was the controversial and polarizing former first lady, now significantly older than in the days of her husband's reign, now a grandmother but still feared, still at war with the ways of God, and still seen by God's people as being as dangerous as ever.

> The two will represent diametrically opposed values and visions for the nation. The warrior will speak of the Lord and claim to be fighting for God and His people. The former first lady will see deep-seated religious belief in God as a threat to be dealt with and eradicated.

In the account of Jehu's campaign for the throne we have a high frequency of instances in which the Lord's name is mentioned. He was fulfilling the will of God and seeking to protect God's people. Jezebel, on the other hand, represented an agenda that was in direct opposition to the ways of God.

In the modern case whatever Donald Trump may have done and been before the campaign, he was now speaking more and more of the Lord. He promised believers that he would fight for religious liberty and protect persecuted believers around the world. Hillary Clinton, as we have seen, was saying, in effect, the opposite, calling for religious belief to be altered. Beyond the personalities, the worldviews presented by the two candidates, their sets of values, visions, and agendas, were in diametric opposition.

> In the midst of his campaign the warrior will speak against the former first lady's sins and her corruption.

In the midst of his race to the throne Jehu speaks of Jezebel's harlotries and witchcraft. So in the midst of Trump's race to the throne he would accuse the former first lady of dishonesty and wrongdoing. He would call her "Crooked Hillary."[7] This is not to judge the charge as true or not but simply the fact that Trump did as Jehu did. In the midst of his campaign he would speak of the former first lady's sins and corruption.

> The campaign will cause the two, the warrior and the former first lady, to confront each other face-to-face.

Jehu's campaign would bring him face-to-face in confrontation with Jezebel. So in the modern case the campaign would bring Trump face-to-face in confrontation with Hillary Clinton. Jehu and Jezebel's confrontation was recorded in Scripture for the nation to know. Trump and Clinton's confrontation would take place during the presidential debates, which would be televised for the nation to see.

> The warrior will speak against the morality and practices that the former first lady champions. This will involve the anti-biblical morality that includes the offering up of children.

When Jehu accused Jezebel of harlotries and witchcraft, he was referring to the pagan practices she indulged in and promoted, the worship of Baal. This of course included the sacrifice of children. So in the last of the presidential debates Trump would confront the former first lady in front of the nation for her championing of the practice of killing unborn children even up to the moment of their births.

Heading to the election Donald Trump's chances of winning the presidency against Hillary Clinton appeared hopeless. Every major poll showed a massive victory for the Democrats. But the paradigm showed something else:

> The rise of the warrior will end in the defeat of the first lady.

When Jehu entered Jezreel to confront Jezebel, there could only have been one outcome, the victory of Jehu and the defeat of Jezebel. Thus despite every poll showing her victory, the paradigm would determine that Hillary Clinton would be defeated. For in the paradigm the former queen is defeated by the warrior. So at the end of the reign of the heir, in the days of the warrior's uprising, in the confrontation between the modern antitypes of Jehu and Jezebel, Trump and Clinton, it will be the antitype of Jehu that will defeat the antitype of Jezebel.

> The former first lady will adorn herself as a queen on the day of her downfall.

As Jehu approaches, Jezebel prepares herself to appear in royal array and glory as queen, adorning her head most likely with a royal crown. And yet it will be the day of her downfall. So too Hillary Clinton on election night would prepare herself to become the first woman to rule over America. She would prepare an elaborate celebration complete with a massive glass ceiling and fireworks display over New York. Reports in the media would describe it as the first lady preparing her own coronation. The word *coronation* literally means to put on a crown or garland, just as it appears that Jezebel did as she adorned her head on the day of her downfall. And so too it would be for the former first lady—the day she prepared her own coronation, the day she adorned herself to appear as queen would turn out to be the day of her downfall. Thus one headline would read, "How the Clinton Victory Party Went From Coronation to Despair."[8]

> After calling for the queen's judgment and after her downfall, the warrior will show a measure of mercy or softening with regard to his stand against her.

Jehu had called for Jezebel's judgment and saw that it was executed. But after it was accomplished, he softened his stand against her and ordered that her body be treated with dignity worthy of a king's daughter. So too Donald Trump had called for the judgment of the former lady, promising to prosecute her for her crimes. But after her downfall he would soften his stand against her.

> The former queen will have managed to remain in the center of the nation's political stage through her husband's reign and the reigns of the two leaders who succeeded him. But at the end of the third ruler's reign she will be dramatically cast down.

Jezebel had managed to stay in the center of Israel's royal stage through the reigns of three kings, starting with that of her husband, Ahab, and ending with that of Joram. But in the last days of the third king came her downfall. So too Hillary Clinton had managed to stay in the center of America's political stage through the reigns of three presidents, starting with that of her husband, Bill Clinton, and ending with that of Barack Obama. But in the last days of the third presidency, that of Barack Obama, she would be dramatically cast down.

> The two archenemies, the warrior and the former first lady, will be present in the nation's chief northeastern city on the day that will determine their fate. It will become the city of her defeat and downfall and the city of his victory, where the warrior will become the prospective new king of the land.

Two cities would be central to the rise of Jehu and the fall of Ahab's house—Samaria, the capital, and Jezreel, the nation's chief northeastern city. On the day of Jezebel's downfall both Jezebel and Jehu would be together in the northeastern city, Jezreel. So in the modern case, on the day of the first lady's downfall, both Jehu's and Jezebel's antitypes, Trump and Clinton, would be in the same place, the nation's chief northeastern city, New York City. As Jezreel would become the site of Jezebel's fall and Jehu's victory, New York City would become the site of Clinton's fall and Trump's victory.

> The former first lady will be defeated in the city connected to the blood of the innocent—and her sin.

Jezreel was the site of Jezebel's downfall because it was marked by the blood of the innocent, that of Naboth and his family. Their blood was spilled because of the queen's plot. Thus Jezreel was especially the city of her sin. So Jezebel is defeated in the city linked to the blood of the innocent and her sin. Of course Jezebel had much more blood on her hands than that. Her sins included the blood of the nation's children who had been sacrificed to Baal.

New York City was the site of Clinton's defeat. As in the ancient case, it too was especially linked to blood and specifically to the blood of the innocent. New York was the place where abortion on demand was inaugurated in America. And it was New York City that was the abortion capital of America. More unborn babies were killed there than in any other place in America.[9] And it was this particular sin that was especially linked to Hillary Clinton.

The political victories, defeats, and overthrows that took place in the days of Ahab's house transpired through violence. We can be thankful that the political victories and defeats that took place in the modern scenario came about through far less violent means. Hillary Clinton was reportedly stunned by her defeat. She would go on. In fact, just a few months after her defeat she received an honor. In May 2017 in New York City the nation's largest abortion performer, Planned Parenthood, paid her homage for her championship of the killing of unborn children. She was honored as "Champion of the *Century*."[10] In other words, she had championed and advanced the practice of abortion more than anyone else in modern history. It was a revealing moment. It joined her once more to the queen of the ancient template who championed the offering of children more than anyone else of her time.

As for Jehu, his victory at Jezreel would establish his kingship. But he wasn't finished. In order to seal his position and ascend the throne, he would have to go to Samaria.

> Upon his victory the warrior will become the pro-
> spective ruler of the land. Yet neither his mission nor
> his battles will be complete. In order to ascend the
> throne of the highest office in the land, he will have
> to enter the capital city.

So too Trump's victory on election night would establish his presidency. But there were of course still many battles to be fought. And to assume the office of the presidency, he would have to go to the nation's capital. The focus of his story and his battle would now shift to Washington, DC.

―――

Before we continue on Jehu's journey, we have another mystery to open. Now that the template of Joram is completed, could the paradigm contain the mystery of his days? Could it have foretold the time given to Joram's modern antitype? Could the days of the ancient king hold the key to the days of the twenty-first-century president?

We will now see.

Chapter 24

The DAYS of the HEIR

WE HAVE SEEN the paradigm reveal not only the events of modern time but the timing of those events. What about the template of Joram? What happens if we open it in view of its timing, the days given the ancient king? Could it contain any revelation concerning Joram's modern antitype, Barack Obama?

To set the stage, we must again note that while the reigns of the ancient kings had no set term limits, the reigns of American presidents do. On the other hand, unlike the ancient case where kings typically came to the throne suddenly upon the death of another, most American presidents have been on the national stage or in national office years before the start of their presidencies. Their rise to power is in most cases gradual.

In the paradigm of Ahab are found the parameters of his antitype, Bill Clinton. Clinton's time on the national stage was twenty-two years. The years of the ancient king, his prototype, were likewise twenty-two years. The years of the modern ruler conformed to the years of the ancient ruler. What about Obama? Could the paradigm of Ahab's heir, Joram, reveal the time parameters given to Barack Obama? Could the years of the modern president have followed and conformed to the years of the ancient king? Let's first look at the years of Obama.

Barack Obama graduated from Columbia University in 1983. He then worked as a community organizer in Chicago. In late 1988 he entered Harvard Law School. After graduating in 1991, he returned to Chicago, where he worked for the University of Chicago Law School. In 1995 Obama announced his candidacy for the Illinois State Senate. He was elected in 1996. He served as an Illinois state senator from 1997 to 2004.

There are few political careers so strongly demarcated as that of Barack Obama. In his case the turning point is so clear that it leaves virtually no room for interpretation. Up to the year 2004 Barack Obama's political career had taken him only as far as the state level, as one of many other Illinois state senators. Speaking of his time in politics up to that moment, the *New York Times* described him as "a virtual unknown outside his home base on Chicago's South Side."[1] In other words, he was not even generally recognized on a state level. He was known in Chicago and not all of Chicago but just the South Side.

But in 2004 all that would change. In the summer of that year was the Democratic National Convention. The Democratic candidate for president, John Kerry, chose Obama to give the keynote speech. Obama gave his address on the convention's second night. It was that address that marked his emergence onto the national stage. It was that moment that changed everything.

Overnight Barack Obama's name was known across the nation. There was even talk that he might one day become president—and yet up to that moment he had never held any national office and had hardly been known outside Chicago. It was said that the convention would be remembered for two people, John Kerry and Barack Obama. An article in the *New York Times* entitled "The Speech That Made Obama" said of the address: it "would form the foundation of his 2008 presidential campaign."[2] It was that speech and that moment more than anything that catapulted him onto the national stage and began his rise to the presidency.

Obama's ascent to power and fame was exceedingly rapid. In November of that same year, he was elected to the US Senate. He was sworn into the US Senate on January 3, 2005. It was the first time he had ever held national office. Two years after that he had already launched his campaign for the American presidency. And two years after that, in January of 2009, he became the forty-fourth president of the United States. He went from someone virtually unknown beyond the South Side of Chicago to the forty-fourth president of the United States in the span of just over four years.

What happens if we take the same standards as we applied to the years of Bill Clinton and apply them to the years of Barack Obama?

The first question we must ask is when did Obama enter the national stage? When did he assume public office on a national or nationally recognized level? When did he begin his rise to the presidency?

Obama won his first seat in public office on a national level when he was elected to the US Senate. That happened on November 2, 2004.

He assumed his first public office on a national level when he was sworn in as a US senator. That took place on January 3, 2005.

Both of these are landmark events in Obama's rise to the national stage and then to the presidency. But even these are overshadowed by the seminal event that changed everything and caused everything else to take place—the night he addressed the Democratic National Convention. When was it? It happened on July 27, 2004.

If we now look at the first measure, his time in national public office, what was the span of that time period? It began the day he was sworn in as US senator and ended on the last day of his presidency—from January 3, 2005, to January 20, 2017.

It was twelve years.

What about the time span between the election that first brought him into national public office and the election that marked the end of his time in national public office? It would begin on November 2, 2004, and end November 8, 2016.

It was twelve years.

And what about the span of time between the convention that launched his rise to the presidency and the convention that would nominate another to replace him as president? The first convention, in Boston, began on July 26, 2004. The last, in Philadelphia, began on July 25, 2016. What was the time span?

Twelve years.

Obama's rise to power presents one of the clearest of political trajectories in American presidential history. On every count it comes out to the same span of time—*twelve years.*

The Heir's Paradigm of Days

If Barack Obama is Joram's antitype, or the Joram of the paradigm's modern replaying, is it possible that the years of his prototype would hold the mystery of his years in power?

The years of Obama are framed by four national conventions and three terms of office, one as senator and two as president—twelve years. In the case of Joram's time in power, as with Ahab, it had no connection to any such cycles. It was determined solely by three deaths—the death of his father, Ahab, the death of his brother Ahaziah, and his own death at the time of Jehu's rising.

So what was the length of Joram's reign? What was the time span in between the death of his brother and his own?

The answer appears in the Book of 2 Kings chapter 3:

> "Now Jehoram [Joram] the son of Ahab became king over Israel at Samaria in the eighteenth year of Jehoshaphat king of Judah, and reigned *twelve years*."[3]

Twelve years: the years of King Joram and the years of Barack Obama— another exact match. The time on the national stage allotted to the heir is twelve years.

As Bill Clinton's time on the national stage followed the exact same parameters of his ancient prototype in the paradigm, King Ahab, so Barack Obama's time on the national stage follows the exact same parameters of his prototype in the paradigm, Joram, the heir and son of Ahab. Or it could be said that the time given in Joram's paradigm would determine the time given to Barack Obama.

As Obama approached the end of his presidency, the twelve years of his paradigm were unavoidably prominent. He was scheduled to give his farewell speech to the Democratic party at the convention that would nominate his successor—the former first lady. It was the first Democratic National Convention since the one that lifted him into the national spotlight and began his rise to the presidency, and it would fall at the end of July.

He was scheduled to address the convention on the third night. The date was July 27. The day of his first convention speech, the one that launched his rise to the presidency, happened on the same date—July 27. So it was now *twelve years to the day* from the moment his rise to the presidency began.

And now the torch was to be passed. The two moments, twelve years apart, would serve as the bookends to his days on the national stage. Because of the convergence the twelve-year span became all the more unavoidable. The press was forced to see it and take note:

> "Speaking to what's likely to be the largest remaining audience of his presidency, Obama recalled the moment *twelve years* ago to the day that thrust him onto the national stage."[4]

In fact, Obama's speech that night was opened with two words, "*Twelve years . . .* "

> "*Twelve years* ago tonight, I addressed this convention for the very first time."[5]

And then news commentator upon commentator repeated it:

> "Barack Obama entered the national spotlight with his rousing 2004 speech at the Democratic National Convention, so it seems fitting that he appears at the DNC once again—*twelve years to the day* after he gave the keynote address as a Senate candidate from Illinois—as he attempts to pass the political baton to Hillary Clinton."[6]

It didn't all have to converge on the exact same date it all began. But in view of the importance of Joram's twelfth year as revealed in the paradigm, the fact that all this converged exactly twelve years to the day of Obama's rise to power is most striking. It marked and highlighted the years in the paradigm given to the heir.

It could also be taken as an omen. The Democrats were confident of a massive victory in the coming presidential election. But the paradigm spoke otherwise. In the ancient template the twelfth year was not a portent of coming victory for the house of Ahab but of coming defeat.

> The showdown between the forces of the warrior and the house of the heir will take place in the heir's twelfth year on the national stage.

Obama's rise to the presidency and his time on the national stage began in 2004. The paradigm would thus mark 2016 as the year in which the showdown between the two forces, that of the warrior and that of the house of Ahab, would take place. And so it was.

> In the twelfth year of the heir the warrior will defeat the queen.

The paradigm would thus ordain that the warrior's victory and defeat of the former queen would take place in 2016, the twelfth year of the heir. And so 2016 would be the year that Trump defeated Clinton.

> In the twelfth year the heir's reign will come to its end, and the warrior will ascend the throne to replace him as ruler of the land.

Obama was first sworn into national office in January 2005. Twelve years from that inauguration brings us to another inauguration, that which would bring his days in power to an end. It was in January 2017, at the end of his twelfth year in national office, that Obama stood on the Western Terrace of the Capitol Building and watched as Donald Trump was inaugurated as president in his place.

———

Summing up the days of the heir, we have this paradigm:

> The heir, the third king of the paradigm, who will continue leading the nation on a course of apostasy and whose reign will be characterized by hostility to the ways of God, will be on the national stage for twelve years.

Again we have two figures, an ancient king and a modern president, whose worlds could not have been more different. The twelve years of Joram were determined almost entirely by the death of his family members at the beginning of his reign and his own death at its end.

The twelve years of Obama were determined by entirely different factors. Had he not decided to run for the US Senate in 2004, and then against a large field of candidates won the nomination, had he not then been chosen to address the Democratic National Convention, had he not won the Senate race, had he not announced his candidacy for the presidency two years into his term, had he not won the presidential race, and had he not been reelected to a second term, if any of those details had not taken place, it would not have matched the parameters of time contained in the paradigm.

Only with all these factors working together did his time on the national stage end up matching the exact number of years given to his prototype in the paradigm of King Joram. Only with *every* event and quirk materializing, moving, and coalescing together could the years of Obama follow the years of his ancient forerunner. But just as all the countless quirks and turns and decisions and actions in the political career of Bill Clinton ended up conforming to the days of his royal prototype in ancient times, so it was for Barack Obama. The days allotted him on the national stage would conform to the days given the ancient king, whose reign would be brought to a dramatic end with the rise of the warrior.

We are now about to encounter perhaps the most mysterious figure in the paradigm, as Jehu comes upon a fellow traveler on the way to the nation's capital city.

Chapter 25

The HOLY MAN

DONALD TRUMP'S ELECTORAL victory could not have taken place without the votes of one particular portion of the American population. It was this most crucial and decisive segment that was also the most deeply conflicted over his candidacy.

Is it possible that even this facet of the story is contained and revealed in the paradigm?

The figure we are about to encounter is one of mystery. He appears in the biblical template with no background information, no details, and no explanation. The details and clues would come but many years later.

His appearance in the account will form another template, that of the holy man, the man called Jehonadab, the mysterious figure Jehu encountered on the way to the capital city.

"Now when he departed from there, he met Jehonadab the son of
Rechab, coming to meet him."[1]

Who was Jehonadab? The account in 2 Kings gives us virtually nothing
to go on except for one clue: he was the son, or descendant, of Rechab.
The house of Rechab is mentioned in 1 Chronicles as linked to a people
called the Kenites. The Kenites were a nomadic tribe that accompanied the
Hebrews into the land of Israel.

What we know of Jehonadab comes hundreds of years later in the Book
of Jeremiah:

"Thus we have obeyed the voice of Jonadab [Jehonadab] the son of
Rechab, our father, in all that he charged us, to drink no wine all our
days, we, our wives, our sons, or our daughters, nor to build ourselves
houses to dwell in; nor do we have vineyard, field, or seed.

"But we have dwelt in tents, and have obeyed and done according to
all that Jonadab [Jehonadab] our father commanded us."[2]

Putting the pieces together, the picture we have of Jehonadab is that of
a godly man, a leader, an ascetic, a holy man. His impact is so great that
it endures for centuries after his lifetime and becomes the moral code for
an entire people who will call him father. Jehonadab taught his children
and presumably his followers to avoid drinking wine, dwelling in houses,
or planting fields. Jehonadab was leading his people to live an ascetic life, to
seek purity and holiness. He would have clearly been opposed to the rule of
Joram and Jezebel and the spiritual and moral damage that had been done
to the nation through the house of Ahab.

One commentator says this of Jehonadab and Elisha:

"Both appear to have stood morally apart from their generation, Elisha
in his service, and Jonadab [Jehonadab] in his testimony. The days
were evil, and he was not at home in them."[3]

Jehonadab and his people would stay separate from the culture that surrounded them, from its spiritual corruptions and defilements. In such times
of moral apostasy, the pursuit of holiness required a form of separation. In
the case of Jehonadab and his people that separation would manifest in
their abstaining from worldliness.

Upon seeing Jehonadab, Jehu pauses his race. It is apparent that Jehonadab
is not only well known but highly revered. Only that could explain such

deference on the part of the military commander. At the same time, it is Jehonadab who has come to meet Jehu. Why? He would have undoubtedly been deeply grieved by the idolatry and immorality that surrounded him, the cult of Baal, and the overall spiritual and moral decay of the culture in which he lived. As a man of God living in the midst of apostasy, he would have been praying for his nation's revival. He would have hoped that in Jehu was a chance to stop or slow Israel's spiritual descent and perhaps even help turn the nation back to God. One commentator explains Jehonadab's interest in Jehu this way:

> "Accordingly, Jehonadab was extremely interested in Jehu's reputed desire to purge the nation of its heathenism. Perhaps he hoped that in Jehu a sense of national repentance and longing for the Lord God of Israel would now take place."[4]

At that moment in Israel's history there were only two choices, the change promised by the warrior or the nation's continued apostasy as led by the house of Ahab. Even if Jehonadab saw Jehu as the lesser of two evils, there was no choice. The only alternative to the nation's continued descent and the rule of the house of Ahab was offered in Jehu. In this, Jehonadab would have found a common cause, as the commentaries explain:

> "The Rechabite sheikh was . . . apparently one of the leaders of those who had not 'bowed the knee to Baal.'"[5]

> " . . . he accepted Jehu as a servant of Jehovah, hence an adversary of Ahab. As an adversary of Ahab, he led the religious community in worshiping Jehovah . . . "[6]

Jehu more than anyone else of his time appeared positioned to end the evil of Ahab's dynasty. Jehonadab would have hoped that Jehu would be an instrument for national redemption. At the same time, he must have been torn by Jehu's nature and ways and wondered if such a person could be used for God's purposes.

As far as Jehu was concerned, Jehonadab would be an invaluable asset to his campaign. So the commentators explain:

> "Jehonadab was just the kind of man Jehu needed to make his crusade look credible."[7]

> " . . . Jehu, it would seem, desired the sanction of Jehonadab to the proceedings upon which he was about to enter, as calculated to legitimate them in the eyes of some who might otherwise have regarded them with disapproval."[8]

As a man of holiness revered by the people, Jehonadab's support would give sanction to his campaign and legitimacy to his future kingship. The timing of their meeting was critical. Jehu was about to enter the nation's capital. Jehonadab's support would make it all the more likely that his kingship would be accepted as legitimate. Thus one commentator writes:

> "Jehu was no doubt glad to have the countenance of Jehonadab on his
> public entrance into Samaria. The ascetic had a reputation for sanctity,
> which could not fail to make his companionship an advantage to the
> but half-established monarch."[9]

This is not to say that Jehu didn't sincerely respect or agree with Jehonadab, only that the alliance would have been of great benefit to his campaign.

> " . . . and he greeted him and said to him, 'Is your heart right, as my
> heart is toward your heart?'"[10]

Jehu is expressing his support for Jehonadab and asking if he can count on his support in return.

> "And Jehonadab answered, 'It is.' Jehu said, 'If it is, give me your hand.'
> So he gave him his hand, and he took him up to him into the chariot."[11]

The commander and the holy man join themselves together in the objective of a common goal—to end the evil of Ahab's dynasty.

> "Then he said, 'Come with me, and see my zeal for the LORD.'"[12]

Jehu is eager to prove to Jehonadab that his faith is sincere, his motives, pure, and his passion, genuine. He seeks to convince him that he too is a man of God. Over two and a half thousand years later that question is still a matter of debate.

> "So they had him ride in his chariot."[13]

So Jehonadab joins Jehu's campaign and his race to the throne—two people who could have hardly been more different in nature and ways but joined together in an alliance forged by a common purpose. The two will ride together into the capital city, where Jehu will ascend to the throne.

The Paradigm of the Holy Man

Now the paradigm of Jehonadab.

Jehonadab represented a specific portion of the nation's population, the Rechabites and those associated with them. Who were the Rechabites? The commentators say this:

> "We may therefore count his kinsmen as among the more faithful portion of the people of Israel."[14]

> " . . . the Rechabites represented the *conservative* defenders of Israelite traditions which were also represented by Elijah . . . "[15]

> "Rechabite, member of a *conservative*, ascetic Israelite sect that was named for Rechab, the father of Jehonadab."[16]

Jehonadab was a leader of those who would today be called conservatives. But it was more than that:

> " . . . the Rechabites are described as a religiously conservative group . . . "[17]

> "Jehonadab is the leader of the Rechabites, a rather obscure clan in Israel that apparently lived an ascetic lifestyle and was known for its commitment to a seminomadic existence . . . and for its religious conservatism . . . "[18]

The people Jehonadab represented would best be described as "religious conservatives." And thus the paradigm:

> In the days of the warrior's rise, in the midst of national apostasy, there will be a portion of the nation's population who will resist the moral and spiritual decay taking place around them and will seek to hold faithful to God's Word—the religious conservatives.

As it was at the time of Jehu, so at the time of Donald Trump's rise to power there was a portion of the American population that sought to resist the moral and spiritual decay happening around them and to hold true to God's ways. They would be known as religious conservatives.

> They will be grieved over the moral and spiritual state of their nation, its continuing descent into apostasy. They will pray for their nation's return to God and for spiritual revival.

So too at the end of the Obama years and at the time of Donald Trump's rise this was the burden of religious conservatives, evangelical believers all over America. They were grieved over what they saw happening to America and were praying for their nation's spiritual revival.

The ancient account does not go into the thoughts of Jehonadab or of God's people concerning Jehu. But for those who sought to live in accordance with God's will, Jehu would not only have inspired hope but concern. The concern comes out later in the words of the chronicler himself. Undoubtedly the righteous would have been torn between the ways of Jehu and the promise of his reign.

> Those faithful to God will have to deal with the nature and ways of the warrior versus the promise of his reign. They will wonder if such a person could be used for the purposes of God.

So too religious conservatives and evangelicals would be torn over Donald Trump. His actions and ways would prove troubling. They would wonder if someone who showed little evidence of having known God could be used for God's purposes.

> Even with their concerns the people of God will hope that the warrior will be used as an instrument to stop or at least slow the nation's descent. They will see in him, even with all their concerns, the only alternative to a future of progressive apostasy and godlessness.

So even with all the concerns that religious conservatives and evangelicals held concerning Donald Trump, they saw in him the only alternative to what would surely come if the other side had prevailed—the sealing of America's spiritual descent. They hoped that even in all his unlikelihood he could still be a vessel to slow or reverse the nation's descent.

> In the midst of his race to the throne the leadership
> of religious conservatives will seek to meet with the
> warrior to see if he will uphold the ways of God and
> if they can support him.

As Jehonadab approached Jehu in the midst of his race to the throne, so
evangelical and religious conservative leaders approached Donald Trump
in the midst of his race to the White House. They sought to find out if he
was truly committed to the ways of God and thus if they could support him.

> The warrior will court and seek the support of reli-
> gious conservatives, whom he will see as an invalu-
> able asset to his campaign. He will meet with their
> leadership.

As Jehu sought the support of Jehonadab and his people, so Trump
would seek the support of evangelical and religious conservatives and meet
with their leaders. He would see their support as crucial to the success of
his campaign. He would meet with them on several occasions. The meetings would be crucial in giving assurance to those who were struggling over
whether or not to give him their support.

> The warrior will use his meeting with the leadership
> of religious conservatives to assure them that his
> faith is sincere, his motives are pure, and his zeal for
> the Lord's ways is genuine and strong.

"See my zeal for the LORD," Jehu told Jehonadab. So in his encounters
with religious conservatives Trump would seek to assure them that his faith
was real and his zeal for the Lord was genuine.

One month before his nomination as the Republican candidate for president, Trump spoke before roughly a thousand conservative Christian
leaders at what would prove to be a pivotal meeting held in New York City.
As with the meeting between Jehu and Jehonadab, the purpose of the event
was to see if those representing the ways of God could support the campaign of the man vying for the nation's highest position.

"...and he greeted him and said to him, 'Is your heart right, as my heart is toward your heart?'"[19]

In the case of the ancient meeting, Jehu did more than tell Jehonadab of his zeal for God; he assured the holy man that he was on his side.

> In the meeting between the warrior and the holy man, the warrior will assure the holy man that he is on his side.

Though Trump's meeting with evangelical leaders was a closed-door event, it wasn't long before report got out as to what was said that day. In fact, it made headlines: "Donald Trump Swears to Christian Leaders, 'I'm So On Your Side.'"[20]

It had been reported that Trump had assured the religious conservatives of his support with these words:

"I'm so on your side, I'm a tremendous believer, and we're gonna straighten it out."[21]

Note that the quote contains both a declaration of zeal for God and a pledge of support for the people of God—as in the ancient words that Jehu spoke to Jehonadab.

Jehu had followed his assurance with a request for the holy man's support:

> The warrior will ask the religious conservative leader to join him in his race to the throne.

So too Trump would ask religious conservatives and evangelical leaders to join him in his race to the presidency.

> For the people of God, the only alternative to the warrior will be the consigning of the nation to apostasy, the sealing and deepening of its moral and spiritual descent. The choice will be between the warrior or the house of apostasy—as represented by the heir and the former first lady.

Jehu had set himself against the house and the ways of Baal and the sin of the house of Ahab—so had Jehonadab. The commentaries note their agreement:

> "We see also that Jehonadab was thoroughly at one with Jehu in the destruction of Baal-worship."[22]

To Jehonadab it was either Jehu or the house of Ahab. So for religious conservatives, in the presidential race of 2016 it was either Donald Trump or the former first lady Hillary Clinton, who represented the furthering of America's moral descent and the consigning of the nation to perpetual apostasy.

> In view of the alternative and in the hope that the warrior could be used in turning the nation's course, religious conservatives and their leaders will say yes to supporting the warrior in his campaign. Thus there will be an alliance between the warrior and the religious conservatives of the land.

As with Jehonadab and Jehu, the majority of religious conservatives saw no alternative but to support Donald Trump. So as it was with Jehonadab and Jehu, religious conservatives rode together with Trump in his race to the White House in the cause of a common objective.

> The joining of the religious conservative and warrior will take place not at the beginning of the race but in its latter part.

When did Jehonadab, leader of the religious conservatives, join Jehu in his campaign? It took place in its last phase, the homestretch. So too the majority of religious conservatives and evangelical leaders would join Trump, not at the beginning of his race and campaign, but in its last phase, its homestretch.

Jehonadab was representative of the religious conservatives of his time. But he was also an individual. No one person in the modern replaying embodies everything that was Jehonadab. And in Trump's race to the White House there were several prominent religious conservative leaders who joined him in the race and who, by doing so, bore a resemblance to Jehonadab. But was there anyone who especially stood out among them? Let's look at the paradigm of the holy man in a nutshell:

> To join his race to the throne, the warrior will ask a leader, a religious conservative, respected, known for his virtue, a man of piety and holiness, to join his race to the throne. The leader's devotion to the ways of God will cause him to be deeply burdened over his nation's moral and spiritual decay. He will maintain a strict moral code of behavior, being extra careful to abstain from anything that might cause him defilement. The warrior will seek his partnership out of reverence and in the belief that it will help strengthen his campaign and convince others to lend their support.

Among the religious conservatives who joined Trump in his campaign, one stood out as preeminent—the one whom Trump asked to be his partner in the race, to ride with him to the throne. It was Mike Pence. Pence was a religious conservative. He defined himself as a Christian first, a conservative second, and a Republican third.[23] He was well respected, a leader known for his virtue. Though imperfect, just as was Jehonadab, Pence had a reputation for piety and holiness. His devotion to God had caused him to be deeply grieved over America's moral and spiritual decay. As Jehonadab would have been strongly opposed to the ways of Baal, so Pence was strongly opposed to the killing of the unborn and the promotion of immorality.

As Jehonadab was known for maintaining a strict moral code of behavior, so too was Pence. He was careful to abstain from anything that might cause defilement, temptation, or the appearance of evil. The media even attacked and ridiculed him over it.[24] As Jehu asked Jehonadab to come aboard his chariot to join him in the race to the throne, so Trump asked Pence to come on board to be his running mate, to join him in the race to the White House.

As Jehu knew that Jehonadab's partnership would help give legitimacy to his campaign and help convince the holy man's people to support him, so Trump knew that Pence's partnership would help give legitimacy to his campaign and help convince religious conservatives across the country to support him.

Now listen to the words of the commentaries concerning the alliance. Jehonadab was...

> "A person who, from his piety and simple primitive manner of life was highly esteemed, and possessed great influence in the country. Jehu saw in a moment the advantage that his cause would gain from

the friendship and countenance of this venerable man in the eyes of the people, and accordingly paid him the distinguished attention of inviting him to a seat in his chariot."[25]

This is not to say that Jehu didn't genuinely respect Jehonadab. And in the case of Trump, the evidence suggests a genuine respect for the religious leaders with whom he was allied.

So as it was with Jehu and Jehonadab, the two men who could hardly have been more different in manner, temperament, ways, and lifestyle, the warrior and the holy man, Trump and Pence, two men who likewise could not have been any more different, now rode together on a journey to the nation's throne.

> The religious conservative and the warrior will ride together into the capital city. There the warrior will approach the throne. And the religious conservatives will pray for God's will and blessing.

And as with Jehonadab and Jehu, the journey would culminate as the two rode into the city of Samaria, Israel's capital. So Donald Trump would enter Washington, DC, with Mike Pence and religious conservatives to assume the office of the presidency.

The presence of Jehu and Jehonadab together in the capital city would have presented the most unlikely of images. So too the presence of Donald Trump and religious conservatives together in America's capital city would form an image that not long before would have been almost unthinkable.

But as it was in the ancient case, the joining of the warrior and the holy man was a sign of the dramatic nature of the times and the critical nature of the juncture at which the nation now stood. So America was now standing at one of the most critical junctures in its moral and spiritual trajectory.

The warrior is now about to enter the capital city. He has just put an end to the days of one of the most polarizing figures of his time and of all times—Jezebel. This opens another mystery. We have found an amazingly consistent phenomenon: the days given to each leader in the paradigm conforms to the days given their ancient prototype.

Could this mystery apply as well to the time span of the queen? Could the paradigm reveal the days of Hillary Clinton? Could her ancient prototype hold the key? We will now open up the days of the queen.

Chapter 26

The DAYS of the QUEEN

WE HAVE LOOKED at the paradigm of reigns, the time parameters of the ancient kings. We have seen that the years of the modern leaders have conformed to the years of the corresponding ancient prototypes—the years of Bill Clinton conformed to the years of his ancient prototype, King Ahab, and the years of Barack Obama conformed to the years of his ancient prototype, King Joram. But what about Hillary Clinton? Could her years on the national stage conform to the years of her ancient prototype?

With leaders in the modern era we are concerned with their entrances onto the national stage and their rising to power on a national level. Let us now take the same standards we have used before and see if we find any correspondence.

———

After graduating from Yale Law School in the early 1970s, Hillary Clinton became a member of the impeachment inquiry staff, researching impeachment procedures for the House Committee on the Judiciary concerning President Richard Nixon. Finishing her work in Washington, DC, she relocated to Fayetteville, Arkansas, where she married Bill Clinton. During the next few years she worked as an attorney in the Rose Law Firm and in various legal advocacy groups.

But as with the others connected to the paradigm, there exists a clear turning point marking the moment of entrance onto the national stage and the point where the rise to national power begins. For Hillary Clinton it came with the election of Bill Clinton to the Arkansas governorship. It was then that she first assumed the role of first lady. She was her husband's political partner, his strategist, and his fellow campaigner—not only in the governorship but in their larger goal, to obtain the American presidency. She would go from first lady of Arkansas to first lady of the United States. As we have seen, during the Clinton years she was a different kind of first lady, a political partner and activist working from her offices in the White House.

Then came the next major marker and divide. The Clinton presidency approached its end. It was then that Hillary Clinton set out to launch her own solo political career—the first time in American history a former first lady had done so. She served as a US senator from New York for two terms. As her second term drew near to its end, she ran for the presidency. But she lost the nomination to Barack Obama. She was then asked by Obama to serve as secretary of state, which she did for his first term.

She then resigned from the administration. Many believed it was to prepare for another run for the presidency. She withdrew from political and public life. Unlike the time when Bill Clinton lost a term as governor of Arkansas and both Bill and Hillary Clinton began immediately strategizing and laboring to regain the governorship, this was now a true break from public life. There was no campaigning, no political work, nothing. As several commentators noted, it was the first time in decades that Hillary Clinton had retired from public view to become a private citizen.[1]

But in the spring of 2015 she announced that she was again running for president. She reentered public life, the national stage, and the battle for the presidency with a vengeance. She would thus remain on the public stage through her campaign and her defeat, to the inauguration, and into the start of 2017, when she announced that she would not run again for public office.

The Queen's Paradigm of Days

What happens now if we apply the same questions and standards as in the rise of Bill Clinton and Barack Obama?

When did Hillary Clinton enter the national stage?

Clearly it happened when she became the first lady of Arkansas, when her husband became the governor of Arkansas. When was that? It was January of 1979. She would remain first lady of Arkansas and then of the United States until the end of her husband's presidency—the next turning point.

When did her solo political career begin? It happened in January 2001, when she left the White House to become a US senator.

Thus the first period and major divide of her public life began in January 1979 and went to January 2001. The time period is *twenty-two years*.

She continued her solo career from senator to secretary of state, with a presidential campaign in between the two. This lasted until the next turning point, when she resigned as secretary of state and retired from public life to become a private citizen. That took place in February of 2013.

Thus the first part of her solo career was from January 2001 to February 2013—*twelve years*.

She then lived as a private citizen until announcing her second campaign for the presidency. That took place in April 2015.

She then resumed her public life, her time on the national stage, and her campaign for the presidency. It would end with her defeat in the election of November 2016 and then when she announced publicly that she would likely never run for office again in the spring of 2017. It had lasted *two years*.

So the years of Hillary Clinton are *twenty-two years*, *twelve years*, and *two years*—a total of *thirty-six years* on the national stage and in public life.

The *thirty-six years* can be divided into two parts: *twenty-two years* alongside her husband in his reign as governor and then president—and *fourteen years* of her solo career in the halls of power.

Her solo career can be further divided up into *twelve continuous years* on the national stage—and then a return to the national stage after a two-year hiatus in private life for *two more years* on the national stage.

If Hillary Clinton has followed the paradigm of Jezebel, is it possible that the years of her prototype would hold the mystery of her own years?

The Scriptures speak of Ahab and Jezebel as acting as one. Ahab did evil in the sight of the Lord, but Jezebel incited him. We can assume they shared the national stage and the throne from the beginning:

> "Ahab the son of Omri reigned over Israel in Samaria *twenty-two years.*"[2]

So the first part of Jezebel's time in power is *twenty-two years*—thus *twenty-two years* of reigning alongside her husband.

Ahab is killed. The twenty-two years come to an end. What comes next? Jezebel's career enters its second part. She will act as a political force in her own right, dwelling in the halls of power. But for how long?

The major part of Jezebel's time after Ahab will take place in the reign of Joram. How long were the days of Joram?

> "Now Jehoram [Joram] the son of Ahab became king over Israel at Samaria in the eighteenth year of Jehoshaphat king of Judah, and reigned *twelve years.*"[3]

So after the end of Ahab's reign we have *twelve years* for Jezebel. But there was another son who also reigned during Jezebel's days after Ahab— but only for the shortest of times, Ahaziah.

> "Ahaziah the son of Ahab became king over Israel in Samaria in the seventeenth year of Jehoshaphat king of Judah, and reigned *two years* over Israel."[4]

So we have another two years for Jezebel. *Two* plus *twelve* equals *fourteen years*. So after the end of Ahab's reign, Jezebel's time comes to *fourteen years*.

We will now bring it all together: the ancient queen, the paradigm, and the modern leader.

Jezebel's time on the national stage comes out to a total of *thirty-six years*.

> The first lady's time in power and on the national
> stage will come out to a period of thirty-six years.

Hillary Clinton's time on America's national stage and in power, from the time she became first lady of Arkansas to the time when, after defeated by Donald Trump, she announced she would likely never run again—minus a two-year retirement into private life, comes out to *thirty-six years*—an exact match to the Jezebel paradigm.

Jezebel's thirty-six years are divided into two parts; the first contains the years she reigned alongside her husband, King Ahab—*twenty-two years*.

> The first lady will reign alongside her husband, the
> king, for *twenty-two years*.

So Hillary Clinton's *thirty-six years* are divided into two parts; the first part comprises the years she governed alongside her husband first as first lady of Arkansas and then America. That period lasted *twenty-two years*.

The second part of Jezebel's thirty-six years comprises the years she acted of her own authority and dwelt in Israel's halls of power without Ahab. The period is *fourteen years*.

> The first lady will then pursue her own power as she
> continues to dwell in the nation's halls of power and
> at the center of its political stage for a period of *four-
> teen years*.

After the end of her husband's presidency Hillary Clinton would act on her own authority and pursue her own political career. She would dwell in the highest places of government without her husband for a period that comes out to *fourteen years*. It is another exact match with the paradigm of Jezebel.

Jezebel's *fourteen years* after the reign of Ahab will be divided into two parts, the major part and the much smaller part. The major part will consist of the *twelve years* of Joram's reign. The much smaller part will consist of the *two years* of Ahaziah's reign.

> The first lady's fourteen years beyond the reign of her husband will be further divided up into two periods—a *twelve-year period* and a *two-year period*.

So Hillary's *fourteen years* on the national stage after her husband's reign would be divided up into two parts: a *twelve-year period* as senator and secretary of state—and a *two-year period* separated from the *twelve-year period* constituting her second attempt at becoming president. It is again another exact match to Jezebel's paradigm.

There are some interpreters who believe that because of varying ways of dating and the possibility of co-regencies the numbers given for the kings of Israel may not always be sequential and may sometimes represent small portions of a particular year. Whatever one's interpretation, we have used the pure, literal, and exact time parameters as given in the Bible. And the results are stunning.

To sum up the convergences of the years of Jezebel and the years of Hillary Clinton:

- Jezebel's time on the public stage totaled *thirty-six years*. Hillary Clinton's time on the national stage totaled *thirty-six years*.

- Jezebel's time was divided up in two periods, the time alongside her husband on the national stage and the time she occupied the national stage without her husband.

- Clinton's time was divided up in two periods, the time alongside her husband on the national stage and the time she occupied the national stage without her husband.

- Jezebel's time alongside her husband on the national stage added up to *twenty-two years*.

- Clinton's time alongside her husband on the national stage added up to *twenty-two years*.

- Jezebel's time, beyond the end of her husband's reign, as a political player on her own on the national stage was *fourteen years*.

- Clinton's time, beyond the end of her husband's reign, as a political player on her own on the national stage was *fourteen years*.

- Jezebel's time of fourteen years on her own was broken up into two periods: *twelve years* and *two years*.

- Clinton's time of fourteen years on her own was broken up into two
  periods: *twelve years* and *two years*.

Beyond all the convergences of the modern figures and their ancient prototypes, the fact that even their years and the division of their years converge one with the other is astonishing. The time parameters of the modern
leaders follow the time parameters of their ancient counterparts. And those
parameters were already there in the paradigm and had been there for
almost three thousand years.

Jehu now readies to enter the nation's capital city, Samaria, the city to
which he must go if he is to reign on the nation's throne.

Chapter 27

The WARRIOR KING

J EHU HAD WON his most critical battle. The king and queen mother were dead. But the victory would not be sealed until he entered the capital city. In order to take the throne, he had to go to Samaria.

But Samaria was the stronghold of the old regime—the house of Ahab. The city would be filled with its officials, its royal heirs, and its partisans. As long as Ahab's supporters and potential successors were alive, Jehu and his revolution would be in danger. And beyond the political and tactical considerations Jehu's mission was to end the reign of Ahab's house. Thus he would have to enter hostile territory.

Time would again be of the essence. As he had done in his race to Jezreel, he moves again with extreme speed. He sends an ultimatum to the leaders of Samaria. It will result in the destruction of the dynasty. Jehu's tactics remained brutal, but had the evil of the old regime remained, the nation would be lost. There had been countless chances given. But the long-prophesied judgment had finally come. And Jehu was the agent through which it came.

With Ahab's dynasty removed, Jehu readies to leave Jezreel for the capital city. The sins of the royal house are still impacting the nation. The cult and practices of Baal are still entrenched in Israel's culture and centered in the capital city. So Jehu journeys to Samaria with a mission to cleanse the capital of Baal and then the nation.

Jehu enters Samaria with Jehonadab representing those who had remained faithful to God. The entrance must have been especially dramatic. The capital, like the nation, was undoubtedly polarized into two camps: those who were for Jehu, and those who were for the house of Ahab and Baal. So Jehu's approach would have brought both fear and resentment to some and relief and joy to others. As it was an entrance into largely hostile territory, it would have had the trappings of a military operation, as in the ending of a war or a revolution—which it was.

Jehu goes to work immediately. He summons the priests of Baal to a festival in honor of their god. But upon their assembling he has them executed. At that he begins dismantling the system that Jezebel and Ahab had put in place. He had judged Jezebel for her witchcraft. Now all who practiced such things would see themselves at war.

The dichotomy between Jehu's mission and his means of accomplishing it remains great. His purpose is to cleanse the nation of the evil that had corrupted it, but his ways of accomplishing his ends are often ruthless. The verdict on his actions as a revolutionary and then as king are as divided and contradictory as the man himself. The contradictions are evident in the commentaries:

> "His energy, determination, promptness, and zeal equipped him for the work he had to do. It was rough work and was executed with relentless thoroughness. Gentler measures probably would have failed to eradicate Baal worship from Israel. His impetuosity was demonstrated in his furious driving. He was bold, daring, unprincipled, masterful, and astute in his policy. But one seeks in vain in his character for any touch of magnanimity or of the finer qualities of the ruler."[1]

Despite his nature and his ways it was through this unlikely and controversial figure that the irrevocable sealing of the nation's descent to apostasy and judgment was for a time averted. The evil of Ahab's house was checked; the worship of Baal, rolled back. The killing of the nation's children was no longer championed by the government but now opposed by it. The nation's apostasy was slowed. The highest leader of the land no longer warred against the ways of God, nor did he sanction the persecution of God's people. Rather, he sought to defend them.

At the end of the process it would have been hard for God's people to answer the question as to whether Jehu was a man of God or not. But as to whether he had been used as an instrument for the purposes of God, there could be no denying that he had been.

The Paradigm of the Warrior King

> Having defeated the former first lady in the northeastern city, the warrior will turn his attention to the nation's capital, which he must enter in order to be installed as ruler of the land.

After defeating Joram and Jezebel at Jezreel, Jehu turns his focus to the capital city in view of beginning his reign. So after defeating Hillary Clinton while in New York City, Donald Trump turns his attention to Washington, DC, in view of beginning his presidency.

> The capital city will in many ways be a stronghold for the institutions and establishments the warrior has risen against. It will largely represent hostile territory. He will go there to bring shaking.

As Samaria was the stronghold of Ahab's house and represented largely hostile territory, so too Washington, DC, would represent the stronghold for the establishment and institutions Trump had spoken and campaigned against. It would in many ways be hostile territory. He would go there, as did Jehu, to bring shaking.

> The warrior will enter the nation's capital with an agenda to purge the nation's leadership of corruption. He will seek to remove from government those who stand against the ways of God. He will go to the capital city with a specific mission: to "drain the swamp."

As Jehu's mission was from the beginning to purge the nation's leadership, and as the capital city would be the focus of that purging, so too Jehu's antitype, Donald Trump, would go to Washington, DC, with the mission of Jehu, to purge the nation's leadership of corruption and, in his own words, to "drain the swamp."

> The warrior will come as both an agent of judgment and hope—judgment to the establishment and to the forces that are at war against the ways of God, and hope to those upholding the ways of God.

As Jehu was both an agent of judgment and a vessel of hope, so in the modern replaying Trump was a threat, a danger, and a calamity to those of the Clinton camp and those who supported its objectives. He was a blow to their agenda. But to those who sought to be faithful to God's ways, to most religious conservatives, he offered a ray of hope in the face of America's spiritual darkening.

> On the day of the warrior's ascent to the throne the nation and its capital will be polarized into two camps. The warrior will proceed to the throne alongside God's people. To those of the opposing camp his arrival in the city will produce dread, resentment, hostility, and anger. The day of his entrance will have the trappings of a military operation.

As was Jehu's entrance into the capital city of Samaria, Trump's inauguration in Washington, DC, was a day of polarization. Washington was a city divided in two camps, a microcosm of the nation. Thousands gathered to celebrate and witness the event, and thousands gathered to oppose it. Surrounding Trump were people of God and religious and nonreligious conservatives. But opposing Trump were demonstrations of protesters vowing to resist the new administration. Soldiers blanketed the city to contain the conflict. It had the appearance of a military operation.

> Those engaged in the practice of witchcraft will see themselves at war with the new king.

When Jehu spoke of Jezebel's connection to pagan practices, he used the Hebrew word *keshaf*, meaning to whisper a spell and to practice witchcraft. Jehu had declared war on sorcery and witchcraft. Those engaged in such practices would have seen the new king as their archenemy. And those witches and sorcerers who believed themselves able to cast spells would undoubtedly have done their best, or worst, to have stopped him.

For this facet of the paradigm to have any fulfillment in the modern case or the modern world would be stunning—but it did. After Trump's ascension to the presidency a strange phenomenon took place. One month after the inauguration, all over America and the world witches gathered together at midnight under the crescent moon to cast spells against him. The gatherings were to take place continuously under every crescent moon until they achieved their results. They invited all of like mind and practice to join them. As one article reported:

> "This is not an exclusive witches-only event . . . with . . . shamans . . . sorcerers and sorceresses . . . occultists . . . also invited and urged to take part."[2]

Occult ceremonies would be performed:

> "Mass rituals have also been planned in multiple covens, during which men and women will perform a spell to bind President Trump and all those who abet him by delivering a chant and holding a brief ceremony."[3]

Never in American presidential history had such a phenomenon taken place across the nation or world—but a war involving witches and witchcraft was part of the template of Jehu, and never in American presidential history had there been a figure who fulfilled that ancient template until Trump.

> The warrior's most radical enemies will be found among the supporters of the royal house and the priests and priestesses of the pagan gods.

Among the groups that saw Jehu as a threat to their interests and themselves as his enemy were those closest to the house of Ahab, along with the priests and priestesses of Baal and Ashtoreth who attended them. So in the case of Trump it was of course not only witches who viewed themselves as his enemies. There were many. Foremost among them were those opposed to biblical values, those who supported and allied themselves with the house of Clinton, and the modern equivalents of the ancient pagan priests. The day after Trump's inauguration the modern priestesses of Ashtoreth, leaders of

radical feminism, and others with anti-biblical agendas took part in ral-
lying multitudes to the Washington Mall in a gathering designed to show
their rage over the change that had taken place in the nation's government.

And then of course were the modern-day priests of Baal, the nation's
abortion organizations, advocates, and practitioners. As the priests of
Baal would have seen Jehu as their archenemy, so the proponents of abortion would see themselves as Trump's enemy and set themselves at war
against him. They had poured massive amounts of money to stop him from
becoming president. Now they would pour massive amounts of money to
stop him from taking any action that might impede their practices.

> The warrior will remain a figure of controversy and
> an enigma. His nature will remain contentious, and
> his ways, questionable. Yet the question will also
> remain whether someone of a less radical nature or
> combative nature would have accomplished what
> was called for in view of the radical nature of the
> times.

Jehu would remain a controversial figure for over two and a half thousand years. The biblical record would commend him for overcoming the
foremost evil of his day. But that didn't mean that everything he did was
commended—far from it. Jehu would also be rebuked in the Scriptures for,
among other things, the bloodiness of his means.

So Donald Trump would remain a controversial figure. He could be
commended for the good he had done in opposing evil. But not everything
could be commended—just as not everything could be commended in the
case of Jehu, his ancient prototype. Likewise it remained a question, as in
the case of Jehu, as to whether someone of a less radical nature and less
radical means would have accomplished the radical intervention that was
required.

> Despite his ways it will be through the warrior that the sealing of the nation's course to apostasy will be averted, at least for a time. The war against God's ways as waged by the royal house will be checked. The killing of the nation's children will no longer be championed from the throne but opposed by it. The nation's accelerating apostasy will be slowed. And the highest leader of the land will no longer sanction the persecution of God's people but will seek to defend them.

In the enigma of Jehu this was the larger story. And so it was with the enigma of Donald Trump, or at least with regard to his stated agenda. The sealing of America's apostasy was for a time averted, the killing of the unborn was no longer championed from the White House, the persecution of God's people was no longer sanctioned, and policies that warred against the ways of God were overturned.

The following was written of the enigma and contradictions of the ancient warrior:

> "He is exactly one of those men whom we are compelled to recognize, not for what is good or great in themselves, but as instruments for destroying evil, and preparing the way for good."[4]

For many the same exact words could have been said of his modern antitype.

We will now open a very different facet of the paradigm—one that will involve an ancient structure halfway across the world that will eerily coalesce with the paradigm's mystery.

Chapter 28

The TEMPLE

AFTER DEALING WITH the priests of Baal, Jehu set out to dismantle the institutions and infrastructure by which the cult of Baal had thrived. Foremost among these was the Temple of Baal, the center of the cult. As with much else in the paradigm, its origins are found with Ahab. He was its builder:

> "Then he set up an altar for Baal in the temple of Baal, which he had built in Samaria."[1]

Up to that point the cult of Baal would have functioned mostly in secret or outside the parameters of the public square. Its rites would have been performed on mountaintops, in groves, and in the shadows of Israel's cultural underground. But by building the Temple of Baal in the capital city, Ahab was allying the state with the Phoenician deity and against God and His people. Under the reign of Joram the temple and cult would continue to operate in the nation's capital.

Jehu knew that if he was going to cleanse the nation of Baal and all its horrific practices, he had to destroy the center of its worship, its temple:

> "And they brought the sacred pillars out of the temple of Baal and burned them. Then they broke down the sacred pillar of Baal, and tore down the temple of Baal and made it a refuse dump to this day. Thus Jehu destroyed Baal from Israel."[2]

The destruction of Baal's temple was the defining moment of Jehu's reformation, the most visual, concrete, permanent, and iconic act of his revolution. It would epitomize his cleansing of the land and set him apart from all the other monarchs of the northern kingdom.

He not only tore down the edifice but converted it to serve another purpose—it would become a *refuse dump*. It could have been used as the city dump, as one commentator puts it, as a "depository for all the filth of the town."[3] But the Hebrew word *makharah* goes farther. It could more literally be translated as outhouse or latrine. Jehu was making sure that the site would never again be used for worship but would serve as a reminder. One commentary explains why:

> "*And brake down the house of Baal*—i.e. partially ruined it, but still left portions of it standing, as a memorial of the sin and of its punishment—a solemn warning, one would have thought, to the people of the capital—and made it a draught-house unto this day . . . "[4]

So the ruins of Baal's temple would stand as a permanent testament to the evil of Baal worship and its resulting judgment. It would serve as well as a memorial to what Jehu had accomplished. He was the instrument God had used to cleanse the land of evil. The rise of Jehu meant the fall of Baal's temple.

The Paradigm of the Temple

As Ahab allied the state to Baal worship and thus to the sacrificing of children, so his modern antitype, Bill Clinton, was the first president in American history to ally the state to the practice of abortion.

> The nation's capital will become the central site
> from which the practice of child sacrifice will be
> championed.

As Ahab championed Baal worship from the capital city of Samaria, so Clinton championed abortion from the capital city of Washington, DC. From there he issued presidential orders, directives, and vetoes to guard, advocate for, and expand the practice. Under the Clinton administration Washington, DC, became the city from which the practice of abortion was championed from the highest echelons of power.

But the practice was not only promoted through government. As Israel's capital served as the center of Baal's cult, so Washington, DC, has served as the headquarters of the nation's largest abortion performer, Planned Parenthood. Its other headquarters was New York City. It was in New York where abortion was first legalized in America and Washington where it was first legalized throughout the nation. The paradigm likewise centers on the nation's capital and its chief northeastern city.

> Once in the capital the warrior will make it his goal
> to end the cult of child sacrifice. He will cut off the
> support and resources that sustain and empower it.
> He will dismantle the structures that allow for its
> continuance.

So as Jehu cut off the priests of Baal and began dismantling their Temple, the first thing Trump would do upon entering the capital city and assuming the presidency was to begin undoing the practice of killing unborn children. As Jehu had replaced the government's previous support of Baal worship with opposition, so Trump would seek to reverse the government's prior support and funding of abortion organizations such as Planned Parenthood.[5]

As Jehu dismantled the Temple of Baal that Ahab had built and which had continued to function in Joram's reign, so Trump began dismantling the legal structures first put in place by Bill Clinton and later reinstated by Barack Obama for the promulgating of abortion. Thus he reversed the executive orders first put in place by Clinton and then again by Obama, which had wiped away the safeguards concerning the practice.[6] And he began doing so immediately upon coming to power—just as Jehu had done.

But could there be more to the mystery? If the rise of Donald Trump is a manifestation of the template of Jehu, and if the rise of Jehu was linked to the Temple of Baal, could there be another manifestation linked to the rise of Donald Trump that somehow involves the Temple of Baal?

The answer will take us into another realm and to a land far from American shores.

Most of the temples of the ancient world have long since crumbled to dust. A few world-famous structures have remained standing, such as the Parthenon of Greece and the Pantheon of Rome. But as for Baal, a deity unknown to most people of the modern world, we would not expect there to be many traces left of his worship. The idea that a Temple of Baal, as in the ancient paradigm, could still in some way be standing in the modern world would seem extremely unlikely.

But the surprising answer is that there has existed a Temple of Baal dating back to ancient times and surviving into the modern world. It has stood in the Middle Eastern city of Palmyra, Syria. In fact, for almost two thousand years, Palmyra was the site of not one, but two surviving temples of the Middle Eastern deity.

The first, known as the Temple of Bel, or Temple of Baal (the name *Bel* being another version of *Baal*), was dedicated in AD 32. The second, known as the Temple of *Baalshamim* (or Baal of the Heavens), was built in the second century AD.

We have seen the correspondence between the Temple of Baal in ancient Israel and the modern-day structures dedicated to the killing of the unborn. But now we have an actual Temple of Baal, and more than one, standing in the modern world with origins dating back to ancient times.

Since the Temple of Baal is so central to the paradigm, is it possible these ancient structures could somehow have a part in the paradigm's modern replaying? The paradigm:

> In the days of the unfolding of the paradigm the Temple of Baal will be destroyed.

As Ahab will always be linked to the building of the Temple of Baal, Jehu will always be linked to its destruction. The rise of Jehu meant the Temple of Baal had to fall. And its fall would be the most concrete sign of his rising, the most permanent testament of his mission.

Though these two temples of Baal have stood largely undisturbed since ancient times and in a Middle Eastern city obscure and unknown to most people in the world, could they now become part of the modern replaying of the mystery? If Trump is the Jehu of the template, then could the time of his rising be connected to any event of significance concerning the two surviving temples of Baal?

According to the paradigm, the rise of the warrior means the destruction of the temple. Though after surviving two thousand years of history, we would not naturally expect anything to happen to the two ancient structures, much less anything that would bring them into the news—something did.

ISIS happened. With the destabilization and fighting in western Iraq and eastern Syria, the terrorist organization began taking over land and cities in the region to establish its "Islamic caliphate." One of those cities was Palmyra. A few months after its conquest of Palmyra members of ISIS approached the Temple of Baalshamim. They placed explosives within its columns and detonated them. The ancient building was destroyed.[7] The Temple of Baal had fallen.

One week later it was reported that ISIS had detonated explosives inside the Temple of Bel. After reviewing satellite pictures taken of Palmyra, the United Nations issued its report:

> "We can confirm destruction of the main building of the Temple of Bel
> as well as a row of columns in its immediate vicinity."[8]

So now the Temple of Bel, Baal's other sanctuary, had fallen as well.

The ancient paradigm tells of the fall of the Temple of Baal. And now, in the midst of the paradigm's unfolding, comes the fall of the Temple of Baal.

What about the timing of the destruction? In the paradigm the temple falls at the rise of Jehu. The rise of Jehu is marked by the fall of the Temple of Baal, or the fall of the temple marks the rise of Jehu:

> The rise of the warrior will be linked to the destruction of the Temple of Baal. When the warrior rises, the Temple of Baal must fall.

When were the two temples of Baal destroyed?

ISIS captured the city of Palmyra in 2015. In the same year, its agents destroyed the two temples. Thus the temples of Baal, having survived for two thousand years, fell in the year 2015.

So when did the rise of the modern counterpart to Jehu, the man whose rising marks the fall of Baal's temple, begin? The rise of Donald Trump to the presidency began in the year 2015—the year of the fall of the temples of Baal. The paradigm is fulfilled—the warrior rises and the Temple of Baal falls.

When specifically were the temples of Baal destroyed? The destruction was verified at the end of August but possibly began earlier that summer. Either way, the destruction took place in the summer of 2015.

When did Trump's rise begin? He announced his candidacy for the presidency in the summer of 2015.[9]

> Once the warrior begins his race to the throne, the days of the Temple of Baal are numbered.

Jehu began his race to the throne, and soon after, the Temple of Baal was destroyed. Trump announced his race for the presidency, and approximately two months after announcing his race for the presidency both temples of Baal had been destroyed.

Does this mean that the temples of Baal were destroyed because of Donald Trump? No. As noted, the manifestations of the paradigm rarely come about through direction causation. Rather they represent the interweaving and coalescing of events. The paradigm operates in the realm of signs. And within that realm these facts remain:

- The paradigm involves the Temple of Baal.
- In the paradigm the Temple of Baal is destroyed.
- The temple's destruction is linked to the rise of the warrior.
- In the paradigm's modern-day replaying, one fulfilling the template of the warrior, Jehu is Donald Trump.
- In the paradigm, when the warrior rises, the Temple of Baal must fall.
- The year of Donald Trump's rising was 2015. In 2015 the temples of Baal came crashing down.

So as it was in the days that saw the fall of the house of Ahab and as it is in the paradigm, the ancient mystery replayed itself on the stage of the twenty-first century world—the warrior again arose, and the pillars of Baal again came crashing down as his temple collapsed into ruins.

What of things to come? We now turn to the future.

Chapter 29

The HARBINGERS of DAYS to COME

W HAT ABOUT THE future?
Does the paradigm contain any revelation concerning what lies ahead?

On one hand, with the ascent of the warrior, the saga of Ahab's house, its rise and fall, attains resolution. What began with the rise of Ahab and Jezebel is finally undone and resolved with the rise of Jehu. The manifestations of the paradigm do not necessarily have to continue. On the other hand, the history does continue. Therefore could there be in its continuance a revelation or glimpse of what the future holds? Could its details still contain clues as to where we are heading?

We begin with Jehu. What happened to the warrior after his rise to power?

Though he had done right in bringing the evil of Ahab's house to an end, his reformation was imperfect. It only went halfway. The words of the biblical account contain a rebuke:

"Yet Jehu was not careful to keep the law of the LORD, the God of Israel, with all his heart. He did not turn away from the sins of Jeroboam, which he had caused Israel to commit."[1]

Jehu was wholehearted in his war against Baal. But he was less than wholehearted in following God. He had cleansed the land of Baal worship, but he didn't depart from the "sins of Jeroboam."

What were the sins of Jeroboam? Jeroboam set up two golden calves and led Israel to worship them. Though it wasn't Baal worship, it was idolatry. Jeroboam told the people that to worship the golden calf was, in effect, to worship the God who brought them out of the land of Egypt. Thus the people may have been convinced that they were still worshipping the God of Israel. Nevertheless they were now following idols. Jeroboam's sin represented a mixing of truth and falsehood. It was a corruption. So Jehu warred against the pure evil of Baal but walked in a mixture of truth and falsehood. Why?

The worship of Baal that Ahab and Jezebel championed had been brought into the nation from a foreign land. But the golden calves, on the other hand, had become a part of Israel's culture. They were emblems of the northern kingdom's independence from the southern kingdom. So it appears that Jehu's campaign was not only built on opposition to godlessness and immorality but also on nationalism and a rejection of foreign influence as embodied by Jezebel. Baal worship was ungodly, and it was also foreign; the worship of the golden calves was ungodly but was linked to nationalism. Jehu opposed the more blatant and foreign-based sin but continued in the national and by comparison the lesser sin. One commentator explains it this way:

> "Jeroboam's false worship had been around a lot longer than the Baalism introduced by Ahab and Jezebel. Jeroboam's false worship was not a 'foreign import,' as Baalism was. He introduced a counterfeit version of the only true religion, the worship of Yahweh . . . the worship that Jeroboam established was now 'the national religion' of the northern kingdom . . . One may be reluctant to deal with religious error because it is a part of one's culture and national identity."[2]

So Jehu opposed the deep evil of Ahab's house but walked in a path of compromise in line with the nation's long-term drift from God. He was, again, a mix. Beyond the spiritual realm the Bible records that Jehu's reign saw trouble and conflicts with the surrounding nations. And through these conflicts God would reduce the nation's borders. Israel would be diminished.

And so under the reign of Jehu Israel's apostasy was slowed but not reversed. So the nation's short-term danger was averted, but the long-term danger was not.

Could these elements of Jehu's reign give us revelation into what the future may hold for America and the world?

Beyond the fact that after Jehu's rise there would be no necessity for the manifestations of the paradigm to continue, we must also remember that even if they did, there is no formula dictating which details of the template must manifest. On the other hand, since the account continues, could it contain more keys, revelations, clues, or even warnings? We will now open up and explore some of these clues, not as what must be but as that which could be. Thus they will be presented as possibilities—and warnings.

> The warning of the paradigm is that as king the warrior will not be careful to follow the ways of God—that his reformation will be partial and selective, that he will oppose some aspects of the nation's apostasy but continue in others.

As with Jehu, Donald Trump would be an enigma to those who followed and prayed for God's ways. He had promised to do the will of God, but there was always a concern that his reformation would be inconsistent. As with Jehu, Trump appeared strong on some of the issues concerning the ways of God but weak on others.

> As king, he will oppose the most blatant practices associated with the apostasy, as in the sacrifice of children, but other practices of the apostasy he will not oppose.

In his first days as president Trump took initiative to oppose the sin associated with Baal, the offering up of children. He spoke and acted for the protection of the unborn. But on other issues he appeared much less strong.

> The warrior's championing the cause of nationalism will at times compete with his intentions to carry out God's will.

As with Jehu, Trump's cause was also one of nationalism. At times that cause could be consistent with Scripture but not always. Thus it would at times compete with his ability and intentions to fulfill the will of God.

> The hope for the days in which the warrior reigns will be that they will not only slow the nation's descent but also that they will provide the chance for a massive spiritual and cultural returning to God. Apart from such a return the nation's overall course of apostasy and descent will continue.

What Jehu had done in ending the reign of Ahab's house and rolling back the cult of Baal was a major accomplishment. The government no longer warred against God's ways or persecuted His people. Thus there would have been hope among God's people that his reign could foster a spiritual revival. And yet in the long run the nation would resume its downward course of apostasy.

Trump's victory in the presidential election represented a profound change. It averted the sealing of America's apostasy. And it provided a wide-open door for evangelical leaders and believers to impact the nation. Thus there would likewise be the hope of a wide-scale return to God. On the other hand, the weight and inertia of America's moral and spiritual descent would mean that for such a return to take place would be nothing short of miraculous and that apart from such a return there would be nothing but descent.

Did it have to be that way? Since Jehu's actions were inconsistent, did it mean that the same would have to be true of Donald Trump? No. As noted earlier, there is no formula in the continuation of the dynamics. Is it possible that Trump could depart from the example of Jehu's latter days and rise above it? It is. Is it possible that he could do worse than Jehu or fail to finish his term or terms in office? That too is possible. And if so, would that change the purpose he served in his rising? No. No more so than Jehu's subsequent failure in governing in any way negated the purpose he had served in the time of his rising. Despite the fact that Jehu didn't continue in the ways of God, his initial victory against the house of Ahab had averted disaster.

On the other hand, is it possible that Hillary Clinton or a candidate representing a similar agenda could in future days run for office and win? The paradigm would ordain that in the days of the warrior's rise, the former first lady would be defeated. After that her time in the paradigm is finished. Yet anything is possible. But barring a complete reversal of her positions on biblical issues or the positions of a similar candidate, such an event would represent the nation's definitive rejection of God's ways and the sealing of its apostasy.

Is there a possibility that, unlike what happened or didn't happen in the days of Jehu's kingship, America and the world could witness a massive spiritual reawakening? That too is possible. And it is that possibility that constitutes the heart of the matter.

The context of the paradigm is the accelerating fall of a nation that had once known God, a process that reaches a critical juncture where apart from some form of intervention the nation is in danger of being irrevocably sealed in a course of apostasy.

America was at a similarly critical juncture in the election of 2016. And then, as with Jehu's surprise ascendancy, everything was turned on its head. What does it mean for America? What did it mean for ancient Israel?

There are patterns in Scripture concerning a nation's progression to judgment: The nation in apostasy from God is given warning, even shaking, but also reprieves. In the southern kingdom of Judah the reprieve was given in the reign of the righteous king Josiah. Josiah sought to lead his nation back to God. The judgment that had already been decreed was held back. After Josiah's death the nation's downward course resumed and judgment fell.

Likewise the rise of Jehu provided a reprieve for Israel. But what was the purpose of that reprieve? It was to give the nation a chance to turn back from its course, to avert judgment, and to return to the God of its foundation. It was to give God's people a period of time in which to call to the Lord as many as would come.

The issue was not Donald Trump any more than the issue in ancient times was Jehu. Jehu was a flawed vessel with flawed motives and tactics. But he was nevertheless a vessel, an instrument of purposes higher than his own intentions or knowledge. So too what happened in the election of 2016 was not ultimately about Donald Trump but about something much higher, the purposes of God, the purpose of a reprieve. Such reprieves may come, as they did in ancient times, shortly before a nation's judgment. They may at times be accompanied by national crises. They may even come in the midst of divine correction—as the purpose of both reprieves and corrections are the same—to turn a nation or a people back to God.

In the case of ancient Israel some undoubtedly saw Jehu's rise as a calamity. Others saw it as the answer. It was neither. It was a window. So in the present case the answer was not an election, a man, a party, or a political agenda. A political answer cannot solve a spiritual problem. But it can open a window through which that answer can come. On the other hand, a political turning without a corresponding spiritual turning will end up in failure or calamity. As for the desire to make America great again, the only way America can be great again is for America to return to the God who made America great in the first place. The answer is in repentance, return, and revival.

Jehu's reign would provide a window for revival, but the revival that should have come through that window never did. Though the descent had slowed, the people never turned back to God.

> Without a return to God the nation that has been given the reprieve will progress to judgment and destruction.

What about America? The template ultimately warns of national judgment. A nation that has especially known God but now stands in defiance of His ways stands also in danger of His judgment. And a nation that has been given a reprieve for the purpose of turning back but spurns that chance will have nothing left but the prospect of judgment.

And it is in judgment that two biblical and prophetic templates come together. After the end of Jehu's reign the nation would continue down its spiral of apostasy until the day of its destruction. But before the coming of that day God would warn them and call them back. He would give them signs of coming judgment, harbingers. This is the template of judgment revealed in *The Harbinger*. In the last days of the northern kingdom of Israel nine harbingers, or prophetic signs, appeared in the land. The harbingers warned of approaching judgment. The nation had rejected God's warnings. And when the judgment came, it would be wiped off the face of the earth.

The revelation of *The Harbinger* is that these same nine harbingers of coming judgment that appeared in the last days of ancient Israel have now appeared on American soil. Some have appeared in New York City; some, in Washington, DC; some have involved prophetic objects; some, prophetic events; and some, national leaders, even leaders pronouncing prophetic words of judgment on the land. Since the time *The Harbinger* was written until the writing of this book, the signs and warnings of judgment have not stopped their manifesting, just as the nation has not yet stopped in its defiance and war against God's ways.

The templates of *The Harbinger* and *The Paradigm* are joined together. Both originate from ancient Israel and specifically from the northern kingdom of ancient Israel. Both originate from the land of Jehu. The events of *The Paradigm* lead up to Jehu's reign. Jehu's reign ultimately leads up to the events of *The Harbinger*. The two templates and mysteries are connected.

The template of *The Paradigm* identifies a nation progressing to judgment. So too does that of *The Harbinger*. What is especially ominous is that both templates converge on one specific nation—America. And lest one take comfort in the fact that the nation's final judgment came many years after Jehu's reign, one must note that both templates have *already begun* to manifest and have done so, in large part, simultaneously.

As to when the judgment will come, we cannot be dogmatic, except to say that such things are ultimately dependent on the mercy and long-suffering of God. As to how one can be safe in the face of such judgment, this will be given in the last part of the coming chapter.

As for those who know the Lord, what this tells us is that the time is late. The window is temporary. We must not waste it. Without revival there can be no hope. Is there any hope of revival? If there were no hope, what would be the point of such prophetic warnings? If there is warning, there is hope. So a promise was given to ancient Israel to be applied even in days of the nation's apostasy and judgment. It was this:

> "If My people who are called by My name will humble themselves, and
> pray and seek My face, and turn from their wicked ways, then I will
> hear from heaven, and will forgive their sin and heal their land."[3]

As of the time of this writing the turning that is necessary for revival and restoration has not yet come. And if the nation's culture remains unchanged, if its youngest generation remains untouched, if its progression of sin and defiance remains unbroken, then its ultimate destination will also remain unchanged. But if ever there was a time for God's people to apply that ancient promise given to Israel and to humble themselves and pray and seek the face of God and turn from their sinful ways, in the confidence of His mercy and His power to heal and restore—it is now.

So we must take account of the critical nature of our days. And we must all the more pray for revival, believe for revival, work for revival, and speak the truth for revival. And most importantly we must not only pray for revival, but we must actually start living in revival.

We must use every moment to the best of our abilities for the will and purposes of God. We must make the most of the days we have. For we will not always have them.

———

As we now come to the end of the revelation, there remains one last paradigm to open. And it will be this paradigm that will give us the blueprint and the answer concerning our own ways, lives, and destinies. It is the paradigm given to those who seek to stand strong in such a time as this, to live in the will of God, and to fulfill the purpose for which they were placed on earth. It is the template that concerns more than any single person of modern times. It is the template given for the one reading this book. One might even say it is the paradigm of you.

Chapter 30

The ELIJAH PARADIGM

ND NOW THE missing paradigm . . .

It has been there in one form or another from the beginning, from the time of Ahab. But it is time now that we open it.

Behind the rise and fall of the paradigm's rulers lies another realm—the prophetic realm. Much of what takes place in the paradigm, from the throne to the battlefield, is the specific outworking of prophecy. And the key prophetic figure of the paradigm is one of the most famous of all prophetic figures—Elijah.

The second key prophetic figure is his apprentice, Elisha. We will count it as one ministry, one function, and one role as Elisha was carrying out the continuation of Elijah's ministry. He would anoint those Elijah was called to anoint, be part of the fulfilling of Elijah's prophecies, and even minister in Elijah's anointing.

It was Elijah who was there from the beginning to challenge Ahab and Jezebel. It was Elijah who anointed Elisha, who would minister at the time of the paradigm's resolution. It was Elijah who was first told to anoint

Ben-Hadad and Hazael, key players in the paradigm's resolution. And it was Elijah's prophecy that would be fulfilled in the judgment of Ahab, Joram, and Jezebel.

He would enter the biblical account in this way:

> "And Elijah the Tishbite, of the inhabitants of Gilead, said to Ahab, 'As the LORD God of Israel lives, before whom I stand, there shall not be dew nor rain these years, except at my word.'"[1]

He comes on the stage as if out of nowhere. We know little about him, yet he seems from the start to be a major figure, an equal to the king. It is no accident that his first appearance in Scripture directly follows that of King Ahab. For Elijah would be God's answer to the house of Ahab and its evils. It is as Ahab and Jezebel embark on their campaign of apostasy and their agenda to stamp out the ways of God that God raises up Elijah.

He would speak boldly to the throne. He would stand resolute against their evils. He would challenge their god Baal. He would close and open the heavens. He would confront the nation with its sin and call it to repentance. He would expose the sins of the royal house. His apprentice, Elisha, would prophesy to Joram, Hazael, and indirectly to Jehu. By this kings would rise and fall. It all began with Elijah. His impact on Israel, directly and indirectly, cannot be overstated. Virtually every facet of the paradigm bears some connection to this fiery prophet.

He was radical, dramatic, unafraid, bold, and powerful. And it was just such a figure that was required for the challenge of the times. He would stand as a counterforce to the nation's apostasy. He would be hated by the priests of Baal and their followers and by Jezebel, who would threaten his life. Yet he would confront the king face-to-face. He would refuse to bend to the times or give any ground to the dictates of the apostasy. He would not be intimidated but would stand unyielding, uncompromised, and unashamed for the ways of God. And his life and ministry would be used to change the course of his nation's history.

So who is Elijah?

The Paradigm of Elijah

For the answer we must go back to the big picture with which we began at the paradigm's opening—that of the massive falling away of Western civilization from its biblical foundations and its war against biblical morality and faith.

We have seen the same elements of this war in the apostasy of modern times. Western civilization is replaying the fall of ancient Israel. And it is this paradigm that forms the stage for the prophet Elijah. Elijah's calling took place in the midst of a civilization once established for the purposes of God and once saturated with the knowledge of His ways. But it had fallen away. And now its fall was deepening and accelerating.

If Ahab, Jezebel, and Joram represent the darkness of the paradigm, then Elijah, along with Elisha, represents the light. Thus the paradigm of Elijah is the paradigm of the righteous and particularly of the righteous who live in the days of apostasy. And since the apostasy of Elijah's day is the paradigm of the present apostasy, the paradigm of Elijah speaks especially to our day and is critical in revealing how God's people are to stand, act, bear witness, overcome, and be a light to the days and world in which they live.

The witness of Elijah was unlike that of the righteous before him. In earlier ages, as in that of King David, the ways of God represented the ruling principle of the nation's culture. Biblical faith was society's reigning worldview, and biblical morality represented its prevailing code of ethics. There were always those who violated such codes, but the codes themselves remained in place. But in the days of Elijah all that was turned upside down. With the rise of Ahab and Jezebel the culture's reigning worldview and principle was no longer biblical faith but paganism and pagan practices, its code of morality.

The days in which biblical faith constitutes the ruling principle of civilization are not the days of the prophet Elijah but the days of King David. But the days in which civilization is ruled by that which is anti-biblical are not the days of David but the days of Elijah. In the days of David biblical faith is a cultural phenomenon as it is largely joined to and one with the nation's culture. It is established and part of the status quo. But in the days of Elijah biblical faith is not a cultural phenomenon. It becomes, instead, a countercultural phenomenon. It is disestablished. And it is not part of the status quo but is radical and revolutionary.

In the days of David the faith is royal. But in the days of Elijah the faith becomes prophetic. Or to put it another way, in the days when a civilization is characterized by the reign of Ahab, then the people of God must, in turn, be characterized by Elijah.

> As the culture's reigning principle changes from biblical to anti-biblical, the faith must change from a cultural phenomenon to a countercultural phenomenon, from that which is status quo to that which is radical and revolutionary. It ceases from being a ruling or royal phenomenon and becomes a prophetic phenomenon.

In past ages the Judeo-Christian faith in many ways constituted the reigning principle of Western civilization. This was the David stage. Church and state were in many ways joined. Christianity appeared as a cultural phenomenon and part of the status quo. But with the apostasy of Western civilization all that has been reversed. As in the paradigm biblical faith is no longer the culture's reigning principle. Western civilization has moved to the Ahab stage. Thus God's people must, in turn, move to the Elijah stage. The Judeo-Christian faith must change from functioning as a cultural phenomenon to a countercultural one. Its people must increasingly become a revolutionary people, a prophetic people.

"Then it happened, when Ahab saw Elijah, that Ahab said to him, 'Is that you, O troubler of Israel?'"[2]

Ahab called Elijah the "troubler of Israel." Yet Elijah had simply remained faithful to the Lord's ways. It was the nation that changed. And so for simply holding true to that which at one time the entire nation had held to, he was considered a radical. In the days when a nation becomes radically immoral, the moral will appear to be radical. So it was with Elijah. His refusal to go along with the apostasy made him a living witness, a reminder of what the nation had forsaken and that from which it had fallen. So he troubled it. A civilization that sees evil as good will now see good as evil. So those who in times past would have been looked upon as heroes and role models were now seen as enemies of the state. Thus the paradigm:

> Those who refuse to go along with the culture's apostasy, those who remain faithful to God's ways, will now be labeled as radical, troublemakers, dangerous, even enemies of the state. Their very existence will bear witness of what the culture had once upheld but had now forsaken.

When a "Christian culture" apostatizes into a post-Christian or anti-Christian state, those who refuse to go along with the apostasy, those who remain Christian, who hold true to the Word and ways of God, become the Elijahs of the age. As it was with Elijah, their very existence will constitute a witness and reminder that will trouble the civilization in which they live concerning that from which it has fallen. As was Elijah, they will increasingly be labeled as radical and dangerous.

> "And he answered, 'I have not troubled Israel, but you and your father's
> house have, in that you have forsaken the commandments of the LORD
> and have followed the Baals.'"[3]

Ahab has led the nation in redefining what is good and evil. Now he seeks to redefine the righteous, namely Elijah. But Elijah refuses to be redefined. He sees the new morality, with its newly fabricated values and new dictates of political correctness, for what it is, a rebellion against the eternal laws of God. It is not Elijah but Ahab who is the troubler of the kingdom. And Elijah is not afraid to tell him so. For in the days of apostasy it is the lawless who judge and the criminals who reign.

> A civilization in apostasy will attempt to redefine not only good and evil but the people of God themselves. Therefore the righteous must reject all redefinition. They must refuse to be redefined by the apostasy. They must hold unshakably to the eternal laws of God.

So in the modern apostasy of America and the West the culture will not only seek to redefine values and morality but also those who remain faithful to God. Therefore the righteous must do as did Elijah and reject all of the apostasy's redefinitions. And they must themselves refuse to be redefined. They must hold unshakably to the eternal laws of God.

God always provided for Elijah. Even in days of famine his needs were attended to. Thus Elijah was never dependent on the culture that surrounded him. That was a crucial dynamic. Only by standing independent of the surrounding culture was he able to be a light into its darkness.

> In the days of apostasy the people of God must
> become increasingly independent of the culture that
> surrounds them, especially separated from its cor-
> ruptions. Only then will they be able to bring light
> into its darkness.

So in the midst of the apostasy those who hold true to God's Word will have to increasingly wean themselves from any dependency on the surrounding culture, especially from its corruptions. But as with Elijah, this separation and independence is not to be sought for the purpose of withdrawal but rather for the impacting and engaging of the surrounding culture for God. Only those who are not *of* the darkness can become a light *to* the darkness.

In order to become independent of the corruption of his times, Elijah had to become all the more dependent on God. He was thus a man of deep prayer and communion with God.

> The ability of God's people to become indepen-
> dent from the corruption and defilement of the
> surrounding culture will be proportionate to their
> increasing dependence on God.

In order to be unplugged from the darkness, one must become all the more plugged in to the light. So in the days of apostasy it is all the more critical for believers to become all the more plugged in to God through prayer and communion in His presence. The more dependent they are on Him, the more independent they will become of the surrounding culture. Their power and effectiveness will depend on it.

Elijah was a man uncompromised, undivided, single-minded, and focused. Others had compromised with the evil of their day and had disqualified themselves from being used of God. But Elijah went in the opposite direction. The more evil the culture became, the more strongly he stood. And it was this radical and uncompromised stand that allowed him to change the course of his nation.

> In the days of increasing apostasy those who com-
> promise with evil will fall. But the one who will most
> commit to living undivided, uncompromised, and
> wholeheartedly for God will also be the one most
> powerfully used by God for His purposes.

In the days when immorality becomes a culture's ruling principle, the temptation for God's people will be to soften their stands, to bend under the pressure, and to compromise with the dark. But those who do so will disqualify themselves from being used of God as they were meant to be used. The righteous must instead commit to living as did Elijah and to resist all temptation to compromise and all pressure to soften their stand. Rather, they must move in the opposite direction. When the dark grows increasingly darker, it is then that the lights must grow increasingly bright. When evil goes from bad to worse, the righteous must go from good to great. In a Christian civilization the candles shine in the light of the sun. But in a post-Christian civilization they shine in the darkness of the night. They become lights of contradiction. But it is the contrary light that changes the history of lives and nations. It is the radical light, the light of the candle in the night, that lights up the world.

Elijah was a man of faith and confidence, of boldness and courage against all odds, of a stubborn hope that would not yield in spite of all that was arrayed against it. Despite his circumstances and despite those who sat on his nation's throne, he knew who was King above all kings and which side it was that would prevail in the end.

> In days when darkness rules, the righteous must
> see beyond the dark and hold by faith to a stubborn
> unyielding hope, seeing above all powers to the reign
> of the true King and to the assurance of the victory
> that waits at the end. They must be bold, courageous,
> and fully confident of the good.

In the days of the paradigm Elijah stood in the minority. Those who pursued evil or who simply accepted it and went along with it were the majority. The fight must have often looked hopeless. Yet Elijah stood and acted as if he was on the winning side—and he was.

So in the days of mass apostasy it will often look as if God's people are on the losing side. But they must be all the more stubborn in faith, all the more bold in truth, and all the more confident of victory. They must resist the temptation to be silent. They must be as Elijah and fight their good fight and take up their stand as if they are on the winning side—as, in fact, they are.

"Then Elijah said to all the people, 'Come near to me.' So all the people came near to him. And he repaired the altar of the LORD that was broken down."[4]

In the days of Ahab, Elijah summoned the nation to Mount Carmel in an attempt to break the curse that rested on the land. For the curse to be broken, the people had to choose which God they would serve, the Lord or Baal. But before that choice could be made, the altar of the Lord that had been broken down had to be repaired.

> In the apostasy the Lord's altar is broken. For there to be restoration and revival, there must be a return to that altar. And that altar must be repaired.

What is an altar? It is that upon which a sacrifice is killed. The faith on which America and Western civilization was founded doesn't have an altar—or does it? At the spiritual foundation of American and Western civilization lies an altar—the cross. What is the cross? It is that upon which the sacrifice was killed. The cross is an altar—the altar of the Lord.

According to the paradigm, in the days of apostasy the altar of the Lord is neglected and broken down. So in the present apostasy the cross, the altar of Western civilization, has likewise become neglected and broken down. For a civilization given to idolatry and materialism will ultimately devalue the altar of the cross. A culture obsessed with self-gratification and self-worship will reject that which epitomizes self-sacrifice. Thus it will disparage and break down the Lord's altar. The pursuit of prosperity, success, and self-realization has caused the cross to be neglected and broken down as well in many of the houses that bear His name.

Revival could not come in the ancient case apart from a return to the Lord's altar. Neither can revival come in the present case without the same. It can only come in a return to the foundation, to the cross, to Jesus. And it must be the Elijahs of this age who first return to that altar, who build it up, and who, as did Elijah, call back to that altar the civilization in which they live. Only then can there be true revival.

"And Elijah came to all the people, and said, 'How long will you falter between two opinions? If the LORD is God, follow Him; but if Baal, follow him.'"[5]

Elijah called the nation to make a decision once and for all. Without that decision there could be no restoration.

> For there to be revival and restoration, there must be repentance. And for there to be repentance, there must be decision.

On April 29, 2015, I stood in the US Capitol Building and spoke to a gathering of leaders and members of Congress. When I sought the Lord as to what message I should give, I was led to Elijah's moment on Mount Carmel. I gave this word:

"We have come to a most critical moment. As Elijah stood on top of Mount Carmel and cried out to Israel in its hour of decision, in between two altars and two gods, his voice now cries out to America and says to us, 'Choose you this day whom you will serve.' Seventy years ago, the chaplain of the United States Senate cried out in the same voice and said to this nation, 'If the Lord be God, then follow Him! But if Baal, then follow him . . . and go to hell.'

"Tonight, America stands at the crossroads. And as Elijah came to the summit of Mount Carmel to make a declaration, we have come this night to Capitol Hill to declare that our God is not Baal . . . We have come to this hill to declare that there is only one God . . . the God of Abraham, Isaac, and Jacob . . . the God of Israel and of all nations . . . He alone is the Rock upon which this nation has come into existence . . . We will not bow down to Baal."

I was led to speak of America standing at the crossroads in between God and Baal. What was in the paradigm had not yet come to me. Two weeks before I gave that word, Hillary Clinton had declared her candidacy for the presidency. Less than a week before I spoke, she issued her proclamation that deep-seated religious beliefs would have to be changed. The day before I spoke, the Supreme Court heard the case that would decide the future of marriage in America. Two months after I spoke, Donald Trump declared his candidacy for the presidency. And two months after that the ancient sanctuaries of the god against whom I specifically spoke, the temples of Baal, would come crashing down.

America is still at this writing standing at the crossroads in between God and Baal. And only through repentance can there be revival. And only through decision can there be repentance.

We stand in the most critical of times, the days of Elijah. We must pray for our civilization's Mount Carmel moment and call for the decision that must be made. But we ourselves must likewise have our own Mount Carmel moment. We must each bring to an end any lingering indecision or wavering that still remains. We must each choose whom we will serve. For the one who serves the Lord completely, wholeheartedly, and with no reservations will be the one whom God will anoint, as He anointed Elijah, for the purpose of great and mighty things, even for the changing of the history of nations.

We have uncovered the template of Elijah. It is time now that we become part of it. It is time we become the Elijah of the paradigm.

Or, in other words, if these are the days of Elijah—it is time that we become the Elijahs of the day.

As for the one who reads these words and ponders the question as to how one can be safe in the approach of judgment or how one can be saved in the approach of eternity—the answer is found in the same place—in the altar of the Lord, in the cross. Outside of that altar there is no safety or hope. Inside of it there is no fear or judgment.

It is written, "There is no other name under heaven given among men by which we must be saved."[6] That name, which we know as *Jesus*, in its original form is *Yeshua*. *Yeshua* means God is salvation. That is the crux of the matter—not religion or culture—but the love of God—that God Himself would place Himself in our place and take upon Himself our judgment and overcome death, that we could be saved. It remains, from ancient times to now, the greatest manifestation of love we could possibly fathom. There is no greater love and in the end no other hope.

It is the love of God, the mercy of God, and the forgiveness of all sins. And it is only in that love and mercy that we find new life and new birth. And it is only in that new birth that one can be saved—as it is written, in order to enter the kingdom of heaven, one must be born again. It is eternal life; it is the peace and joy of heaven now and forever.

It is given freely and without condition to all who will receive it. It is received by faith. It can begin wherever one is with a simple prayer of one's heart to receive the love and mercy of His sacrifice and the power of His resurrection. It begins by receiving His presence into one's heart and life—then following in His footsteps every day and every moment as His disciple.

As Elijah's call to the people required a decision, so does salvation. To not decide is to decide against it. To delay or postpone making that decision is to not decide. So it is written, "Choose you *this day*." For it is "this day" that is the only day it can be chosen. Today is the only day in which salvation can take place…and the only moment is now.

Chapter 31

CONCLUSIONS

W‍HAT HAVE WE seen?

- A blueprint that dates back almost three thousand years and yet that contains the mystery of our times
- A paradigm that reveals or determines the rise and fall of leaders and governments
- A template that lies behind world events into the twenty-first century
- A mystery that involves in one way or another the lives of everyone on earth
- A paradigm that reveals...

    ...not only the events of our times but the timing of those events, the years and in some cases even the exact dates on which they were to take place.

...the people of our times, the leaders and players, the figures on the modern world stage, their natures, their actions, their personalities, and even, in at least one case, a name.

...the parameters of time each of the modern leaders are allotted to remain on the world stage.

...the outcomes of current events, even those of presidential elections.

...the meaning and significance behind the events of our time.

What, then, are the implications of the paradigm?
They are these...

- God is real.

- God is over all things.

- He works all things—His will and all that wars against His will, the good and the bad, the holy and the profane—together for His ultimate purposes.

- The God of the Bible, who was actively and dynamically involved in the events of the ancient world, is just as actively and dynamically involved in the events of the modern world and of our day.

- His workings take place not only in the sacred realm but in the secular realm, the political realm, the economic realm, the cultural realm, the spiritual realm, the natural realm—in every realm and in all things.

- The Bible is the Word of God, so much so that its patterns, keys, and templates reveal, illuminate, foretell, if not determine even the events and details of the present day.

- The Word of God is beyond time. That which was written nearly three thousand years ago is as relevant now as when it was first written.

- What we are now witnessing is a massive metamorphosis of Western civilization, a metamorphosis of values, morality, culture, society, and nations—the metamorphosis of apostasy. This metamorphosis is affecting the entire world.

- The metamorphosis is taking place according to an ancient template, the paradigm of ancient Israel.

- The paradigm is manifesting not only on a global scale but on the smallest of scales and in the most intricate of details.

- It involves modern leaders walking in the footsteps of ancient rulers and following the patterns and courses of an ancient template.
- The ancient leaders were part of a paradigm of apostasy and judgment. We are thus now living likewise in the days of apostasy and progressing to judgment.
- God is slow to judge. Yet He must and will ultimately bring all that is evil into judgment. It is His necessity to bring judgment, but it is His heart to show mercy. Thus He calls all to repentance and salvation.
- God hears the prayers of His people and moves on their behalf.
- God's workings are so precise that they determine even the smallest moments of world history—and of our lives.
- We are living in biblical times.

The events of the paradigm are separated by almost three millennia. No figure from the modern story was alive at the time of the ancient account. And all those who lived and moved in the ancient account are long gone.

So who was it that put it all together? Who was it that was alive at both times, in both ages, three thousand years apart? There is only One.

Thus the Paradigm reveals that in the end all kings and queens, all prophets and priests, all holy men and warriors, all leaders and followers, all saints and sinners, all cultures and nations, all kingdoms and empires, all struggles and tears, all evil and darkness will pass away. All things pass away but God and His love. And the one who takes refuge within that love will abide with Him forever.

For above all kings, above all kingdoms, above all powers, and above all thrones, only One is King. And thus to Him is the kingdom, the power, and the glory yesterday, today, and forever.

NOTES

Chapter 2: Metamorphosis

1. 1 Corinthians 10:11.
2. 2 Kings 17:17.
3. Jeremiah 19:4–5.

Chapter 3: Days of the Gods

1. Fish Eaters, accessed June 24, 2017, www.fisheaters.com/forums/index. php?topic=2871173.0, emphasis added. The site includes this citation: Patricia Baird-Windle…quoted in an August 29, 1999 interview with *Florida Today*, and in "The 'Sacrament' of Abortion: An Interview With a Retired Abortionist." LifeSite Daily News at http://www.lifesite.net, August 31, 1999.
2. Ginette Paris, *The Sacrament of Abortion*, translated by Joanna Mott (Washington, DC: Spring Publications, 1992), 56, accessed June 5, 2017, https://books.google.com, emphasis added.
3. Ibid., 92, emphasis added.
4. Ginette Paris, *The Psychology of Abortion: Second Edition* (originally published as *The Sacrament of Abortion*) (Washington, DC: Spring Publications, 2007), 70, accessed June 5, 2017, https://books.google.com, emphasis added.

Chapter 4: The King

1. Richard D. Patterson and Hermann J. Austel, *1 and 2 Kings: The Expositor's Bible Commentary, Revised Edition* (Nashville, TN: HarperCollins Christian Publishing, 2017), accessed June 17, 2017, https://books .google.com/books?id=g8ESDgAAQBAJ.
2. Dick Meyer, "What 'Culture War'?" *Los Angeles Times*, August 27, 2008, accessed June 7, 2017, http://www.latimes.com/la-oe-meyer27-2008aug27-story .html.
3. Ibid.
4. Patrick J. Buchanan, "Culture War Speech: Address to the Republican National Convention," Voices of Democracy, August 17, 1992, accessed June 7, 2017, http://voicesofdemocracy.umd.edu/buchanan-culture-war-speech -speech-text/.
5. Bill Clinton, *My Life: The Early Years* (New York: Vintage Books, 2005), 29, 38.
6. 1 Kings 16:30.

Chapter 5: The Queen

1. Patrice Taddonio, "WATCH: For Hillary in Arkansas, First Came Rejection. Then Came Rebranding," *Frontline*, September 22, 2016, accessed June 17, 2017,

http://www.pbs.org/wgbh/frontline/article/watch-for-hillary-in-arkansas-first-came-rejection-then-came-rebranding/.

2. Sarah Ellison, "How Hillary Clinton's Loyal Confidants Could Cost Her the Election," *Vanity Fair*, December 2015, accessed July 30, 2017, http://www.vanityfair.com/news/2015/10/hillary-clinton-inside-circle-huma-abedin.

3. Peter Baker and Amy Choznik, "Hillary Clinton's History as First Lady: Powerful, but Not Always Deft," *New York Times*, December 5, 2014, accessed June 7, 2017, https://www.nytimes.com/2014/12/06/us/politics/hillary-clintons-history-as-first-lady-powerful-but-not-always-deft.html.

4. William H. Chafe, *Bill and Hillary: The Politics of the Personal* (New York: Farrar, Straus and Giroux, 2012), 230, accessed July 31, 2017, http://tinyurl.com/yd9x3b8j.

5. Geoffrey W. Bromiley, *The International Standard Bible Encyclopedia*, vol. 2 (Grand Rapids, MI: Wm. B. Eerdmans, 1982), accessed June 7, 2017, http://tinyurl.com/ybwqoxek.

Chapter 6: King and Queen

1. 1 Kings 18:19.

2. 1 Kings 21:25.

3. Michael A. Genovese, *Encyclopedia of the American Presidency* (New York: Facts On File, 2004), 99.

4. Amy Chozick, "Sara Ehrman, Outspoken Feminist With Deep Ties to Clintons, Dies at 98," *New York Times*, June 3, 2017, accessed June 26, 2017, www.nytimes.org.

5. Marielle Segarra, "A Look at Women Who've Had a Strong Influence Over the Presidency," Newsworks, July 28, 2016, accessed June 26, 2017, http://www.newsworks.org/index.php/local/item/95225-as-dnc-approaches-a-look-at-women-whove-had-a-strong-influence-over-the-presidency.

6. Peter Baker and Amy Chozick, "Hillary Clinton's History as First Lady: Powerful, but Not Always Deft," *New York Times*, December 5, 2014, accessed July 27, 2017, https://www.nytimes.com/2014/12/06/us/politics/hillary-clintons-history-as-first-lady-powerful-but-not-always-deft.html.

7. "Bill Clinton on Abortion," On the Issues, accessed June 26, 2017, http://www.ontheissues.org/celeb/Bill_Clinton_Abortion.htm.

8. "Clinton Health Care Plan of 1993," Wikipedia, accessed July 3, 2017, https://en.wikipedia.org/wiki/Clinton_health_care_plan_of_1993.

9. "Bill Clinton on Abortion," On the Issues, accessed July 3, 2017, http://www.ontheissues.org/celeb/Bill_Clinton_Abortion.htm.

10. "Partial-Birth Abortion Ban Act of 2003," NRLC.org, accessed July 3, 2017, https://www.nrlc.org/archive/abortion/pba/partial_birth_abortion_Ban_act_final_language.htm.

11. "Clinton Makes Keynote Speech Before Gay-Lesbian Group," CNN, AllPolitics, November 8, 1997, accessed July 3, 2017, http://www.cnn.com/ALLPOLITICS/1997/11/08/clinton.gays/index.html.

12. "Presidential Documents," *Federal Register*, June 6, 2000, accessed July 3, 2017, https://www.gpo.gov/fdsys/pkg/FR-2000-06-06/pdf/00-14440.pdf.

13. Andrew Gimson, "Hillary Clinton as Lady Macbeth," *Telegraph*, April 17, 2008, accessed July 3, 2017, http://www.telegraph.co.uk/news/worldnews/1895909/Hillary-Clinton-as-Lady-Macbeth-Democratic-debate.html.

14. Edward B, Coe, "Jezebel," accessed July 3, 2017, https://www.scribd.com/document/92464891/JEZEBEL.

15. "A Comparison of Shakespeare's Lady Macbeth and Biblical Jezebel," Kibin, accessed July 3, 2017, https://www.kibin.com/essay-examples/a-comparison-of-shakespeares-lady-macbeth-and-biblical-jezebel-mCiZpWBT.

16. *Ellicott's Commentary for English Readers*, Bible Hub, accessed July 3, 2017, http://biblehub.com/commentaries/1_kings/16-31.htm.

Chapter 7: The Goddess

1. 2 Chronicles 33:6.

2. Mary Emily O'Hara, "Hillary Clinton Draws Cheers and Criticism for 'Future Is Female' Line," NBC News, February 7, 2017, accessed July 3, 2017, http://www.nbcnews.com/news/us-news/hillary-clinton-draws-cheers-criticism-future-female-line-n717736.

3. Joseph Berger, "Performing Seances? No, Just 'Pushing the Membrane of the Possible,'" *New York Times*, June 25, 1996, accessed July 3, 2017, http://www.nytimes.com/1996/06/25/us/performing-seances-no-just-pushing-the-membrane-of-the-possible.html.

4. Kenneth L. Woodward, "Soul Searching," *Newsweek*, July 7, 1996, accessed July 3, 2017, http://www.newsweek.com/soul-searching-179536.

5. Ibid.

6. "Performing Séances?," *New York Times*.

7. Jean Houston, *The Passion of Isis and Osiris* (New York: Wellspring/Ballantine, 1998), 21.

8. Ibid., emphasis added.

9. Richard Lieby, "Marianne Williamson, Hollywood Self-Help Guru, Wants to Heal Washington," *Washington Post*, March 11, 2014, accessed July 3, 2017, https://www.washingtonpost.com/lifestyle/style/marianne-williamson-hollywood-self-help-guru-wants-to-heal-washington/2014/03/11/378b0d02-a85f-11e3-b61e-8051b8b52d06_story.html?utm_term=.2a3e782862cf.

10. Houston, *The Passion of Isis and Osiris*, 20.

11. E. A. Wallis Budge, "Neter. The Egyptian Word for God" *Monist*, Vol. 13, No. 4 (July 1903), 481, accessed July 3, 2017, https://www.jstor.org/stable/27899432?seq=1#page_scan_tab_contents.

12. Houston, *The Passion of Isis and Osiris*, 21.

13. Ibid., emphasis added.

14. Mark Ellis, "Hillary Clinton: Has Her Methodism Been Influenced by Séances, Spiritism, and New Age Spirituality?" *Christian Post*, March 22, 2016, accessed July 3, 2017, http://devblogs.christianpost.com/post/hillary-clinton-has-her-methodism-been-influenced-by-seances-spiritism-and-new-age-spirituality.html.

15. Houston, *The Passion of Isis and Osiris*.

16. Ibid.

Chapter 8: The Days of the King

1. 1 Kings 16:29, emphasis added.

Chapter 9: The Nemesis

1. 1 Kings 20:38–42.
2. "Osama Bin Laden: A Chronology of His Political Life," *Frontline*, accessed July 3, 2017, http://www.pbs.org/wgbh/pages/frontline/shows/binladen/etc/cron.html.
3. Ibid.
4. Ibid.
5. Ibid.
6. Glenn Kessler, "Bill Clinton and the Missed Opportunities to Kill Osama Bin Laden," *Washington Post*, February 16, 2016, accessed July 3, 2017, https://www.washingtonpost.com/news/fact-checker/wp/2016/02/16/bill-clinton-and-the-missed-opportunities-to-kill-osama-bin-laden/?utm_term=.2ddfa5eca9af.
7. Dan Good, "Bill Clinton, Hours Before 9/11 Attacks: 'I Could Have Killed' Osama Bin Laden," ABC News, August 1, 2014, accessed July 3, 2017, http://abc-news.go.com/US/bill-clinton-hours-911-attacks-killed-osama-bin/story?id=24801422.
8. 1 Kings 20:42, emphasis added.

Chapter 10: The Vineyard

1. 1 Kings 21:1–2.
2. vv. 3–4.
3. v. 7.
4. v. 7.
5. v. 8.
6. v. 14.
7. v. 15.
8. vv. 17–18.
9. "Whitewater Time Line," *Washington Post*, accessed July 3, 2017, http://www.washingtonpost.com/wp-srv/politics/special/whitewater/timeline.htm.
10. "Whitewater Controversy," Wikipedia, accessed June 28, 2017, https://en.wikipedia.org/wiki/Whitewater_controversy.
11. Dan Froomkin, "Untangling Whitewater," *Washington Post*, accessed July 3, 2017, http://www.washingtonpost.com/wp-srv/politics/special/whitewater/whitewater.htm.
12. Ibid.
13. "Whitewater Controversy," Wikipedia.
14. Ibid.
15. "Vince Foster," Wikipedia, accessed July 3, 2017, https://en.wikipedia.org/wiki/Vince_Foster.
16. "Whitewater Time Line," *Washington Post*.
17. "Foster Origins," The Foster Name Website, accessed July 31, 2017, http://www.fostername.com/england.htm.

Chapter 11: The Prophecy

1. Exodus 20:17, CSB.
2. 1 Kings 21:9–10.
3. Exodus 20:16.
4. 1 Kings 21:13.
5. Exodus 20:13.
6. 1 Kings 21:19.
7. vv. 20–22.
8. v. 22.
9. vv. 23–24.
10. v. 27.
11. vv. 28–29.
12. Steven Nelson, "Bill Clinton 15 Years Ago: 'I Did Not Have Sexual Relations With That Woman,'" *US News & World Report*, January 25, 2013, accessed July 3, 2017, https://www.usnews.com/news/blogs/press-past/2013/01/25/bill-clinton-15-years-ago-i-did-not-have-sexual-relations-with-that-woman.
13. "House Brief for Impeachment Trial," *Washington Post*, January 11, 1999, accessed July 3, 2017, http://www.washingtonpost.com/wp-srv/politics/special/clinton/stories/housetext011199.htm.
14. Julia Maues, "Banking Act of 1933 (Glass-Steagall)," Federal Reserve History, accessed July 3, 2017, https://www.federalreservehistory.org/essays/glass_steagall_act.
15. Ryan Chittum, "Bill Clinton on Deregulation: 'The Republicans Made Me Do It!'" *Columbia Journalism Review*, October 1, 2013, accessed July 3, 2017, http://archives.cjr.org/the_audit/bill_clinton_the_republicans_m.php.
16. Bill Medley, "Riegle-Neal Interstate Banking and Branching Efficiency Act of 1994," Federal Reserve History, accessed July 3, 2017, https://www.federalreservehistory.org/essays/riegle_neal_act_of_1994.
17. Steven A. Holmes, "Fannie Mae Eases Credit to Aid Mortgage Lending," *New York Times*, September 30, 1999, accessed July 3, 2017, http://www.nytimes.com/1999/09/30/business/fannie-mae-eases-credit-to-aid-mortgage-lending.html.
18. "Bill Clinton on Deregulation," *Columbia Journalism Review*.
19. "This Day in History," December 19, 1998, accessed July 3, 2017, http://www.history.com/this-day-in-history/president-clinton-impeached.
20. "Bin Ladin Preparing to Hijack US Aircraft and Other Attacks," Central Intelligence Agency Memo, December 4, 1998, Declassified and Approved for Release July 12, 2004, accessed July 3, 2017, https://www.cia.gov/library/readingroom/docs/DOC_0001110635.pdf.
21. "Ahab," Smith's Bible Dictionary, accessed July 3, 2017, http://www.christianity.com/bible//dictionary.php?dict=sbd&id=151, emphasis added.
22. Tokunboh Adeyemo, ed., *Africa Bible Commentary* (Nairobi, Kenya: WordAlive Publishers, 2006), 441.

Chapter 12: The End

1. 1 Kings 22:3–4.
2. vv. 29–30.

3. v. 31.

4. vv. 34–35.

5. 1 Kings 21:19.

6. 1 Kings 22:35–38.

7. Helen Kennedy, "President Clinton Admits He Lied Under Oath About His Affair With Monica Lewinsky in 2001," *Daily News*, January 19, 2016 (originally published January 20, 2001), accessed July 3, 2017, http://www.nydailynews.com /news/politics/bill-feds-cut-dealsurrenders-law-license-escape-ind-article-1.904790.

8. Tom Rosenstiel and Amy S. Mitchell, eds., *Thinking Clearly: Cases in Journalistic Decision-Making* (New York: Columbia University Press, 2003), 26, accessed July 26, 2017, http://tinyurl.com/ycwc5pfq.

9. "Controversial Article Regarding Kenneth W. Starr, Independent Counsel," Government Publishing Office, June 24, 1998, accessed July 3, 2017, https://www .gpo.gov/fdsys/pkg/CREC-1998-06-24/html/CREC-1998-06-24-pt1-PgH5252-9 .htm.

10. 1 Kings 22:1–2, emphasis added.

Chapter 13: The Day

1. 1 Kings 21:27.

2. v. 29.

3. 1 Kings 20:42.

4. Steven Nelson, "Bill Clinton 15 Years Ago: 'I Did Not Have Sexual Relations With That Woman,'" *US News & World Report*, January 25, 2013, accessed July 3, 2017, https://www.usnews.com/news/blogs/press-past/2013/01/25/bill-clinton-15 -years-ago-i-did-not-have-sexual-relations-with-that-woman.

5. David Maraniss, "First Lady Launches Counterattack," *Washington Post*, January 28, 1998, accessed July 3, 2017, http://www.washingtonpost.com/wp-srv /politics/special/clinton/stories/hillary012898.htm.

6. "President Bill Clinton," CNN, All Politics, August 17, 1998, accessed July 3, 2017, http://www.cnn.com/ALLPOLITICS/1998/08/17/speech/transcript.html.

7. Ibid.

8. Ibid.

9. "Transcript of President's Remarks to Religious Leaders at Prayer Breakfast," *Los Angeles Times*, The Starr Report, September 12, 1998, accessed July 3, 2017, http://articles.latimes.com/1998/sep/12/news/mn-21961.

10. 1 Kings 21:29, 22:1–2, emphasis added.

11. "President Bill Clinton: I Have Sinned," The History Place, accessed July 3, 2017, http://www.historyplace.com/speeches/clinton-sin.htm.

Chapter 14: The Shadow Queen

1. Terence P. Jeffrey, "Hillary Clinton on Partial Birth Ban," CNSNews.com, August 31, 2016, accessed July 3, 2017, http://www.cnsnews.com/commentary /terence-p-jeffrey/hillary-clinton-partial-birth-ban.

2. Patrick Healy, "Clinton's Announcement Makes Waves in '08 Field," *New York Times*, January 20, 2007, accessed July 3, 2017, http://www.nytimes.com /2007/01/20/us/politics/20cnd-clinton.html.

Chapter 15: The Heir

1. Zeke J. Miller, "Axelrod: Obama Misled Nation When He Opposed Gay Marriage in 2008," *TIME*, February 10, 2015, accessed July 3, 2017, http://time.com/3702584/gay-marriage-axelrod-obama/.

2. "Clinton Makes Keynote Speech Before Gay-Lesbian Group," CNN, AllPolitics, accessed July 30, 2017, http://www.cnn.com/ALLPOLITICS/1997/11/08/clinton.gays/index.html.

3. Brooks Jackson, "Obama and the 'Christian Nation' Quote," FactCheck.org, August 26, 2008, accessed July 3, 2017, http://www.factcheck.org/2008/08/obama-and-the-christian-nation-quote/.

4. Ibid.

Chapter 16: The Hostile Kingdom

1. 2 Kings 6:30–31.

2. vv. 32–33.

3. 2 Kings 3:13.

4. Geoffrey W. Bromiley, *International Standard Bible Encyclopedia,* vol. 2 (Wm. B. Eerdmans Publishing, 1995), 977, accessed July 3, 2017, http://tinyurl.com/y7mn7b2n.

5. Ben Smith, "Obama on Small-Town Pa.: Clinging to Religion, Guns, Xenophobia," Politico, April 11, 2008, accessed July 3, 2017, http://www.politico.com/blogs/ben-smith/2008/04/obama-on-small-town-pa-clinging-to-religion-guns-xenophobia-007737.

6. Zeke J. Miller, "Axelrod: Obama Misled Nation When He Opposed Gay Marriage In 2008," *TIME*, February 10, 2015, accessed July 3, 2017, http://time.com/3702584/gay-marriage-axelrod-obama/.

7. Adam Liptak, "Supreme Court Ruling Makes Same-Sex Marriage a Right Nationwide," *New York Times*, June 26, 2015, accessed July 3, 2017, https://www.nytimes.com/2015/06/27/us/supreme-court-same-sex-marriage.html?_r=0.

8. Allie Malloy and Karl de Vries, "White House Shines Rainbow Colors to Hail Same-Sex Marriage Ruling," CNN, June 30, 2015, accessed July 3, 2017, http://www.cnn.com/2015/06/26/politics/white-house-rainbow-marriage/index.html.

9. "Freedom of Access to Clinic Entrances and Places of Religious Worship," The US Department of Justice, updated August 6, 2015, accessed July 3, 2017, https://www.justice.gov/crt-12.

10. Igor Volsky, "Obama at HRC Dinner: GOP Presidential Candidates Must 'Stand Up' for Gay Soldiers," ThinkProgress, October 1, 2011, accessed July 3, 2017, https://thinkprogress.org/obama-at-hrc-dinner-gop-presidential-candidates-must-stand-up-for-gay-soldiers-6d2f48be13b4.

11. Billy Hallowell, "Obama's 5 Most Controversial Statements About Abortion and 'Women's Rights' During His Planned Parenthood Speech," The Blaze, April 26, 2013, accessed July 3, 2017, http://www.theblaze.com/news/2013/04/26/obamas-5-most-controversial-statements-about-abortion-and-womens-rights-during-his-planned-parenthood-speech/.

12. "America's Most Biblically-Hostile U.S. President," Wall Builders, December 29, 2016, accessed July 3, 2017, https://wallbuilders.com/americas-biblically -hostile-u-s-president/#edn1.

13. "Trump Executive Order Reverses Foreign Abortion Policy," BBC News, January 23, 2017, accessed July 3, 2017, http://www.bbc.com/news/world-us -canada-38724063.

14. "Obama Pick: Taxpayers Must Fund Abortions," World Net Daily, January 27, 2009, accessed July 3, 2017, http://www.wnd.com/2009/01/87249/.

15. Sarah Pulliam Bailey, "Obama Admin. Changes Bush 'Conscience' Provision for Health Workers," *Christianity Today*, February 18, 2011, accessed July 3, 2017, https://www.christianitytoday.com/news/2011/february/obama-admin -changes-bush-conscience-provision-for-health.html.

16. Steven Ertelt, "Obama Administration Announces $50 Million for Pro-Forced Abortion UNFPA," *LifeNews*, March 26, 2009, accessed July 3, 2017, http:// www.lifenews.com/2009/03/26/int-1138/.

17. Steven Ertelt, "Pro-Life Groups Left Off Obama's Health Care Summit List, Abortion Advocates OK," *LifeNews*, March 5, 2009, accessed July 3, 2017, http:// www.lifenews.com/2009/03/05/nat-4888/.

18. Jim Iovino, "Jesus Missing From Obama's Georgetown Speech," NBC Washington, April 17, 2009, accessed July 3, 2017, http://www.nbcwashington.com/news /local/Jesus-Missing-From-Obamas-Georgetown-Speech.html.

19. Steven Ertelt, "Obama Admin Terrorism Dictionary Calls Pro-Life Advocates Violent, Racist," LifeNews, May 5, 2009, accessed July 3, 2017, http://www .lifenews.com/2009/05/05/nat-5019/.

20. Johanna Neuman, "Obama Ends Bush-Era National Prayer Day Service at White House," *Los Angeles Times*, May 7, 2009, accessed July 3, 2017, http:// latimesblogs.latimes.com/washington/2009/05/obama-cancels-national-prayer-day -service.html.

21. Matt Cover, "Obama's EEOC Nominee: Society Should 'Not Tolerate Private Beliefs' That 'Adversely Affect' Homosexuals,'" CNSNews.com, January 18, 2010, accessed July 31, 2017, http://www.cnsnews.com/news/article/obama-s -eeoc-nominee-society-should-not-tolerate-private-beliefs-adversely-affect.

22. "White House Spent $23M of Taxpayer Money to Back Kenyan Constitution That Legalizes Abortion, GOP Reps Say," *Fox News*, July 22, 2010, accessed July 3, 2017, http://www.foxnews.com/politics/2010/07/21/gop-lawmaker-blasts-white -house-m-spent-kenya-constitution-vote.html.

23. Steven Ertelt, "Obama, Congress Cut Funding for 176 Abstinence Programs Despite New Study," LifeNews, August 26, 2010, accessed July 3, 2017, http://www.lifenews.com/2010/08/26/nat-6659/.

24. Steven Ertelt, "President Barack Obama's Pro-Abortion Record: A Pro-Life Compilation," LifeNews, November 7, 2010, accessed July 3, 2017, http://www .lifenews.com/2010/11/07/obamaabortionrecord/.

25. Meredith Jessup, "Obama Continues to Omit 'Creator' From Declaration of Independence," TheBlaze, October 19, 2010, accessed July 31, 2017, http://www .theblaze.com/news/2010/10/19/obama-continues-to-omit-creator-from -declaration-of-independence/.

26. LadyImpactOhio, "Feds Sued by Veterans to Allow Stolen Mojave Desert Cross to Be Rebuilt," RedState, January 14, 2011, accessed July 3, 2017, http://www .redstate.com/diary/ladyimpactohio/2011/01/14/feds-sued-by-veterans-to-allow -stolen-mojave-desert-cross-to-be-rebuilt/.

27. Marianne Medlin, "Amid Criticism, President Obama Moves to Fill Vacant Religious Ambassador Post," Catholic News Agency, February 9, 2011, accessed July 3, 2017, http://www.catholicnewsagency.com/news/amid-criticism-president -obama-moves-to-fill-vacant-religious-ambassador-post/.

28. Brian Montopoli, "Obama Administration Will No Longer Defend DOMA," CBS News, February 24, 2011, accessed July 3, 2017, http://www.cbsnews.com /news/obama-administration-will-no-longer-defend-doma/.

29. Chris Johnson, "ENDA Passage Effort Renewed With Senate Introduction," Washington Blade, April 15, 2011, accessed July 3, 2017, http://www.washington blade.com/2011/04/15/enda-passage-effort-renewed-with-senate-introduction/.

30.   Chuck Donovan, "HHS's New Health Guidelines Trample on Conscience," Heritage Foundation, August 2, 2011, accessed July 3, 2017, http://www.heritage .org/health-care-reform/report/hhss-new-health-guidelines-trample-conscience.

31. "Wounded, Ill, and Injured Partners in Care Guidelines," Family Research Council, accessed July 31, 2017, http://downloads.frc.org/EF/EF11L05.pdf.

32. "Maintaining Government Neutrality Regarding Religion," Military Reli- gious Freedom Foundation, accessed July 31, 2017, https://www.militaryreligious freedom.org/docs/gen_schwartz_letter_religion_neutralilty.pdf.

33. Hillary Rodham Clinton, "Remarks in Recognition of International Human Rights Day," U.S. Department of State, December 6, 2011, accessed July 31, 2017, https://2009-2017.state.gov/secretary/20092013clinton/rm/2011/12/178368.htm.

34. Ted Olsen, "Church Wins Firing Case at Supreme Court," *Christianity Today*, January 11, 2012, accessed July 3, 2017, http://www.christianitytoday.com /ct/2012/januaryweb-only/church-firing-case-supreme-court.html.

35. Geoff Herbert, "Air Force Unit Removes 'God' From Logo; Lawmakers Warn of 'Dangerous Precedent,'" syracuse.com, February 9, 2012, accessed July 3, 2017, http://www.syracuse.com/news/index.ssf/2012/02/air_force_rco_removes _god_logo_patch.html.

36. Markeshia Ricks, "Bible Checklist for Air Force Lodges Going Away," *First- Principles Press*, accessed July 31, 2017, http://firstprinciplespress.org/2012/04/26 /bible-checklist-for-air-force-lodges-going-away/.

37. Patrick Goodenough, "White House 'Strongly Objects' to Legislation Pro- tecting Military Chaplains from Doing Same-Sex Weddings or Being Forced to Act Against Conscience," CNS News, May 16, 2012, accessed July 3, 2017, http:// www.cnsnews.com/news/article/white-house-strongly-objects-legislation -protecting-military-chaplains-doing-same-sex.

38. "Military Logos No Longer Allowed on Troop Bibles," CBN News, June 14, 2012, accessed July 3, 2017, http://www.cbn.com/cbnnews/us/2012/june/military -logos-no-longer-allowed-on-troop-bibles/?mobile=false.

39. Billy Hallowell, "Obama Opposes NDAA's 'Rights of Conscience' for Military Chaplains and Members, Vows to Protects Rights of Gays," The Blaze, January 4, 2013, accessed July 3, 2017, http://www.theblaze.com/stories/2013/01/04/obama

-opposes-ndaas-rights-of-conscience-for-military-chaplains-members-vows-to
-protect-rights-of-gays/.

40. Steven Ertelt, "Obama Admin's HHS Mandate Revision Likely Excludes Hobby Lobby," LifeNews, February 1, 2013, accessed July 3, 2017, http://www.lifenews.com/2013/02/01/obama-admins-hhs-mandate-revision-excludes-hobby-lobby/.

41. Tony Perkins, "Obama Administration Begins Training Homosexual Activists Around the World," LifeSiteNews, June 6, 2013, accessed July 31, 2017, https://www.lifesitenews.com/opinion/obama-administration-begins-training-homosexual-activists-around-the-world.

42. Stacie Ruth and Carrie Beth Stoelting, *Unite the USA: Discover the ABCs of Patriotism* (Bloomington, IN: WestBow Press, 2013).

43. Jack Minor, "Military Warned 'Evangelicals' No. 1 Threat," World Net Daily, April 5, 2013, accessed July 3, 2017, http://www.wnd.com/2013/04/military-warned-evangelicals-no-1-threat/.

44. "Liberty Institute Calls On U.S. Department of Defense to Abandon Shift in Military's Proselytizing Policy," PR Newswire, May 7, 2013, accessed July 3, 2017, http://www.prnewswire.com/news-releases/liberty-institute-calls-on-us-department-of-defense-to-abandon-shift-in-militarys-proselytizing-policy-206486691.html; Ken Klukowski, "Pentagon May Court Martial Soldiers Who Share Christian Faith," Breitbart, May 1, 2013, accessed July 3, 2017, http://www.breitbart.com/national-security/2013/05/01/breaking-pentagon-confirms-will-court-martial-soldiers-who-share-christian-faith/.

45. "Obama Administration Ignores Outcries, Finalizes HHS Mandate Targeting Religious Freedom," Liberty Counsel, June 30, 2013, accessed July 31, 2017, http://www.lc.org/newsroom/details/obama-administration-ignores-outcries-finalizes-hhs-mandate-targeting-religious-freedom; Tom Strode, "Moore, Others: Final Mandate Rules Fail," Baptist Press, July 1, 2013, accessed July 31, 2017, http://www.bpnews.net/40659/moore-others-final-mandate-rules-fail.

46. Todd Starnes, "Obama 'Strongly Objects' to Religious Liberty Amendment," Townhall.com, June 12, 2013, accessed July 3, 2017, https://townhall.com/columnists/toddstarnes/2013/06/12/obama-strongly-objects-to-religious-liberty-amendment-n1618769.

47. Chad Groening, "Attorney Demands Answers for Air National Guard Sergeant Punished for Beliefs," OneNewsNow, July 15, 2013, accessed July 3, 2017, https://www.onenewsnow.com/culture/2013/07/15/attorney-demands-answers-for-air-national-guard-sergeant-punished-for-beliefs#.UeapQFNXyRS.

48. Steven Ertelt, "Army Briefing Tells Soldiers Christians and Pro-Lifers are a 'Radical' Threat," LifeNews, October 23, 2013, accessed July 3, 2017, http://www.lifenews.com/2013/10/23/army-briefing-tells-soldiers-christians-and-pro-lifers-are-a-radical-threat/.

49. "White House on Kim Davis: The Rule of Law Is Central to Our Democracy," RawStory, September 3, 2015, accessed July 3, 2017, http://www.rawstory.com/2015/09/white-house-on-kim-davis-the-rule-of-law-is-central-to-our-democracy/.

50. "America's Most Biblically-Hostile U. S. President," WallBuilders.

51. Ibid.

52. Penny Starr, "Civil Rights Commission: 'Religious Liberty,' 'Religious Freedom' Code Words for Intolerance, Homophobia, and 'Christian Supremacy,'" CNSNews.com, September 9, 2016, accessed July 3, 2017, http://www.cnsnews.com /news/article/penny-starr/civil-rights-commission-religious-liberty-religious -freedom-code-words.

Chapter 17: Heir and Queen

1. *The Open Door: A Pocket Magazine for Trolley of Train,* vol. 8 (New York Public Library, 1911), 17, accessed July 30, 2017, https://books.google.com/books? id=46ZVAAAAYAAJ&printsec=frontcover&dq=The+Open+Door:+A+Pocket+M agazine+for+Trolley+of+Train,+Volume+8&hl=en&sa=X&ved=0ahUKEwi54YKF mLPVAhWh1IMKHSAkCfMQ6AEIKDAA#v=onepage&q=After%20Ahab's%20 death&f=false.

2. John Kitto, ed., *A Cyclopaedia of Biblical Literature*, vol. 2 (London: W. Clowes and Sons), 112, accessed July 30, 2017, http://tinyurl.com/ycuqglxm.

3. Don Fleming, "Jezebel," *Bridgeway Bible Dictionary*, accessed July 3, 2017, http://www.studylight.org/dictionaries/bbd/j/jezebel.html.

4. Peter Baker and Helene Cooper, "Clinton Is Said to Accept Secretary of State Position," *New York Times*, November 21, 2008, accessed July 3, 2017, http:// www.nytimes.com/2008/11/22/us/politics/22obama.html.

Chapter 18: The Assassin

1. 2 Kings 8:7–8.

2. vv. 9–10.

3. vv. 11–13.

4. v. 14.

5. v. 15.

6. Mark Mazzetti, Helene Cooper, and Peter Baker, "Behind the Hunt for Bin Laden," *New York Times*, May 2, 2011, accessed July 3, 2017, http://www.nytimes .com/2011/05/03/world/asia/03intel.html.

7. 2 Kings 6:11-12.

8. 2 Kings 8:8.

9. Keith Bodner, *Elisha's Profile in the Book of Kings: The Double Agent* (Oxford: Oxford University Press, 2013), 133–134, accessed July 3, 2017, http:// tinyurl.com/yau52xlr, emphasis added.

10. Mazzetti, Cooper, and Baker, "Behind the Hunt for Bin Laden," *New York Times*, accessed July 3, 2017, http://www.nytimes.com/2011/05/03/world/asia /03intel.html.

11. "SEAL's First-Hand Account of Bin Laden Killing," CBS News, September 24, 2012, accessed July 3, 2017, http://www.cbsnews.com/news/seals-first-hand -account-of-bin-laden-killing/.

Chapter 19: The War of Thrones

1. *The Pulpit Commentaries*, StudyLight.org, accessed July 25, 2017, https:// www.studylight.org/commentaries/tpc/2-kings-9.html?print=yes.

2. Merrill C. Tenney, *The Zondervan Encyclopedia of the Bible*, Volume 1: Revised Full-Color Edition (Grand Rapids, MI: The Zondervan Corp., 2009), accessed July 30, 2017, http://tinyurl.com/yavhe7e2.

3. Marc A. Thiessen, "Hillary Clinton Is a Threat to Religious Liberty," *Washington Post*, October 13, 2016, accessed July 3, 2017, https://www.washingtonpost.com/opinions/hillary-clinton-is-a-threat-to-religious-liberty/2016/10/13/878cdc36-9150-11e6-a6a3-d50061aa9fae_story.html?utm_term=.704ae93d2621, emphasis added.

4. James Strong and John McClintock, "Jezebel," *The Cyclopedia of Biblical, Theological, and Ecclesiastical Literature* (New York: Haper and Brothers, 1880), accessed July 3, 2017, http://www.biblicalcyclopedia.com/J/jezebel.html.

5. Amy Chozick, "Planned Parenthood, in Its First Primary Endorsement, Backs Hillary Clinton," *New York Times*, January 7, 2016, accessed July 3, 2017, https://www.nytimes.com/politics/first-draft/2016/01/07/planned-parenthood-in-its-first-primary-endorsement-backs-hillary-clinton/.

6. Daniel Allott, "Democratic Convention a Celebration of Abortion," *Washington Examiner*, July 26, 2016, accessed July 3, 2017, http://www.washingtonexaminer.com/democratic-convention-a-celebration-of-abortion/article/2597792.

7. Jay Hobbs, "4 Ways Hillary Clinton Will Increase Abortion as President," The Federalist, October 19, 2016, accessed July 3, 2017, http://thefederalist.com/2016/10/19/four-ways-hillary-will-increase-abortion/.

8. Ramesh Ponnuru, "Clinton's Only Consistency: Ghastliness on Abortion," National Review, July 26, 2016, accessed July 3, 2017, http://www.nationalreview.com/article/438315/hillary-clinton-abortion-democratic-partys-nominee-far-left-america-abortion.

9. Dave Andrusko, "10 Examples of How Extreme Hillary Clinton Is on Abortion," LifeNews, September 12, 2016, accessed July 3, 2017, http://www.lifenews.com/2016/09/12/10-examples-of-how-extreme-hillary-clinton-is-on-abortion/.

Chapter 20: The Warrior

1. 2 Kings 9:1–3.

2. vv. 4–5.

3. vv. 6–8.

4. Warren W. Wiersbe, *The Bible Exposition Commentary*, vol. 1 (David C. Cook, 2004), 543, accessed July 3, 2017, http://tinyurl.com/y7md2649.

5. Ibid.

6. Michelle Fields, "Former Florida Governor Jeb Bush Went After Donald Trump During Tuesday's GOP Presidential Debate, Calling Him a 'Chaos Candidate,'" Breitbart, December 15, 2015, accessed July 31, 2017, http://www.breitbart.com/big-government/2015/12/15/jeb-bush-calls-donald-trump-chaos-candidate/.

7. 2 Kings 9:6.

Chapter 21: The Race

1. 2 Kings 9:11–13.

2. v. 14.

3. v. 16.

4. v. 20.

5. Matthew Poole, "Commentary on 2 Kings 9:20," *Matthew Poole's English Annotations on the Holy Bible* (public domain, 1685), accessed July 3, 2017, http://www.studylight.org/commentary/2-kings/9-20.html.

6. Dwight L. Moody, T. DeWitt Talmage, and Joseph Parker, *Bible Characters* (public domain, digital format released May 17, 2017), accessed July 3, 2017, https://www.gutenberg.org/files/54736/54736-h/54736-h.htm.

7. 2 Kings 9:14.

8. v. 16.

9. v. 20.

10. Ibid., NET, emphasis added.

11. Ibid., JUB, emphasis added.

12. Ibid., ISV, emphasis added.

13. Ibid., NLT, emphasis added.

14. Ibid., GW, emphasis added.

15. Ibid., NIV, emphasis added.

16. Ibid., YLT, emphasis added.

17. *ESV Global Study Bible* (Crossway, 2012), accessed July 3, 2017, http://tinyurl.com/y8pyx8yk.

Chapter 22: The Overthrow

1. 2 Kings 9:14–15.

2. v. 17.

3. v. 22.

4. v. 23.

5. v. 25.

6. vv. 25–26.

7. John McCormack, "Would Donald Trump Be a Pro-Abortion President?" *Weekly Standard*, January 17, 2016, accessed June 20, 2017, http://www.weeklystandard.com/would-donald-trump-be-a-pro-abortion-president/article/2000619.

Chapter 23: The Downfall

1. 2 Kings 9:22.

2. v. 30.

3. v. 31.

4. v. 32-33.

5. v. 34.

6. Joseph Benson, *Commentary of the Old and New Testaments* (New York: T. Carlton & J. Porter, 1857), accessed July 31, 2017, http://biblehub.com/commentaries/2_kings/9-34.htm.

7. Jenna Johnson, "At Florida Rally, Trump Resumes Attacking 'Crooked Hillary Clinton,'" *Washington Post*, September 27, 2016, accessed July 3, 2017, https://www.washingtonpost.com/news/post-politics/wp/2016/09/27

/at-florida-rally-trump-resumes-attacking-crooked-hillary-clinton/?utm_term
=.93ed5f52d897.

8. Myra Adams, "How the Clinton Victory Party Went From Coronation to Despair," *Washington Examiner*, November 12, 2016, accessed July 3, 2017, http:// www.washingtonexaminer.com/how-the-clinton-victory-party-went-from -coronation-to-despair/article/2607188.

9. Ryan Lizza, "The Abortion Capital of America," *New York*, accessed July 3, 2017, http://nymag.com/nymetro/news/features/15248/.

10. Susan Berry, "Hillary Clinton to Receive Planned Parenthood's 'Champion of the Century' Award," Breitbart, April 11, 2017, accessed July 3, 2017, http:// www.breitbart.com/big-government/2017/04/11/hillary-clinton-receive-planned -parenthoods-champion-century-award/, emphasis added.

Chapter 24: The Days of the Heir

1. Marie Horrigan, "From Relative Obscurity, Obama's Star Rose Quickly," *New York Times*, January 16, 2007, accessed June 20, 2017, http://www.nytimes .com/cq/2007/01/16/cq_2127.html.

2. Mark Leibovich, "The Speech That Made Obama," *New York Times*, July 27, 2016. accessed July 3, 2017, https://www.nytimes.com/2016/07/27/magazine /the-speech-that-made-obama.html.

3. 2 Kings 3:1, emphasis added.

4. Kevin Liptak, "Barack Obama Slams Trump, Makes Appeal for Hillary Clinton," CNN, July 28, 2016, accessed July 3, 2017, http://www.cnn .com/2016/07/27/politics/president-obama-democratic-convention-speech /index.html, emphasis added.

5. "READ: President Obama's Speech at the Democratic Convention," NPR, July 28, 2016, accessed July 3, 2017, http://www.npr.org/2016/07 /28/487722643/read-president-obamas-speech-at-the-democratic-convention, emphasis added.

6. "12 Years Later: Obama's DNC Speeches Then and Now," NBC News, July 28, 2016, accessed July 3, 2017, http://www.nbcnews.com/storyline /2016-conventions/12-years-later-obama-s-dnc-speeches-then-now-n618166, emphasis added.

Chapter 25: The Holy Man

1. 2 Kings 10:15.

2. Jeremiah 35:8–9.

3. W. H. Westcott, "The House of the Rechabites," *Scripture Truth*, vol. 7 (1915), 291, accessed July 3, 2017, http://www.stempublishing.com/authors /westcott/Rechabites.html.

4. "2 Kings Chapter 10," *YORWW Bible Commentary*, June 2, 2012, accessed July 3, 2017, http://yorwwbiblecommentary.com/index.php /historical-books/book-of-second-kings/2-kings-1-12, emphasis added.

5. Alexander MacLaren, *MacLaren's Commentary: Expositions of Holy Scripture* (Delmarva Publications Inc.), accessed July 3, 2017, http://tinyurl.com /y86g95f4, emphasis added.

6. Charles Pfeiffer and Everett Harrison, *The Wycliffe Bible Commentary* (Moody Publishers, 1962), accessed July 3, 2017, https://books.google.com/books?id=r4lLCAAAQBAJ&pg=PT20&dq=The+Wycliffe+Bible+Commentary&source=gbs_selected_pages&cad=3#v=onepage&q=as%20a%20servant%20of&f=false, emphasis added.

7. Warren Wiersbe, *The Bible Exposition Commentary,* vol. 1, 543, accessed July 3, 2017, http://tinyurl.com/ya7bwjgx.

8. "2 Kings 10:15" *Pulpit Commentary,* accessed July 3, 2017, http://biblehub.com/commentaries/2_kings/10-15.htm.

9. "2 Kings 10:16," *Barnes' Notes on the Bible,* accessed July 3, 2017, http://biblehub.com/commentaries/2_kings/10-16.htm.

10. 2 Kings 10:15.

11. Ibid.

12. v. 16.

13. Ibid.

14. Joseph Rawson Lumby, *The Second Book of the Kings: With Introduction and Notes* (University Press, 1887), 103, accessed July 3, 2017, http://tinyurl.com/y94dodww.

15. John L. Mckenzie, *The Dictionary of the Bible* (Simon and Schuster, 1995), 722, accessed July 3, 2017, http://tinyurl.com/yaz9rup8, emphasis added.

16. "Rechabite," *Encyclopaedia Britannica*, accessed June 20, 2017, https://www.britannica.com/topic/Rechabite, emphasis added.

17. David Noel Freedman, ed., *Eerdmans Dictionary of the Bible* (Wm. B. Eerdmans Publishing, 2000), 1112, accessed July 3, 2017, https://books.google.com/books?id=P9sYIRXZZ2MC&printsec=frontcover&source=gbs_ge_summary_r&cad=0#v=snippet&q=the%20rechabites%20are%20described%20as%20a%20relig&f=false.

18. John H. Walton, Victor H. Matthews, and Mark W. Chavalas, *The IVP Bible Background Commentary: Old Testament* (InterVarsity Press, 2012), 398, accessed July 20, 2017, http://tinyurl.com/yaeu2kor.

19. 2 Kings 10:15.

20. Candace Smith, Paola Chavez, and Veronica Stracqualursi, "Donald Trump Swears to Christian Leaders, 'I'm So on Your Side,'" ABC News, June 21, 2016, accessed July 31, 2017, http://abcnews.go.com/Politics/donald-trump-swears-christian-leaders-im-side/story?id=40021097.

21. David Gibson, Aysha Khan and Emily McFarlan Miller, "Trump to Top Evangelicals: 'I'm so on Your Side, I'm a Tremendous Believer,'" Deseret Digital Media, June 21, 2016, accessed July 31, 2017, http://www.deseretnews.com/article/865656629/Trump-to-top-evangelicals-6I7m-so-on-your-side-I7m-a-tremendous-believer7.html.

22. Lumbry, *The Second Book of the Kings: With Introduction and Notes*, 102, accessed July 3, 2017, http://tinyurl.com/ycw8bb2j.

23. "Mike Pence: 'I'm a Christian, a Conservative, and a Republican—in That Order,'" *The Week*, July 20, 2016, accessed July 3, 2017, http://theweek.com/speedreads/637487/mike-pence-im-christian-conservative-republican--that-order.

24. Bradford Richardson, "Shock Over Vice President Pence's Marriage Shows Washington, Media Out of Touch," *Washington Times*, April 6, 2017, accessed

July 3, 2017, http://www.washingtontimes.com/news/2017/apr/6/shock-over-mike
-pences-marriage-shows-washington-m/.

25. "2 Kings 10:16" *Jamieson-Fausset-Brown Bible Commentary*, accessed July
3, 2017, http://biblehub.com/commentaries/2_kings/10-16.htm.

Chapter 26: The Days of the Queen

1. Sam Frizell, "What Hillary Clinton Did Before Her Campaign," *TIME*,
April 12, 2015, accessed July 3, 2017, http://time.com/3774872/hillary-clinton
-campaign-launch/.

2. 1 Kings 16:29, emphasis added.

3. 2 Kings 3:1, emphasis added.

4. 1 Kings 22:51, emphasis added.

Chapter 27: The Warrior King

1. Bromiley, *The International Standard Bible Encyclopedia*, vol. 2, 982,
accessed July 3, 1017, http://tinyurl.com/yby9mcsc.

2. Chris Spargo, "Double, Double, Donald's in Trouble: Witches Including
Lana Del Rey Will Gather at Midnight to Cast a Spell on President Trump AND
His Supporters in Hopes of Banishing Him From Office," Daily Mail, updated
February 25, 2017, accessed July 27, 2017, http://www.dailymail.co.uk/news
/article-4257216/Witches-gather-midnight-cast-spell-Donald-Trump.html.

3. Ibid.

4. "2 Kings 10:31" *Pulpit Commentary*, accessed June 20, 2017, http://biblehub
.com/commentaries/2_kings/10-31.htm.

Chapter 28: The Temple

1. 1 Kings 16:32.

2. 2 Kings 10:26–28.

3. "2 Kings 10:27," *The Pulpit Commentaries*, accessed July 3, 2017, https://
www.studylight.org/commentaries/tpc/2-kings-10.html..

4. Ibid.

5. Maggie Haberman, "Trump Tells Planned Parenthood Its Funding Can Stay
if Abortion Goes," *New York Times*, March 6, 2017, accessed July 3, 2017, https://
www.nytimes.com/2017/03/06/us/politics/planned-parenthood.html.

6. Laurie McGinley and Amy Goldstein, "Trump Reverses Abortion-Related
U.S. Policy, Bans Funding to International Health Groups," *Washington Post*,
January 23, 2017, accessed July 3, 2017, https://www.washingtonpost.com/news
/to-your-health/wp/2017/01/23/trump-reverses-abortion-related-policy-to
-ban-funding-to-international-health-groups/?utm_term=.5df9483b9ec9.

7. Liam Stack, "ISIS Blows Up Ancient Temple at Syria's Palmyra Ruins," *The
New York Times*, August 23, 2015, accessed June 20, 2017, https://www
.nytimes.com/2015/08/24/world/middleeast/islamic-state-blows-up-ancient
-temple-at-syrias-palmyra-ruins.html.

8. Mathew Katz, "Satellite Images Confirm Destruction of Ancient Temple in
Palmyra," *TIME*, August 31, 2015, accessed July 3, 2017, http://time.com/4018108
/satellite-images-temple-destruction-palmyra/.

9. Reem Nasr, "Donald Trump Announces Candidacy for President," CNBC, June 16, 2015, accessed July 3, 2017, http://www.cnbc.com/2015/06/16/donald -trump-announces-candidacy-for-president.html.

Chapter 29: The Harbingers of Days to Come

1. 2 Kings 10:31, NIV.

2. Bob Deffinbaugh, "23. The Life and Times of Elisha the Prophet—Jehu Cleans House (Ahab's House) (2 Kings 10:1–36)," August 24, 2004, accessed July 3, 2017, https://bible.org/seriespage/23-life-and-times-elisha-prophet-jehu -cleans-house-ahab-s-house-2-kings-101-36.

3. 2 Chron. 7:14.

Chapter 30: The Elijah Paradigm

1. 1 Kings 17:1.
2. 1 Kings 18:17.
3. v. 18.
4. v. 30.
5. v. 21.
6. Acts 4:12.

ABOUT the AUTHOR

J ONATHAN CAHN CAUSED a national stir with the release of the *New York Times* best seller *The Harbinger* and his subsequent *New York Times* best sellers. He has addressed members of Congress and spoken at the United Nations. He was named, along with Billy Graham and Keith Green, as one of the top forty spiritual leaders of the last forty years "who radically changed our world." He is known as a prophetic voice to our times and for the opening up of the deep mysteries of God. Jonathan leads Hope of the World, a ministry to the world's most needy—and the Jerusalem Center outside New York City in Wayne, New Jersey. He is a much-sought-after speaker and appears throughout America and the world. He is a Messianic believer, a Jewish follower of Jesus.

For more information; to find out about over two thousand other messages and mysteries from Jonathan, prophetic updates, or free gifts; or to have a part in or contact his ministry, write to:

Hope of the World
Box 1111
Lodi, NJ 07644
USA

Or visit his website at:

HopeOfTheWorld.org

Facebook: Jonathan Cahn

Email: contact@hopeoftheworld.org

CONNECT WITH US!

CHARISMA HOUSE

(Spiritual Growth)

f Facebook.com/CharismaHouse

🐦 @CharismaHouse

📷 Instagram.com/CharismaHouse

SILOAM

(Health)

📌 Pinterest.com/CharismaHouse

MODERN ENGLISH VERSION

(Bible)

www.mevbible.com